Large Scale Structure and Dynamics of Complex Networks

FROM INFORMATION TECHNOLOGY TO FINANCE AND NATURAL SCIENCE

T0331566

Large Scale Structure and Dynamics of Complex Networks

FROM INFORMATION TECHNOLOGY TO FINANCE AND NATURAL SCIENCE

EDITORS

GUIDO CALDARELLI

Centre for Statistical Mechanics and Complexity
CNR-INFM, Department of Physics
University of Rome "La Sapienza", Italy

ALESSANDRO VESPIGNANI

Indiana University, USA
Institute for Scientific Interchange, Italy

 World Scientific

NEW JERSEY · LONDON · SINGAPORE · BEIJING · SHANGHAI · HONG KONG · TAIPEI · CHENNAI

Published by

World Scientific Publishing Co. Pte. Ltd.

5 Toh Tuck Link, Singapore 596224

USA office: 27 Warren Street, Suite 401-402, Hackensack, NJ 07601

UK office: 57 Shelton Street, Covent Garden, London WC2H 9HE

British Library Cataloguing-in-Publication Data
A catalogue record for this book is available from the British Library.

Complex Systems and Interdisciplinary Science — Vol. 2
LARGE SCALE STRUCTURE AND DYNAMICS OF COMPLEX NETWORKS
From Information Technology to Finance and Natural Science

ISBN-13 978-981-270-664-5
ISBN-10 981-270-664-X

Printed in Singapore.

Preface

In the last decade, the increased power of computers and the informatics revolution have made possible the systematic gathering and handling of data sets on several large scale networks, allowing the detailed analysis of their structural and functional properties. In particular, mapping projects of the World-Wide Web and the physical Internet offered the first chance to study the topology and traffic of large scale networks. Gradually other studies followed describing networks of practical interest in social science, infrastructures analysis and epidemiology. The study of these systems involves researchers from many different disciplines such as physics, biology, mathematics, engineering and computer science and has led to a shift of paradigm in which the complexity of networks has become the central issue in their characterization, modeling and understanding. Indeed, the evidence that a complex topology is shared by many complex evolving networks cannot be considered as incidental. Rather, it points to the possibility of some general principle that can possibly explain the emergency of this architecture in such different contexts. In this perspective, it becomes particularly relevant to seek the development of a general methodological and theoretical framework rationalizing the general principles underlying the dynamics and structure of complex networks.

In this context the Information Technology section of the European commission has been a main actor in fostering the development of interdisciplinary researches and collaborations among European institutions with a focus on network science. In particular, the FET open project Coevolution and Self-Organization in Dynamical Networks (COSIN IST-2001-33555)[a] has represented a major initiative tackling a wide spectrum of network research. Different scientists from different fields have decided to collaborate in order to build a common set of knowledge and expertise to be used in the description different phenomena. While the collaboration was intended

---

[a]http://www.cosinproject.org

to principally tackle issues related to networks arising in the information technology domain, it has been fully pursuing an interdisciplinary approach where research activities in the field of ecological, economical and social systems have not been neglected. Results obtained in each of these fields could turn to be applicable or prospect innovative solutions and understanding in the other domains. Indeed, various nodes of the project work on fields as different as Protein Interaction Networks, the network of e-mails, the Internet Graph and the financial networks present in the stock exchange.

The purpose of this volume is twofold. First we intend to provide a snapshot of the forefront research activities in the area of complex networks, provide a good sampling of the disciplines involved, and the kinds of problems that form the subject of inquiry. In doing this, we organized the book in thematic chapter, each one addressing a special area or domain of network science. On the other hand, we want to present the many research achievements obtained within the COSIN project, as well as new identified problems and the various research directions still in their initial stages. In this spirit, chapters will be co-authored by leading scientists who have been involved, in a stage or the other, in the COSIN project. This will also allow us to emphasize the value of the interdisciplinary approach by showing specific pieces of research realized in each particular domain. Despite the contributed chapter format, a specific effort has been put in place to homogenize the various chapters in a general structure providing a coherent and unified framework for the study of networked structure. We hope that this presentation of the field will attract the interest of colleagues within and outside the network community, and serve to further improve our understanding of this fascinating subject.

Many people have contributed to the preparation of this book. First of all we thank all the authors for their extraordinary contributions. We thank all the colleagues that through various scientific interactions have helped all the authors of the book in their scientific activities. We also thank all institutions and funding agencies that along with the European community have generously supported the scientific activity of the authors of the present book. In particular, on top of the support received for the COSIN book, we also acknowledge the support of the Ministerio de Ciencia y Tecnología (Spain) through its program "Ramón y Cajal" and grant BFM 2001-2154; the European project "DELIS". Finally we want to express our gratitude to who helped in the final preparation of the manuscript.

Contents

Introduction

Ralph Dum

*European Commission DG INFSO - F1 (J-54 01/118),
B - 1049 - Brussels, Belgium*

Various types of diverse networks — communication networks, transport networks, global business networks, networks of friends, or the Internet — shape our daily life and the way we think and act. We depend on various social, economic, and technological networks that weave a tissue of businesses, governments, technologies and that contain us as citizens, users, or customers. We only become aware of our dependence if failures occur in these networks: when cities are plunged into darkness because of a breakdown of the power grid like happened recently in New York, when national economies collapse because of a failure of global financial systems like happened in the South-Asian banking crisis, or when computer viruses spread with mind-boggling speed over information networks destroying or, even worse, exposing sensitive data.

Of course networks are not a new phenomenon nor are their influence and our dependence on them. What is new is the extent to which technology allows these networks to take on new roles and ever changing forms. Increasingly, the technologies and social institutions on which we depend for our daily life are explicitly engineered as networks, often with help information and communication technologies. We use information networks to explicitly engineer networks by connecting persons, businesses, and technologies: Sophisticated manufacturing logistics allows on demand supply chains, novel business models use the almost instantaneous access to millions of on-line customers via the Internet. Technology itself is no longer a distinct set of artifacts but an intricate network of connected artefact's. Electric power grids that form a critical part of a nation infrastructure are very large and complex engineered networks logistically connecting power grids across large geographical distances.

The Internet itself is the perhaps most telling example of a network that literally changed our lives. Apart from the already mentioned impact on business the Internet affects the way we access and produce information in general: networked content is being created at a phenomenal rate and the information we deal with is taking on an increasingly networked character. Present IT allows us to represent, index, and access gigantic link structures, such as graphs of citations, collaborations, or even contents of whole libraries (see recent surge in interest in digital libraries).

Networks are indeed everywhere, but it is fair to say that our understanding of networks has not kept up with our dependence on them: while such networks open opportunities they also bear risk. How can we avoid that local failures in one part of such networks lead to a cascade of failures in the whole network? How are decisions made in systems that become more and more open, more and more interconnected, and less and less centralised? How do we design systems — technological or political — that act reliably in such highly dynamic networked environments? How do networks grow, and how does that growth process influence the shape — the pattern of connections — in the network?

A network is essentially anything that can be represented by a graph: a set of generically called nodes connected by links representing some binary relationship. In social networks, the nodes are people, and the ties between them are friendship, political alliance or professional collaboration. In the case of the Internet, the nodes are routers, and they are joined by a link when they are physically tied together. In the case of the World Wide Web, the nodes are Web sites, and they are joined when there is a hyper-link from one to the other. But these social and technological networks are only part of a much bigger variety of networks in nature. A living cell is a fascinating network of molecular events that allow cells to multiply and therefore organisms to grow (metabolic pathways and gene expression networks), that allow inter and intra cell communication (signaling pathways). Organisms themselves form networks of predator and prey in food webs — that has been studied by biologists for a long time.

One might argue that apart from an abstract notion of being connected all these diverse networks have very little in common. Recently, however, inspired by empirical studies of such networks, researchers from the mathematical, biological, physical, and social sciences have made substantial progress on a number of previously intractable problems and uncovering connections between what had seemed to be quite different problems. The result has been called the "science of networks" that is spurred by the bewildering progress in computing power and widely available large-scale electronic datasets. Due to progress in IT, we can now study networks on a scale far larger than previously possible: instead of a few hundreds we now study millions of network nodes and analyse their large-scale statistical properties. What made progress possible as well is that we have today, for the first time, enough data on networks that will allow a systematic study. In the social sciences, we have a wealth of demographic data and data on business processes, in IT itself we have data on the Internet, and in the life science we have data on molecular networks that give us insight into the functioning of life.

Researchers are uncovering general concepts and properties intrinsic to all of these diverse networks. Intrinsic properties of networks studied include robustness of networks to disturbances, or the influence of the topology of the underlying networks in spread of epidemics or in the flow of information. These discoveries are supplemented by a variety of theoretical ideas concerned with the modelling of social networks, including static and dynamical models, graph theory, simulation techniques and computer algorithms, and measures of graph structure. As such networks are the result of interactions between a large number of agents humans, businesses, molecules etc. the science of complex systems that elucidates the emergence of structure in such systems plays therefore an important unifying role in these studies of networks across various domains and disciplines.

The articles in this book will give an account of the variety and unity of networks. They are a result of a multidisciplinary research effort funded by the Future and Emerging Technologies of the European Commission in the focus area of Complex Systems that managed to uncover commonalities across networks a diverse as the Internet, the food webs and networks of board members in companies.

CHAPTER 1

Preliminaries and Basic Definitions in Network Theory

Guido Caldarelli[1] and Alessandro Vespignani[2,3]

[1] *INFM-CNR Centro SMC Dipartimento di Fisica Università di Roma "La Sapienza" P.le A. Moro 5 00185 Roma, Italy*

[2] *School of Informatics & Biocomplexity Center, Indiana University, IN 47406, USA*

[3] *Laboratoire de Physique Théorique (UMR du CNRS 8627), Batiment 210, Université de Paris-Sud 91405 Orsay, France*

1.1. *Introduction*

In very general terms a network can be described as a graph whose nodes (vertices) identify the elements of the system. The set of connecting links (edges) represents the presence of a relation or interaction among these elements. With such a high level of generality it is easy to perceive that a wide array of systems can be approached within the framework of network theory. In this section we provide a basic notation and the definitions needed to describe networks. Not surprisingly, each field concerned with network science introduced its own basic notation and nomenclature. The natural framework for a rigorous mathematical description of networks, however, is found in graph theory and we will stick to it in this Chapter. Note that graph theory consists in an impressive body of work and we are not in the condition to provide a formal and complete presentation of it. Our purpose in this introductory chapter is to provide some notions useful to describe networks and commonly used in the rest of the book. For the interested reader, amongst the various introductory books on graph theory, we suggest to consult those by West,[1] Bollobás,[2] Diestel,[3] and Caldarelli.[4]

1.2. *Basic definitions*

As in any mathematical abstraction, when we describe a systems as a **graph** we decide to discard many of the specific peculiarities of the real phenomena and focus only on a few features of interest. In particular, a graph is essentially a way to code a relation (physical links, interactions etc.) between the elements of a system. The elements of the system identify the set V (set of **vertices**), and the relations among those the set E (set of **edges**). The graph indicated as $G(V, E)$ can be drawn plotting the vertices as points and the edges as lines between them. It is not important how they are actually drawn. Ultimately the only thing that matters is to know which vertices are connected.

- A graph $G(V, E)$ where V has n elements (n vertices) is said to have **order** n. Analogously, the **size** of a graph is the number m of its edges (the number of elements of the set E).
- When an edge e links vertices v_1, v_2 we have that vertices v_1, v_2 are **incident** with the edge e. Alternatively the edge e *joins* v_1, v_2 that are its *endvertices*.
- Vertices v_1, v_2 joined by edge e are **adjacents** or neighbours.
- A *dominating set* for a graph is a set of vertices whose neighbors, along with themselves, constitute all the vertices in the graph.
- A graph with *order* n cannot have more than m_{max} edges where $m_{max} = n(n-1)/2$ (the *size* is smaller than m_{max}). When all these possible edges are present the graph is **complete** and it is indicated with the symbol K^n. The opposite case happens when there are no edges at all. The graph is then *empty* and it is indicated by the symbol E^n.

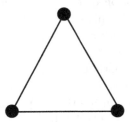 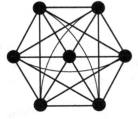

Fig. 1.   Two different examples of a complete graph. On the left K^3 and on the right K^7.

1.3. *Different kinds of graphs*

1.3.1. *Weighted, directed and oriented graphs*

- Whenever a real number can be attached to an existing edge we have that the edge is characterized by a weight w. Note that in this book the weights are (almost exclusively) positive real numbers (i.e. $w > 0$). The graph in this case is a **weighted** graph.
- A **directed** graph $G(V, E)$ is given by two disjoint sets E and V plus two functions $I(E \to V)$ and $F(E \to V)$. The first one assigns to every edge e an initial vertex $I(e)$. The second one assigns to every edge e a final vertex $F(e)$. More simply, every edge e has assigned a direction from one vertex $I(e)$ to another $F(e)$.
- Sometime $I(e)$ and $F(e)$ coincide. In this case e is a **loop**. Moreover, we can have different edges directed between the same two vertices $I(e)$ and $F(e)$. This is the case of **multiple edges**.

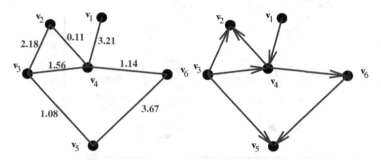

Fig. 2. On the left a realization of a weighted graph. The degree of vertex v_4 is 6.02 (given by $0.11 + 3.21 + 1.14 + 1.56$). On the right an example of an oriented graph. If the weight were the same in this case we would have an in-degree $k^{w,in} = 4.77(3.21 + 1.56)$ and an out-degree $k^{w,out} = 1.25(0.11 + 1.14)$

- Whenever the direction is assigned but neither loops nor multiple edges are present, then the graph is **oriented**. Intuitively oriented graphs are undirected graphs where for every edge one assigns a direction.
- A **multigraph** is a pair of disjoint sets (V, E) together with a map $E \to V \cup [V]^2$ assigning to every edge either one or two vertices (the ends). A multigraph is then similar to a directed graph, with multiple edges and loops but no direction assigned. A sketch of the various kind of graph is presented in Fig. 3.

- The number of edges of vertex v_i in a graph is called **degree** of vertex v_i and it is indicated here by $k(v_i)$. In the case of an oriented graph the degree can be distinguished in *in-degree* $k^{in}(v_i)$ and the *out-degree* $k^{out}(v_i)$. In the case of weighted graphs we will consider the *weighted-degree* $k^w(v_i)$ of a vertex v_i as the sum of the weight of the edges on v_i.
- If the set V in graph $G(V,E)$ is composed by vertices $v_1, v_2, ..., v_n$ then the series $k(v_1), k(v_2), ..., k(v_n)$ is a *degree sequence* of $G(V,E)$. Particular importance in this book is devoted to the statistical properties of such degree sequence.

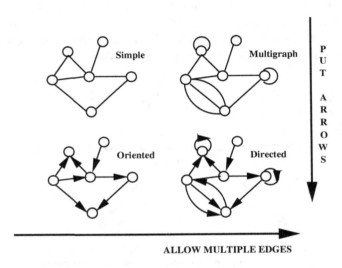

Fig. 3.   The distinction between the various types of graphs.

1.3.2. *Subgraphs*

- Consider two graphs $G(V,E)$ and $G'(V'E')$. We can define a new graph indicated by $G \cap G'$ whose vertices are in the set $V \cap V'$ and the edges in the set $E \cap E'$. If $V \cap V' = \emptyset$ the two graphs are **disjoint**. On the other hand if $V' \subseteq V$ and $E' \subseteq E$ then $G'(V',E')$ is an *induced subgraph* of $G(V,E)$ and we indicate this by writing $G'(V',E') \subseteq G(V,E)$. Finally, if $G'(V',E') \subseteq G(V,E)$ and $V' = V$, $G'(V',E')$ is **spanning** of $G(V,E)$

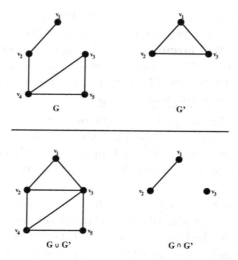

Fig. 4.   The operations of union and intersection of two graphs

- Two graphs are *isomorphic* if you can re-draw one of them so that it looks exactly like the other. An open problem is to determine in a short time whether two graphs are isomorphic or not.

1.3.3. *Partited graphs*

- Let $r \geq 2$ be an integer, a graph $G(V, E)$ is called **r-partite** if it can be divided in r classes such that every edge has its ends in different classes. This means that vertices in the same class cannot be adjacent. If $r = 2$ the graph is also called **bipartite**
- A complete *bipartite clique* $K_{i,j}$ is a graph where every one of i nodes has an edge directed to each of the j nodes.
- A *bipartite core* $C_{i,j}$ is a graph on $i + j$ nodes that contains at least one $K_{i,j}$ as a subgraph.

1.4. *Paths and cycles*

- A **path** is a (not empty) graph $G'(V', E')$ of the form $V' = v_0, v_1, ..., v_n$, $E' = e_1, , ...e_n$ where $v_0, v_1, ..., v_n$ a set of vertices for which e_i is an edge joining vertices v_{i-1} and v_i. Less formally we can say that a series of consecutive edges forms a **path**. The number of edges in a path is called the *length* of the path.

- if $P = e1 + e2 + \dots + e_n$ is a path then if $n \geq 3$ and we add an edge e_0 joining vertices v_n and v_0, we obtain a **circuit**. Put in other words a **circuit** is a path whose endvertices coincide. If in the circuit all the vertices are distinct each other the circuit is a **cycle**. A cycle of length k is indicated as C^k. Note that **a cycle is different from a loop**

  - A *Hamiltonian path* is a path passing once through all the vertices (not necessarily through all the edges) in the graph. A Hamiltonian circuit is a Hamiltonian path which begin and ends in the same vertex. By construction this circuit is also a cycle.
  - An *Eulerian path* is a path that passes once through all the edges (not necessarily once through all the vertices) in the graph. An Eulerian circuit is an Eulerian path which begins and ends in the same edge. If the vertices in the circuit are all different then the circuit is a cycle.

- When a path exists between any couple of vertices v_i, v_j in a graph, the graph is **connected**. This property is called **connectivity**.

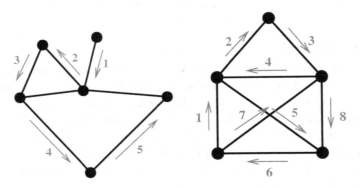

Fig. 5.   Left an Hamiltonian path and right an Eulerian circuit

1.4.1. *Trees*

- A **tree** is a connected graph that also does not contain cycles (also acyclic graph). If the graph is not connected but still acyclic then it is composed by different trees and assume the natural name of **forest**.

- Vertices of degree 1 in a tree are called **leaves**. In any non trivial tree there are at least two leaves.
- It is convenient, in some cases, to consider one vertex of the tree as a special one. This vertex is called **root**. A tree with a fixed root is a *rooted tree*.

1.5. *Statistics on graphs*

One of the elements that has fostered the recent development of network science can be found in the recent possibility for the systematic gathering and handling of data sets on several large scale networks. The large number of elements comprised in these networks prompts us to the use of a statistical analysis as the proper tool for a useful mathematical characterization. Indeed, in large systems, asymptotic regularities cannot be found by looking at local elements or properties. This consideration has led many researchers, particularly in physics and computer science, to use a large scale statistical characterization. This allows to take into account the aggregate properties of the many interacting units that compose large scale networks. In the recent literature on large scale networks the statistical analysis has been initially focused on three main features, namely the small-world, the clustering and the degree distribution properties.

1.5.1. *Small world properties*

The small-world property refers to the the fact that in many large scale networks the average distance between vertices is very small compared to the size of the graphs. The distance between two vertices in a graph is measured as the shortest path length $\langle \ell \rangle$ among them. A global statistical measure of the distance among vertices can then be expressed as the average shortest path length among all possible couples of vertices in the network. The small-world concept describes in simple words a simple fact. It is possible to go from one vertex to any other in the system passing through a very small number of intermediate vertices. To be more precise, the small-world property is present when $\langle \ell \rangle$ scales logarithmically (or slower) with the number of vertices.

The small-world effect has been popularized in the sociological context where it is sometimes referred as "six degrees of separation".[5] A short number of acquaintances (on the average six) is enough to create a connection between any two people chosen at random. Since then, the small-world effect has been observed in many natural networks[6] and appears to characterize several infrastructure networks. As we see in the next chapters, the small-world property can be simply explained by the presence of randomness in the evolution of networks. It finds an elegant mathematical treatment in the celebrated graph model of Erdős and Rényi.

1.5.2. *Clustering coefficient*

The small-world property alone is not the signature of a special organizing principle. More interesting is the fact that, in close analogy to many social and technological networks,[6] the small-world effect goes along with a high level of clustering. The concept of clustering of a graph, also called *transitivity* in the context of sociology,[7] refers to the tendency observed in many natural networks to form cliques in the neighborhood of any given vertex. In this sense, a high clustering implies that, if the vertex i is connected to j, and j is connected to l, then very likely i is also connected to l (the friends of my friends are also friends of mine). The clustering of an undirected graph can be quantitatively measured by means of the *clustering coefficient*. Let us consider the vertex i, with degree k_i, and let us denote by e_i the number of edges existing between the k_i neighbors of i. The clustering coefficient, c_i, of i is defined as the ratio between the actual number of edges among its neighbors, e_i, and its maximum possible value, $k_i(k_i - 1)/2$, i.e.

$$c_i = \frac{2e_i}{k_i(k_i - 1)}. \tag{1}$$

Thus, the clustering coefficient c_i measures the average probability that two neighbors of the vertex i are also connected between them. Note that this measure of clustering has only meaning for $k_i > 1$. For $k_i \leq 1$ we define $c_i \equiv 0$. The finding of many clustered networks with small-world properties raises a very interesting issue: Random graphs feature the small-world effect but are not clustered, while regular grids tend to be clustered but are not small-world. We therefore need to identify the different organizing principles (on their turn related to both hierarchical and geographical factors) that allow the development of both properties at the same time.

1.5.3. *Degree distribution*

The most basic statistical characterization of a graph is given by the sequence of degrees k_i of its vertices i or, (on average) the relative probability distribution of degrees $P(k)$. This degree distribution $P(k)$ for an undirected graph is defined as the probability that any randomly chosen vertex has degree k. In the case of directed graphs, one has to consider two different distributions, the in-degree $P(k_{in})$ and out-degree $P(k_{out})$ distributions, defined as the probability that a randomly chosen vertex has in-degree k_{in} and out-degree k_{out}, respectively. The functional forms generally considered to describe the degree distribution of real networks define two broad network classes. The first one refers to the so-called homogeneous networks. In this case the degree distribution have functional form with light tail such as Poisson's or Gaussian distributions. The second class concerns networks with heterogeneous connectivity pattern usually corresponding to heavy tailed degree distribution. A typical example is the case of scale-free networks with power-law degree distribution[b] that behaves as $P(k) = Ak^{-\gamma}$. The origin of the discrimination of homogeneous

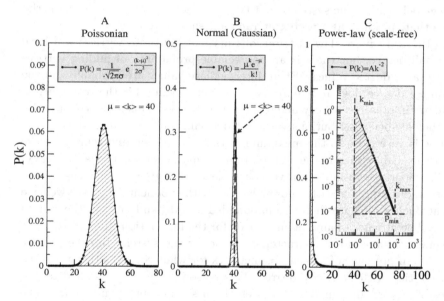

Fig. 6. (A) The plot of a Gaussian Distribution. (B) The plot of a Poisson Distribution. (C) The plot of a Power-law distribution. In the inset of (C) the same plot on a logarithmic scale.

and heterogeneous networks can be understood by looking at the first two moments of the degree distribution. For example we can compute what is the typical value that the degree assumes in the graph. This value will be

---

[b]Power-law distributions are in many cases referred to as Pareto distributions.

indicated by $\langle k \rangle$, where the symbol $\langle ... \rangle$ indicates an average over all the possible outcomes. A measure of the typical error we make if we assume that every vertex has degree $\langle k \rangle$ (thereby neglecting values fluctuations in our system) is given by the standard deviation σ^2. By definition these quantities are expressed as

$$\langle k \rangle = \int k P(k) dk \tag{2}$$

$$\sigma^2 = \int (k - \langle k \rangle)^2 P(k) dk \tag{3}$$

The peculiar fact about a distribution with a heavy tail is that there is a finite probability of finding vertices with degree much larger than the average $\langle k \rangle$. In other words, the consequence of heavy tails is that the average behavior of the system is not typical. The characteristic degree is the one that, picking up a vertex at random, should be encountered most of the times. In power-law distributions most of the times vertices will have a small degree, but there is an appreciable probability of finding vertices with large degree values. Yet all intermediate values are probable and the average degree does not represent any special value for the distribution. We are in presence of very heterogeneous networks. This is clearly opposite to bell-shaped distributions with fast decaying tails, in which the average value is very close to the maximum of the distribution and represents the most probable value in the system. In more mathematical terms the heavy-tail property translates in a very large level of degree fluctuations. In the case of distributions with a power-law tail with exponent $2 \leq \gamma \leq 3$ we have that fluctuations are therefore unbounded and depend only on the system size. The absence of any intrinsic scale for the fluctuations implies that the average value is not a characteristic scale for the system. In other words, we are in presence of a *scale-free* network for what concerns the statistical properties of the vertices' degree. This reasoning can be extended to values of $\gamma \leq 2$, since in this case even the first moment is unbounded. The power-law behavior and the relative exponent thus represent a quantitative measure of the level of *heterogeneity* of the network's degree.

1.6. *Complexity*

While the extreme heterogeneity of networks is a well defined mathematical property, the definition of complex networks implies the distinction of what is "complex" and what is the merely complicated. This distinction is a critical one because the characteristic features and the behavior of complex systems differ significantly from those of merely complicated systems. A general and accepted definition of complexity does not exist. Authors in different context provide different definitions which are often tailored on specific systems or areas of interest. Without entering in the details of such a discussion, however, a minimal definition of complexity may involve two main features: i) the system exhibits complications and heterogeneity that extend virtually on all scales allowed by the physical size of the system; ii) these features are the spontaneous outcome of the interactions among the many constituent units of the system, i.e. we are in the presence of an emergent phenomenon. It is easy to realize that the WWW, the Internet, the airport network are all systems which grow in time by following complicate dynamical rules and without a global supervision or blueprint. The same can be said for many social and biological networks. All these networks are self-organizing systems, which at the end of the evolution show an emergent architecture with unexpected properties and regularities. At the same time, heavy tails and heterogeneity appear to be common to a large number of these networks, along with other complex topological features such the presence of communities, motifs, hierarchies and modular ordering. We are thus in the presence of structures whose fluctuations and complications are unbounded and extend over all possible scales allowed by the physical size of the systems, therefore defining the class of complex networks.

1.7. *What is next*

The characterization of large complex networks goes far beyond the basic properties discussed in the previous sections. Real networks comprises systems of a very different nature that show several other complex structural properties that might differ from case to case. The increasing evidence in networks for the presence of communities, motifs, hierarchies and modular ordering opens a series of important questions and at the same time defines different classes of complex networks. In this perspective, it becomes particularly relevant to develop specific tools for the characterization and analysis of large scale networks as well as a theoretical understanding that might uncover the very general principles underlying the networks formation. In the next chapters the reader will find an extensive review of recent studies concerning the structural analysis of complex networks and the applications of these concepts and models to several real world systems. Chapter 2 presents the basic modeling paradigms for static and evolving networks. Chapter 3 offers a discussion on the empirical analysis and modeling of cor-

relations and clustering in complex networks. In Chapter 4 the reader finds
an introduction to weighted networks and their relevance in the modeling
of real world networks. Chapter 5 is devoted to the analysis of communities and motifs in complex networks and the methods for their detection.
The last methodological Chapter 6 addresses the questions arising in the
visualization of large networks and presents recent tolls and developments
in this area. The remaining chapters are devoted to specific domain applications. Namely Chapter 7 deals with the world-wide web graph; Chapter
8 discusses the analysis of the real Internet; Chapter 9 reviews the use of
networks in the ecological domain; Chapter 10 presents the some recent
applications of network analysis to large scale socio-economical networks.
We are confident that the following part might provide a "state-of-the-art"
discussion of the complex networks research and its application in many
real world instances.

CHAPTER 2

Models of Complex Networks

Paolo De Los Rios

École Polytechnique Fédérale Lausanne, SB ITP LBS, 1015 Lausanne,
Switzerland

2.1. *Introduction*

The renewed interest in large complex networks that has arisen recently
has been fostered on the one hand by the growing availability of large sets
of data, that have allowed for more and more detailed characterizations of
the statistical features of complex networks, and on the other hand by the
formulation of a variety of models able to capture several of the key features
of the data. The modeling effort, in particular, has seen a great contribution from the statistical physics community, that has been ready to lend a
number of computational and analytical skills to the effort of understanding the origin of many of the peculiar features of complex networks. These
contributions are collected in an almost uncountable-countable number of
manuscripts: a simple search in the *condensed matter* section of the on-line
preprint archive (*http://www.arxiv.gov/cond-mat*) in the years 2000–2005
yields a number of papers on complex networks which ranges in the order
of 1000, and which is growing by many units on a weekly basis. Taking into
account that not all the papers on complex networks have been posted on
such a public archive and that a large number of contributions come from
different communities, it becomes evident that it would be impossible to
propose an exhaustive description of all the models for complex networks
presently available in the literature. Among the published material there
are already some good reviews[8–10] and some books[4,11,12] describing in some
detail many network models. Our choice here is rather to give an overview
of the main *classes* of models, that is, those models that embody the main
ingredients that have been used, modified and tinkered with in trying to

develop mathematical schemes able to describe real data in a progressively more detailed way. We prompt the interested reader who is willing to work on networks to refer to the above mentioned reviews and to perform extensive literature searches.

The two principal classes of models that we are going to describe in the following are *static random networks* and *evolving random networks*. Static random networks ought to describe structures where the number of vertices is fixed in time and edges connecting them are assigned according to some probabilistic law once and for all. Whether such networks could describe any real instances is debatable, and yet they clearly represent both a mathematical reference and a tool to create networks satisfying some specific topological properties. Within the class of static random networks we will make unavoidable reference to the forefather of all network models, the celebrated Erdős-Rényi model[13,14] of Random Graphs, and to some recent generalizations. Models for evolving random networks try to capture the very making of the networks and to uncover how the network history sculpts its structure. The ancestor of these models, although still very young, is the Barabási-Albert model,[15] which has spawned countless variations. Some of the clever yet not necessarily realistic ingredients of the Barabási-Albert model can be derived by "first principles" from models based on real observations, such as the Duplication-Divergence model, which plays therefore the double role of a "microscopic" model and of a theoretical basis to reinterpret the Barabási-Albert model. We include the relatively new models for weighted networks in the class of evolving random networks. This is a rather unfair classification, since some static models could legitimately reclaim the "weighted" label for themselves. Yet the newest developments have paid a particular attention on the way weights and topology co-evolve, so that we deem historically more appropriate to deal with weighted networks as a special case of evolving network.

2.2. Random networks

2.2.1. Erdős-Rényi networks

The random network model of Erdős and Rényi[13,14] is perhaps the first model able to coherently describe networks of arbitrary size. The rules to create a graph according to the Erdős-Rényi (ER) prescriptions are simple. The network is a set of N different vertices and E edges joining randomly selected pairs. Since there are $N(N-1)/2$ possible pairs, the number of different realizations of an Erdős-Rényi (ER) network is given by the binomial

$\binom{N(N-1)/2}{E}$, and every network appears with the same probability. An alternative, stochastic, construction can be proposed by letting each edge be present with probability p. The average number of edges over many network realizations is then $\langle E \rangle = \frac{N(N-1)}{2} p$. The relation with an ER network with a specified number of edges E is then fixed by $p = 2E/[N(N-1)]$. For a network of N vertices without self-connections the maximal possible vertex degree is $N - 1$. For stochastic ER networks the probability that a randomly chosen vertex has degree k (that is that only k of its possible edges are present and $N - 1 - k$ are absent) is the binomial distribution

$$P(k) = \binom{N-1}{k} p^k (1-p)^{N-1-k} \tag{4}$$

which is shown in Fig. 7. The average degree is then easily computed as $\langle k \rangle = (N-1)p$, and the clustering coefficient is $c(k) = p$ since it is simply the probability that two nearest neighbors of a vertex of degree k have an edge between them. The average path length l of an ER network, defined as the average over the network of the shortest path lengths between every pair of nodes, grows logarithmically with the number of nodes, $l \sim \ln N$. This can seen by realizing that starting from a given node, the number of nodes that can be reached following its edges is, on the average, $n_1 = \langle k \rangle$. At the following step, the number of new nodes reached is $n_2 = \langle k \rangle n_1$. We assume a negligible probability that a second nearest neighbor had already been counted as a nearest neighbor, which is the case for very large networks with a fixed small $\langle k \rangle$. Iterating the argument it is easy to find that $n_l = \langle k \rangle n_{l-1} = \langle k \rangle^l$, with the hypothesis that cycles are negligible, *i.e.* that all nodes at step l had not been counted before. If we assume that the average path length l and the number of steps needed to find all the N nodes behave in the same way with respect to N, and are numerically close (which is in general true), we then have $n_l = N$. It follows therefore that $l \sim \frac{\ln N}{\ln \langle k \rangle}$ for large networks.

Very large ER networks are composed by a very large number of nodes, $N \to \infty$. Yet it is important that the "local" environment of each node is independent on N, that is, the average degree $\langle k \rangle = (N-1)p$ should not depend on the size of the network. The degree probability distribution for very large networks becomes then the Poisson distribution

$$P(k) = \frac{\langle k \rangle^k}{k!} e^{-\langle k \rangle} \tag{5}$$

which is shown in Fig. 7.

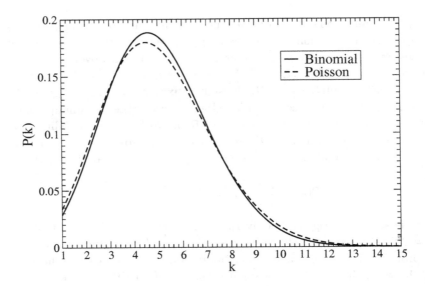

Fig. 7. Binomial and Poisson distributions (Eq. 4 and Eq. 5 respectively) with $p = 5/49$ and $N = 50$ for the Binomial distribution and $\langle k \rangle = 5$ for Poisson distribution.

A binomial (or Poisson) degree distribution is the natural outcome of the binary random process of ER construction. A possible different approach is to use the degree distribution as a starting ingredient, and build a network according to it: given N nodes, their degrees are random numbers taken from a given distribution $P(k)$. The edges are then added by joining pairs of nodes at random until all degrees are satisfied.[16,17] Some special care has to be taken in the construction procedure. First, the sum of all the degrees has to be an even number, since it corresponds to twice the number of edges. Second, if self- and double-edges are forbidden, not all random edge assignments generate legitimate networks, and the procedure must be repeated until all the constraints are fulfilled.

The procedure outlined above, although very effective, has the drawback that it does not allow to change the size of the network during its construction. Indeed, any new vertex added at the end finds no free vertices with which to share edges. The final state of the network is therefore locked. This is at variance with ER networks that, although "static", are yet plastic, in that it is possible to add new nodes at any time, connecting them to already existing ones with probability p.

2.2.2. *Fitness networks*

One simple model that can produce scale-free networks has been proposed by Goh *et al.*[18] In this case to every nodes is assigned an integer index i ($i = 1, \ldots, N$) and a weight $p_i = i^{-\alpha}$, with $0 \leq \alpha < 1$ uniform over the network. Pairs of nodes (i, j) are extracted at random with probabilities proportional, for each node, to its weight, $p_i / \sum_k p_k$ and $p_j / \sum_k p_k$ and they are joined by an edge, unless they already are. A total of mN nodes are added, for an average degree of $2m$. The degree of a node in this model is the number of times it has been picked, which in turn is proportional to its weight. We can therefore write

$$\frac{k_i}{2mN} \simeq \frac{1 - \alpha}{N^{1-\alpha} i^\alpha} \tag{6}$$

from where it is possible, using $P(k)dk = di$, to obtain the degree distribution $P(k) \sim k^{-(1+1/\alpha)}$. The model of Goh *et al* is of particular relevance because it shows that it is possible to generate scale-free networks with arbitrary power-law degree distribution ($2 < 1 + 1/\alpha < \infty$) by using local properties instead of imposing global ones, such as the overall degree distribution.

Recently, Caldarelli *et al*[19] proposed a new model for random networks which naturally produces scale-free networks. Given N vertices, a random variable called "fitness" x_i, $i = 1, \ldots, N$ (taken from an arbitrary probability distribution $q(x)$), is assigned to each of them[c]. An edge is present between two vertices i and j with probability $p \cdot K(x_i, x_j)$. Operatively this is realized by assigning a random variable z_{ij}, uniformly distributed between 0 and 1, to every pair of vertices (i, j). An edge is then present between i and j if $z_{ij} < pK(x_i, x_j)$. The distribution $q(x)$, the probability p and the connection kernel $K(x, y)$ are the shaping ingredients of the networks. A symmetric choice of the kernel, $K(x, y) = K(y, x)$ produces non-directed networks, and in this case the choice $K(x, y) =$ const (const$= 1$ without loss of generality) produces simple ER networks with a governing probability p.

The degree distribution of the network can be computed by finding the relation between the degree k of a vertex and its variable x. On average, it is

$$k(x) = pN \int K(x, y) q(y) dy \tag{7}$$

---

[c]The x_i's have also been called *hidden variables* in some papers.

Networks with a desired degree distribution $P(k)$ can be obtained choosing $q(x) = P(x)$, a given value of p and $K(x_i, x_j) = \frac{x_i x_j}{x_M^2}$ where $x_M = max\{x_1, \ldots, x_N\}$. Equation 7 becomes then

$$k(x) = x \frac{pN\langle x \rangle}{x_M^2} \qquad (8)$$

setting the stage for a simple proportionality between k and x, which also tells that, on average, we can classify vertices either by their degree or by their fitness. Consequently, making use of the relation $P(k)dk = q(x)dx$, we simply find $P(k) = q(k)$. In Fig. 8 we show that a scale-free distribution of exponent $\gamma = 3$ is easily obtained by using $q(x) \propto x^{-3}$. The connection between $q(x)$ and $P(k)$ has been made more formal and it is possible to show, after some straightforward but lengthy calculations, that[20]

$$P(k) = \int_x \frac{e^{-x} x^k}{k!} q(x) dx \ . \qquad (9)$$

Many other exact formulas have been obtained, which allow to use fitness networks to generate networks with a desired degree *and* degree correlation structure.[20,21] Very recently these networks have also been used to derive new approximate expressions for the average path length of random networks, improving pre-existing ones even for the now well-established Erdős-Rényi networks.[22] It is also possible to define *multi-dimensional* fitnesses[23] to take into account more complicated physical situations.

The network is both static and dynamic, since new vertices can be added to the structure at any stage. As new vertices are added to the network, each endowed with its own variable, they are connected with each other and with old ones with probability $pK(x, y)$. If $K(x, y)$ depends on N, as in the case where it depends on x_M, by recording all the z_{ij} values it is easy to decide whether an edge is retained or eliminated as new vertices are added. These networks are therefore the simplest way to generalize ER networks so to obtain networks with pre-set degree distribution. From a mathematical point of view, the choice of the connection kernel $K(x, y)$ and of the variable distribution $q(x)$ can bring to new ways of generating networks with interesting properties, that can be possibly tied to the principles behind some real-world networks.

Note that scale-free networks can arise also from non power-law distributions. A now classical example is given by a fitness exponential distribution $q(x) = e^{-x}$ and a connection kernel $K(x, y) = \theta(x + y - z)$, with z a predetermined threshold. It gives rise to a network with a scale-free degree distribution $P(k) \sim k^{-2}$. As outlined above, the key step to obtain such result is to find the relation between the degree of a vertex and its fitness, that reads

$$k(x) = pN \int_0^\infty e^{-y}\theta(x + y - z)dy = pN \int_{z-x}^\infty e^{-y}dy = pNe^{-z}e^x \quad (10)$$

and using the relation $P(k)dk = q(x)dx$ we finally obtain the desired result $P(k) \sim k^{-2}$ shown in Fig. 8. The threshold mechanism for generating scale-free, or at least heavy-tail distributions is likely to play a role in the appearance of heavy-tail distributions in protein networks, where the fitnesses could represent the propensities for binding ("stickiness") of proteins, capturing some of their physico-chemical properties such as hydrophobicity.[24] Indeed proteins with too many interacting partners are often deleted from the networks being classified as "sticky" and their connections as noninteresting to the goal of protein function prediction.

In a social and technological context, this variables could represent an estimate of some intrinsic property of the vertices such as wealth, quality of facilities (*e.g.*, bandwidth of the connections or speed of the interfaces) and so on. The network would emerge as a consequence of specific connection choices that different vertices take according to the values of their own variables and of the ones of other vertices. Such a mechanism has been proposed to explain the scale-free degree distribution of the Internet at the Autonomous System (AS)[25] level. This takes into account the different sizes of different service providers, that are distributed according to a power-law, as it is often the case in social contexts where it is also known as Zipf's law.[26] Since in these cases and in many other agent based models the establishing of a link is due to the mutual agreement given by the knowledge of the fitness, we prefer the name of fitness with respect to "hidden variables".

The large amount of results that variable networks have allowed in a short time indicate that they are a promising new mathematical framework for random networks.

2.3. *Preferential attachment networks*

Many real networks are not static, but rather they grow and change in time by the addition of new vertices and edges. One of the most successful hypothesis is based on the hypothesis to include the growth of the network by addition of new vertices over time with a connection rule governing the way new vertices establish connections with old ones. The basic properties describing the statistical features of the network topologies can be obtained from dynamical equations of two kinds: master-like equations and *micro-*

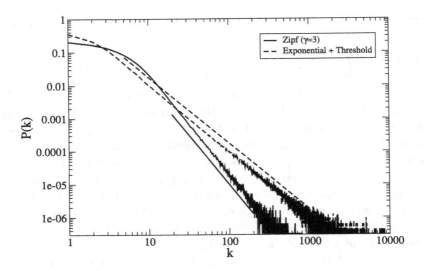

Fig. 8. Degree distribution of a fitness network obtained using (a) the $K(x_i, x_j) = x_i x_j / x_M^2$ connection kernel and $q(x) \propto x^{-3}$ (Zipf distribution) (solid line) and (b) the threshold connection kernel $K(x, y) = \theta(x + y - 9)$, with $q(x) = e^{-x}$ (dashed line). In both cases the networks are made of 10000 nodes and the averages are taken over 1000 realizations. The straight lines (in log-log plot) are power-laws k^{-3} (solid line) and k^{-2} (dashed line).

scopic quantity equations. Master-like equations are functional equations that describe the evolution of some probability distribution. Using the degree distribution as an example, these equations can be written as

$$\frac{dP(k, t)}{dt} = F[\{P(k, t)\}_{k, 1, \infty}] \qquad (11)$$

where $F[\{P(k, t)\}_{k, 1, \infty}]$ is a functional of all the degree probabilities.

Microscopic quantity equations focus rather on the evolution of some specific network property, such as the degree of a specific site i, to infer some general network feature. A typical microscopic quantity equation may read

$$\frac{dk_i}{dt} = \Pi[k_{i=1, N}, t] \qquad (12)$$

where $\Pi[k_{i=1, N}, t]$ is the rate of change of the degree of vertex i as a function of time t and of all the degrees of the N vertices of the network.

Whether one approach or the other is more useful mostly depends on the problem at hand and on the level of detail that is needed in the system description. The next two sections focus on two models for network evolution that have become paradigmatic, namely the Barabási-Albert and the duplication-divergence models.

2.3.1. *The Barabási-Albert model*

Barabási and co-workers,[15,27] have been amongst the first to realize that many real world networks show power-law decreasing degree distributions. They proposed a model that is able to reproduce that feature relying on two simple ingredients: growth and *preferential attachment* (PA). Growth implies that new vertices enter the network at some rate, and PA tells that these new-comers establish their connections preferentially with vertices that already have high degree (*rich-get-richer*).

These two ingredients have, as clear sources of inspiration, the Internet i and the World Wide Web, two networks that have both grown enormously in a relatively short time-span (roughly fifteen years) and where new nodes (routers for the Internet and web-pages for the WWW) tend to connect first with authoritative pre-existing routers and web-pages, where authoritativeness is based on *consensus* and can be weighted by the number of connections.

The mathematical derivation of the degree distribution is easily obtained within the microscopic quantity equation formalism. If new vertices enter the network at a constant rate, and each one makes m connections to pre-existing nodes, the corresponding equation for the degree of site i is

$$\frac{dk_i}{dt} = m\frac{f(k_i)}{\sum_j f(k_j)} \tag{13}$$

where $\frac{f(k_i)}{\sum_j f(k_j)}$ is the probability that a new node entering the network at time t chooses node i as a connection partner for one of its m edges, and $f(k_i)$ is a growing function of k_i in order to capture the PA rule. Equation 13 can be solved only after an explicit expression for $f(k_i)$ has been chosen. The simplest form is $f(k_i) = k_i^\alpha$ with $\alpha \geq 0$, and Eq. 13 becomes

$$\frac{dk_i}{dt} = m\frac{k_i^\alpha}{\sum_j k_j^\alpha} \tag{14}$$

Equation 14 can be simplified by observing that the denominator on its *right hand side (rhs)* grows linearly with t for any $\alpha \in [0,1]$.[28] Indeed, if $\alpha = 0$ it is $\sum_j k_j^0 = \sum_j 1 = m_0 + t$ where m_0 is the number of vertices of the network at time $t = 0$ and the coefficient of time is unitary because time can always be rescaled so that one new node enters the network per unit time. If $\alpha = 1$ it is $\sum_j k_j(t) = A + 2mt$ where $A = \sum_j^{m_0} k_j(0)$ is the sum of the degrees at time $t = 0$ of the vertices present in the network at time $t = 0$; the $2mt$ counts the degrees of all new vertices because every new vertex adds m edges to the network, each of which accounts for an increase of two of the total degree. Given that $\sum_j k_j^\alpha$ is a growing function of both t and α, and that it is linearly bounded in t for both $\alpha = 0$ and $\alpha = 1$, it follows that $\sum_j k_j^\alpha = A(\alpha) + \mu(\alpha)t$ for $0 \le \alpha \le 1$. Equation 14 then becomes

$$\frac{dk_i}{dt} = m\frac{k_i^\alpha}{A(\alpha) + \mu(\alpha)t} \tag{15}$$

whose solution is

$$k_i(t) = \left[m^{1-\alpha} + \frac{(1-\alpha)m}{\mu(\alpha)} \ln\left(\frac{A(\alpha) + \mu(\alpha)t}{A(\alpha) + \mu(\alpha)t_i} \right) \right]^{\frac{1}{1-\alpha}} \tag{16}$$

which has been obtained with the initial condition $k_i(t_i) = m$ where t_i is the time at which vertex i has entered the network. Vertex k_i will henceforth be labeled by means of its entry time t_i rather than by its label i: $k_i(t) = k(t, t_i)$. Importantly, Eq. 16 holds only for $0 \le \alpha < 1$. The distribution of degrees $P(k)$ can be obtained from Eq. 16 by means of

$$P(k) = \frac{1}{t + m_0} \left(\frac{\partial k(t, t_i)}{\partial t_i} \right)^{-1} \Bigg|_{t_i = t_i(k,t)} \tag{17}$$

where $t_i(k, t)$ is the solution of the implicit equation $k = k(t, t_i)$. Using Eq. 16, the Eq. 17 becomes

$$P(k, t) = \frac{A(\alpha) + \mu(\alpha)}{m_0 + t} \frac{1}{m} k^{-\alpha} exp\left\{ -\frac{\mu(\alpha)}{(1-\alpha)m} \left[k^{-(1-\alpha)} - m^{-(1-\alpha)} \right] \right\} \tag{18}$$

which in the $t \to \infty$ limit reaches the stationary state

$$P(k) = \frac{\mu(\alpha)}{m} e^{\frac{\mu(\alpha)}{(1-\alpha)m^\alpha}} k^{-\alpha} e^{-\frac{\mu(\alpha)}{(1-\alpha)m} k^{1-\alpha}} \tag{19}$$

that in turn reduces to a simple exponential for $\alpha = 0$. Solution of Eq. 19 is completely determined by

$$\mu(\alpha) = \frac{1}{t} \sum_i k_i^\alpha(t) = \frac{1}{t} \int_0^t k^\alpha(t, t_i) dt_i \tag{20}$$

which becomes, in the infinite time limit, $\mu(\alpha) = \int_m^\infty k^\alpha P(k) dk$, that is a self-consistent equation for $\mu(\alpha)$, by using (19).

Equation 19 predicts a stretched exponential distribution for any $\alpha < 1$. In the limit $\alpha \to 1$ Eq. 19 becomes $P(k) \sim k^{-3}$. Indeed a full solution of (15) for $\alpha = 1$ gives

$$k(t, t_i) = m \left(\frac{A(1) + 2mt}{A(1) + 2mt_i} \right)^{\frac{1}{2}} \tag{21}$$

from which it can be found, by means of Eq. 17, that $P(k) = 2m^2 k^{-3}$, shown in Fig. 9.

A linear preferential attachment rule ($\alpha = 1$) is therefore the necessary ingredient to find scale-free networks in the Barabási-Albert model. At first sight the exponent $\gamma = 3$ is not satisfactory, since most networks exhibit exponents $2 \le \gamma < 3$ and in some cases even $\gamma > 3$. Yet the good news are that the γ exponent of the Barabási-Albert model is actually sensitive to the details of the preferential attachment rule if $\alpha = 1$. If for example $f(k) = a + k$, with a a constant, the resulting exponent is $\gamma = 3 + a/m$, showing that any exponent $\gamma > 2$ can actually be obtained. The Barabási-Albert model endowed with a linear preferential attachment rule defines therefore a class of scale-free networks of *tunable* degree distribution exponent.

One last comment is necessary for the case $\alpha > 1$. In this case the solution strategy used above is not amenable and it is necessary to use the complete master equation for the probability distribution $P(k, t)$. It is only important to remark here that for $\alpha > 2$ a *winner-take-all* situation emerges, where almost all the vertices of the network are connected to single vertex.[28]

The preferential attachment rule, although simple and nice, poses some problems: new nodes entering the network need to have a complete knowledge of the network in order to make their connection choices. This is unlikely to be realistic, casting a shadow on a direct interpretation of the PA rule. In the next section a different model will be presented, likely to capture some real process behind the formation of the WWW and of protein interaction networks, in which preferential attachment emerges as an effective law from microscopic rules where only a local knowledge of the network is needed.

2.3.2. *Duplication-divergence models*

It has been argued that some networks could be modeled by a growth process where new nodes are generated as copies of older ones. Indeed it has been observed that many existing web-pages in the WWW are often used as

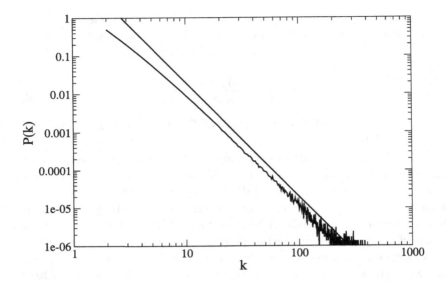

Fig. 9. Degree distribution of a Barabási-Albert model with a linear preferential attachment rule. The distribution is obtained from 100 networks grown for 30000 time steps starting from a core of 5 nodes connected with each other. The value of $m = 2$. The solid line is a power-law k^{-3}.

templates by web-site creators to generate new pages, bringing along their repertoire of hyperlinks.[29,30] The duplication procedure is then followed by some tailoring of the page to suit the interests of the owner of the new page, and as a consequence some old hyperlinks can be lost and some new ones acquired. In the completely different context of protein interaction networks (PIN), the duplication-divergence mechanism fits nicely with the current view of genome evolution.[31,32] As cells divide and organisms reproduce, the duplication of their DNA is accompanied by mutations. Mutations can sometimes entail the complete duplication of a gene. Since in this case the corresponding protein can be produced by two different copies of the same gene, point-like mutations on one of them can accumulate at a rate faster than normal since a weaker selection pressure is applied. Consequently, proteins with new, possibly beneficial, properties can arise by this process. Yet, since new proteins arising by this mechanism still share many *physico-chemical* properties with their ancestors, many of their interactions remain unchanged, with the loss of some old and the acquisition of some new ones. Extensive numerical simulations of such models have shown that the resulting networks are scale-free, or at least heavy-tailed.

The duplication-divergence model is governed by a local rule, where no global knowledge of the network is needed. As such it seems in stark contrast with the preferential attachment mechanism of the Barabási-Albert model. Yet this is not the case. Indeed at every time-step a vertex is chosen at random and its connections are duplicated. Since any vertex can be chosen for duplication, the probability that it is a neighbor of a vertex of degree k is k/N, where N is the number of nodes in the network. Therefore the probability that the degree of a vertex increases by a unit in a time-step is proportional to the degree itself: the preferential attachment rule emerges thus at an effective level from local principles.[33]

A possible formulation of the duplication-divergence model in the context of the World-Wide-Web where edges (hyperlinks) are directed can be given as follows: at every time-step a randomly chosen vertex is duplicated at random. Each of its m out-going connections is either kept with probability $1 - \alpha$ or it is rewired with probability α. The rate of change of the in-degree of a node is then given by

$$\frac{\partial k_{in,i}(t)}{\partial t} = (1 - \alpha)\frac{k_{in,i}(t)}{N} + m\frac{\alpha}{N} \qquad (22)$$

where the first term on the *r.h.s* of Eq. 22 is the probability that a vertex pointing to vertex i is duplicated and its link toward i retained, and the second term on the *r.h.s* represents the probability that the duplicated vertex points toward i by one of its rewired out-going edges. For linearly growing networks is then $N \simeq t$. The solution of Eq. 22 is

$$k_{in,i}(t) = \frac{m\alpha}{1 - \alpha}\left[\left(\frac{t}{t_i}\right)^{1-\alpha} - 1\right] \qquad (23)$$

where t_i is the time when vertex i has entered the network and $k_{in,i}(t_i) = 0$ is the initial condition used to solve Eq. 22. From Eq. 23 it is possible to finally show that $P(k_{in}) \sim [k_{in} + m\alpha/(1 - \alpha)]^{-(2-\alpha)/(1-\alpha)}$.

The case of undirected networks is more complex than the one of directed ones. Indeed, in Eq. 22 the first term on the *r.h.s.* does not change, whereas the second term depends on the degree of the duplicated vertex. Although a rigorous mathematical treatment goes beyond the scope of this chapter, the resulting networks are always characterized by heavy-tail degree distributions, but not necessarily strictly scale-free.[34,35]

P. De Los Rios

2.3.3. *Growing weighted networks*

The BA and DD models neglect the intrinsic relevance of different vertices, that could bias the basic growth rules. At the expense of growth and special dynamical wiring mechanisms, the fitness model tries instead to capture the influence that the properties of individual vertices, described by their variables, have on the structure of the network. Bianconi and Barabási have proposed a model where preferential attachment and fitnesses coexist.[36]

Every node i of the network is assigned a *fitness* $\eta_i > 0$ taken from a probability distribution $\rho(\eta_i)$. The probability that a new node entering the network at time t chooses then node i as a connection partner is given by

$$\Pi_i(t) = \frac{\eta_i k_i(t)}{\sum_j \eta_j k_j(t)} \tag{24}$$

which generalize the preferential attachment rule. The rate equation for the change of the degree of node i is therefore

$$\frac{\partial k_i}{\partial t} = m \frac{\eta_i k_i(t)}{\sum_j \eta_j k_j(t)}. \tag{25}$$

In analogy with the solution of the simpler BA model rate equation, we make the ansatz that the solution can be written as

$$k_i(t, t_0) = m \left(\frac{t}{t_0} \right)^{\beta(\eta_i)} \tag{26}$$

where t_0 is the time at which node i entered the network and $\beta(\eta_i)$ is an exponent possibly dependent on η_i. The ansatz in Eq. 26 has to be eventually verified. The exponent β is bounded in $(0, 1)$ since the degree of a node in general increases, but always less than linearly since it cannot acquire new edges at a rate faster than the one at which new nodes enter the system.

In order to solve Eq. 25, we first need to find an analytical expression for the denominator on its *r.h.s.*. The determination of such a formula is not amenable for a specific realization of the fitness. Therefore we compute its average over many realizations assignments of the η variables:

$$\left\langle \sum_j \eta_j k_j \right\rangle = \int d\eta \rho(\eta) \eta \int_1^t dt_0 k_\eta(t, t_0) = m \int d\eta \rho(\eta) \eta \frac{t - t^{\beta(\eta)}}{1 - \beta(\eta)}. \tag{27}$$

where we labeled nodes according to their entrance time t_0, rather than to their index j.

Since $\beta < 1$, in the limit $t \to \infty$ Eq. 27 reduces to

$$\left\langle \sum_j \eta_j k_j \right\rangle \simeq Cmt \tag{28}$$

where

$$C = \int d\eta \rho(\eta) \frac{\eta}{1 - \beta(\eta)} \qquad (29)$$

Equation 25 becomes finally

$$\frac{\partial k_\eta}{\partial t} = \frac{\eta k_\eta}{Ct} \qquad (30)$$

whose solution is $k_\eta(t, t_0) = m(t/t_0)^{\eta/C}$, consistent with the starting ansatz. The constant C is obtained self consistently using the newly found expression for $\beta(\eta)$ in Eq. 29.

The degree distribution for fixed η can then be found using the usual relation $P(k, \eta)dk = dt_0$, which gives

$$P(k, \eta) \propto \frac{C}{\eta} \left(\frac{m}{k} \right)^{1 + \frac{C}{\eta}} \qquad (31)$$

from which the global degree distribution $P(k)$ can be obtained as $P(k) = \int \rho(\eta) P(k, \eta) d\eta$.

A choice of a constant η, that is $\rho(\eta) = \delta(\eta - \eta_0)$ clearly corresponds to the BA model and gives $P(k) \sim k^{-3}$, as already derived. A power-law degree distribution can also be obtained from a uniform distribution $\rho(\eta) = 1$, $0 < \eta < 1$. Indeed Eq. 29 becomes

$$C = C \int_0^1 d\eta \frac{1}{C/\eta - 1} = -C^2 \left[\ln \left(1 - \frac{1}{C} \right) + \frac{1}{C} \right] \qquad (32)$$

whose solution, obtained numerically, is $C = 1.255$ (and $C > 1$, as needed to avoid singularities in Eq. 29), and $P(k) \propto k^{-(1+C)}/\ln(k)$, that is, scale-free with a logarithmic correction.

Different choices of $\rho(\eta)$ give different degree distributions, not necessarily scale-free (for example, an exponential distribution of η results in a stretched exponential degree distribution). The main message of this model is thus that the precise *real* fitness distribution has to be known if modeling tries to capture the real mechanism of formation of a given network.

It has been shown that the weighted BA model of Bianconi and Barabási[36] allows for very interesting formal connections between the theory of growing networks and more traditional quantum Bose-Einstein statistics.[37] Moreover, some modifications have been proposed where the choice of the connection partners depend both on their degrees and fitness, and on the fitness of the entering node,[38] further showing the sensitivity of these models to the details.

Actually, more recently new models for growing weighted networks have been proposed, where the weights co-evolve with the network structure, yielding results in qualitative agreement with what is observed in real data, in the few cases where weights are known well enough to allow a comparison (the scientific collaboration networks and the world airport network). In these cases weights are also distributed according to power-laws, a strong signature of the dynamical nature of their formation.[39,40]

2.4. *The small-world model*

It is important to give a brief description of the properties of small-world networks and of how they emerge because, although small-world networks are not in general scale-free, many scale-free networks are small-worlds.

Before entering the mathematical details, it is appropriate to recall that the "small-world" property originally refers to the "six degrees of separation" effect in social networks, that is, the surprisingly small average number of acquaintances that are necessary to connect two arbitrary individuals: although societies are pretty well connected on the local geographic and social scale, they also posses some *shortcuts* that allow to readily probe environments that are much farther away.

Mathematically, the small-world effect describes those graphs whose diameter and average path length grow much more slowly than the number of nodes N, typically as $\ln N$, just as in a random, ER, graph. Yet a random graph has a very small local interconnectedness, captured by the clustering coefficient. Watts and Strogatz realized that the good local interconnectedness is typical of regular lattices, whereas ER graphs provide the short distance, and proposed as a consequence an interpolating scheme between the two network classes.[6]

In the Watts-Strogatz small-world model a $d-$dimensional hyper-cubic lattice is augmented by adding new edges to second, third and farther neighbors, up to the $n_t h$ level. All of them become now first neighbours as shown in Fig. 10

These graphs are still regular lattices with an average path length growing as $N^{1/d}$, are are not yet small-world graphs. This second property is gained by adding some degree of randomness by the addition of a few long range edges: each node of the network can establish, with probability p, a long-range connection with a random node of the graph. This new connection can be accompanied by the simultaneous deletion of one local edge, or can be just added. As long as p is small, a condition perfectly compatible

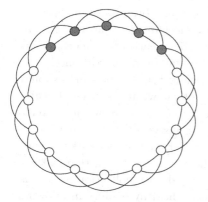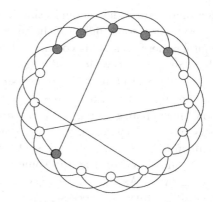

Fig. 10. (Left) A regular one-dimensional lattice with extra links increasing the local connectivity. (Right) the same lattice with shortcuts. In both figures the grey vertices indicate the neighbours of the vertex up in the centre.

with the small-world property, the two alternatives give the same results.

Watts and Strogatz surprisingly found that even very small values of p are sufficient to reduce dramatically the diameter of the network. Using numerical simulation it has been shown that a one dimensional lattice with $N = 1000$ vertices, local connections up to the fifth neighbor and a rewiring probability $p = 1/4$ has diameter 3.6. with no rewiring at all the diameter of the same system is 50. Even with p as small as $1/64$ one still finds a small diameter 7.6. At the same time the clustering coefficient for very small values of the rewiring probability does not change significantly from the one of regular lattices: a few rewired connections are enough to endow the network with both the local connectedness and the short global distance expected to explain the six-degrees-of-separation effect.

As mentioned at the beginning of this section many scale-free networks are also small-world graphs: the average path length and the clustering coefficient of the network are compared with the same quantities calculated over random graphs with the same number of nodes and vertices. If the average path lengths are of the same order but the clustering coefficient of the scale-free network is at least one order of magnitude larger than the one for random graphs, then the scale-free network is also a small-world.

2.5. *Outlook*

In time, we believe that the growth of available data on real networks, and their reliability, will allow a better modelling effort. At the same time new and old models should stimulate the people obtaining real data, to try and shed some light on the microscopic mechanisms that shape large complex networks. This could validate the various theoretical mechanisms that, although very nice and elegant, could be far from the real ones.

Moreover, the distinction between the various types of networks should not be considered a draconian one: we do not know, at the present state, how much real growing networks are also ruled by some of the ingredients of static networks, nor how much static networks, that can form in real time under our very eyes such as protein interaction networks, do not carry, imprinted on them in some ways, their own evolution, that is their own growth. As such we see the theoretical and data-collection efforts as complementary and necessary for each other's healthy evolution, allowing complex network research to join all other scientific research endeavors.

Being exhaustive in the description of network models would have been impossible, due to their large number present in the literature; choosing very specific models among the very many would have been probably unfair to the others. Our choice has been therefore to concentrate on those models that have become *scaffolds* for subsequent ones.

Therefore we apologize with the very many people whose contributions to the developments of network models has not been duly acknowledged in this chapter, but we are confident that interested readers will find the proper route to their works starting from the bibliographical selection that we have made. Hopefully, this fast overview of models is instructive enough to allow the reader to reapply to other models, *mutatis mutandis*, the same concepts and techniques that have been described here.

CHAPTER 3

Correlations in Complex Networks

M. Ángeles Serrano[1], Marián Boguñá[2], Romualdo Pastor-Satorras[3] and
Alessandro Vespignani[1]

[1] *School of Informatics and Biocomplexity Institute, Indiana University,
Eigenmann Hall, 1900 East Tenth Street, Bloomington, IN 47406, USA*

[2] *Departament de Física Fonamental, Universitat de Barcelona,
Martí i Franquès 1, 08028 Barcelona, Spain*

[3] *Departament de Física i Enginyeria Nuclear, Universitat Politècnica de
Catalunya, Campus Nord B4, 08034 Barcelona, Spain*

3.1. *Introduction*

Most real networks exhibit the presence of non trivial correlations in their
connectivity pattern. Indeed, empirical measurements bring evidence to the
fact that, in some instances, high or low degree vertices of the network tend
to preferentially connect to other vertices with similar degree. In this situation, correlations are named *assortative* and are typically observed in social
networks.[41] On the other hand, connections in many technological and biological networks[42] attach vertices of very different degree with stronger
likelihood. Correlations are in this case referred to as *disassortative*. The
overall origin of the appearance of these correlations is not yet completely
understood, neither is the reason for the distinction in real systems between
assortative and disassortative behavior. Correlations, however, drastically
impact the topological properties of networks, encoding the blueprint of
structural organization and are customarily used as a method to classify
real nets. Moreover, correlations do not only have a topological relevance
but may impact a variety of related problems such as percolation phenomena, resilience and robustness, spreading processes, or communication
efficiency, to name just a few. For these reasons, several strategies have been
proposed to model correlated networks. The most general practical algo-

rithms allow the construction of networks matching any desired correlation pattern. Other just generate correlations of a fixed signature.

In the following sections, we will focus on the characterization and modeling of correlations in undirected unweighted complex networks. In particular, we will devote our attention to the statistical characterization of these features in large scale networks. In the section, we review some important and useful general analytical results concerning the topological characterization of random networks. In the third section we recall a number of specific metrics. In particular, two vertices correlations will be characterized by the average degree of nearest neighbors as a function of the vertex degree, $\bar{k}_{nn}(k)$, and correlations among three vertices will be described by several clustering measures, in particular the average clustering coefficient for vertices of a given degree $\bar{c}(k)$. Real networks are discussed in the fourth section, where we present some well-known and representative examples of correlated structures, such as the science collaboration network of physicists submitting papers to a preprint database, the Pretty-Good-Privacy web of trust between users of digital communications, the world-wide air transportation network (all of them assortative), and the Internet at the Autonomous System level, the protein interaction network of the yeast *S. Cerevisiae*, and the world trade web of commercial exchanges between countries in the world (all of them disassortative). Finally, recent developments in the modeling of correlated networks will be discussed in the fifth section. We distinguish between disassortative correlations, derived as an implicit consequence from the formulation of some classical models, and assortative correlations which should be specifically introduced in theoretical constructions. Several more general and rigorous frameworks able to reconstruct a wide range of correlation patterns are also presented. Finally, we conclude by providing an outlook on current and future developments.

3.2. *Detailed balance condition*

Although several possibilities could be considered, the conditional probabilities $P(k', k'', \ldots, k^{(n)} \,|\, k)$ that a vertex of degree k is simultaneously connected to a number n of other vertices with corresponding degrees $k', k'', \ldots, k^{(n)}$ might be the simplest theoretical functions that encode degree correlation information from a local perspective. A network is said to be uncorrelated when the conditionality on k does not apply and, therefore, the only relevant function is just the degree distribution $P(k)$. Otherwise, $P(k)$ cannot be considered in isolation and degree correlations must be taken into account through the conditional probability functions up to the pertinent order. In particular, two vertices and three vertices degree correlations are respectively encoded by the conditional probabilities $P(k' \mid k)$ and $P(k', k'' \mid k)$.

Due to the fact that edges join pairs of nodes, the key functions at the lowest level are $P(k)$ and $P(k' \mid k)$. Theoretically, they can have any form with only two constraints. First, they must be normalized, i.e.

$$\sum_k P(k) = \sum_{k'} P(k' \mid k) = 1. \tag{33}$$

Second, all edges must point from one vertex to another, so that no edges with dangling ends exist in the network. Thus, the total number of edges pointing from vertices of degree k to vertices of degree k' must be equal to the number of edges that point from vertices of degree k' to vertices of degree k. In other words, these functions must obey a degree detailed balance condition:[43]

$$kP(k'|k)P(k) = k'P(k|k')P(k'), \tag{34}$$

stating the closure of the network through the physical conservation of edges among vertices. To prove this condition, we will follow an intuitive derivation.[44]

Let N_k be the number of vertices of degree k, so that $\sum_k N_k = N$, where N is the total number of nodes in the network. In the thermodynamic limit, we can calculate the degree distribution as a frequency distribution[d], that is,

$$P(k) \equiv \lim_{N \to \infty} \frac{N_k}{N}. \tag{35}$$

Additionally, to complete the topological characterization of the network, we need also to specify how the different degree classes are connected to each other. To this end, let us consider the symmetric matrix $E_{kk'}$ accounting for the total number of edges between vertices of degree k and vertices of degree k' for $k \neq k'$. The diagonal values E_{kk} are equal to two times the number of connections between vertices in the same degree class, $k = k'$. This matrix meets the following identities:

$$\sum_{k'} E_{kk'} = kN_k, \tag{36}$$

$$\sum_{k,k'} E_{kk'} = \langle k \rangle N = 2E, \tag{37}$$

---

[d]For the sake of simplicity, in what follows we will obviate the limit.

where $\langle k \rangle$ is the average degree and E is the total number of edges in the network. The first identity simply states that the total number of edges emanating from vertices of degree k is k times the number of vertices in this degree class. The second identity just states that the sum of the degrees of all nodes in the network is equal to two times the number of edges.

The first identity allows to write the conditional probability as

$$P(k' \mid k) = \frac{E_{k'k}}{kN_k}. \tag{38}$$

On the other hand, from the second identity we can define the joint degree distribution as

$$P(k, k') = \frac{E_{kk'}}{\langle k \rangle N}, \tag{39}$$

where the symmetric function $(2 - \delta_{k,k'})P(k, k')$ is equal to the probability that a randomly chosen edge connects two vertices of degrees k and k'. The conditional probability can be easily related to the joint degree distribution, namely

$$P(k' \mid k) = \frac{\langle k \rangle P(k, k')}{kP(k)}. \tag{40}$$

The symmetry of $P(k, k')$ leads directly from the previous equation to the detailed balance condition:

$$kP(k' \mid k)P(k) = k'P(k \mid k')P(k') = \langle k \rangle P(k, k'). \tag{41}$$

The pre-factors k and k' in this equation account for the multiplicative nature of networks as random processes and the whole relation stands as the closure condition for networks with no detached edge ends and with no isolated vertices. On the technical side, the detailed balance condition constraints the possible form of the conditional probability $P(k' \mid k)$ once $P(k)$ is given, and vice versa.

Making use of this important relation and the normalization condition, $P(k)$ can also be written as a function of the joint degree distribution[e]:

$$P(k) = \frac{\langle k \rangle}{k} \sum_{k'} P(k, k'). \tag{42}$$

Among all the networks one can consider, Markovian networks are particularly important.[43] This class of network is completely defined by its

---

[e]Notice that this relation excludes vertices of degree 0, which are never considered in real complex networks.

degree distribution $P(k)$ and the first conditional probability $P(k'|k)$. In other words, such networks belong to a statistical ensemble which is maximally random under the constraint of having a given degree distribution and a given first conditional probability. In this case, the joint distribution $P(k, k')$ conveys all the relevant topological information since both $P(k)$ and $P(k'|k)$ can be derived from it. In turn, all higher-order correlations can also be expressed as a function of these fundamental functions. In particular, the three vertices conditional probability can be written as $P(k', k''|k) = P(k'|k)P(k''|k)$ and the same applies to higher order correlation functions.

The meaning of the term Markovian network that we use in this chapter is borrowed from the theory of Stochastic Processes. In this field, a stochastic process $X(t)$ is called Markovian if the probability to find the process at the position $X(t) = x$ at time t only depends on its position at the previous time $t' < t$. Then, the process is completely characterized by the probability density function $p(x, t)$ of being at x at time t and the transition probability density $p(x, t|x', t')$ of being at x at time t, provided that the process was at x' at time t'. If we identify $P(k)$ with $p(x, t)$ and $P(k'|k)$ with $p(x, t|x', t')$, we can define Markovian networks in a similar manner. One can force even more the analogy and find another connection between Markovian networks and Markovian stochastic processes. Suppose, for instance, a particle that randomly diffuses through the network, uniformly choosing at each time step one of its neighbors to continue its walk. If the underlying network is Markovian, the stochastic process constructed from the sequence of degrees of the visited vertices follows a Markovian jump process with a transition probability given by $P(k|k')$ and a steady state distribution given by $kP(k)/\langle k \rangle$. Notice that the meaning of Markovian network should not be confused with the notion of *Markov graph*.[45]

3.3. *Empirical measurement of correlations*

At the level of two vertices degree correlations, the most straightforward measure consists in a direct inspection of the two-dimensional histograms of the joint degree distribution $P(k', k)$[46,47] or the conditional probability $P(k' \,|\, k)$. However, such histograms in finite size systems are highly affected by statistical fluctuations and are thus not good candidates to evaluate empirical correlations. In order to characterize degree correlations, it is then more convenient to adopt other standards, which nevertheless will eventually depend on these functions. A most useful approach consists in defining a one-parameter function encoding the signature of correlations. In the case of two vertices correlations, such function is defined as the average nearest neighbors degree (ANND) of nodes with degree k, $\bar{k}_{nn}(k)$.[48] It considers the mean degree of the neighbors of a vertex as a function of its degree k. When this function increases with k, the network is named assortative, with vertices associating preferentially to other vertices of similar degree. When $\bar{k}_{nn}(k)$ instead decreases, the network is named disassortative, with high-degree vertices attaching preferentially to other low-degree ones. Hence, this is a representation which gives a clear interpretation of pair correlations and at the same time can provide further information about hierarchical organization in networks. Finally, the scalar Pearson correlation coefficient of the degrees of vertices at the ends of edges is used to summarize the level of correlation with a single number[f].[41,42]

Despite the increasing attention in the literature about the measurement of $P(k', k)$, the first correlation observable appearing in the literature is the network transitivity or clustering coefficient,[6,7] a scalar which quantifies the probability that two vertices with a common neighbor are also connected to each other. This concept has its roots in sociology and, in the language of social networks, it measures the likelihood that the friend of your friend is also your friend. Therefore, it is in fact a measure of three vertices correlations although, curiously, it is among the first studied structural properties of networks, together with the small-world effect or the degree distribution. This definition and other alternatives[49,50] have been broadly used to quantify in a statistical sense the deviation of real networks, strongly clustered, from the behavior of classical random graphs.

Since clustering measures triangles in a network, it seems also natural to pose the question of how to measure higher order loops (closed paths). This issue is particularly important in order to asses if a network can be assumed to be Markovian, since, in this case, the loop structure must be very well described by the two vertices correlations. A number of authors have paid attention to loops of length four and above. However, there are technical difficulties when one tries to separate the independent contributions of the different motifs.[51–55] This is the main reason why triangles –and not higher order loops– have been chosen as a measure of correlations.

In this section we will concentrate on the broadly accepted and used statistical correlation observables in the analysis of large scale networks,

---

[f]The Pearson coefficient is computed as the correlation coefficient of the joint distribution $P(k, k')$.

the average nearest neighbors degree and the degree dependent clustering coefficient, focusing on their theoretical grounds and significance.

3.3.1. *Two vertices correlations: ANND*

The average nearest neighbors degree, $\bar{k}_{nn}(k)$, of vertices of degree k is defined as a smoothed conditional probability:[48]

$$\bar{k}_{nn}(k) = \sum_{k'} k' P(k' \mid k), \qquad (43)$$

so that the statistical fluctuations that usually disturb the evaluation of $P(k' \mid k)$ are damped.

Real networks usually tend to display one of two different patterns: either $\bar{k}_{nn}(k)$ is a monotonous increasing function of k or, on the contrary, it is a monotonous decreasing function of k. At the level of correlation properties, this segregation allows the classification of networks based on their ANND behavior:[41]

- Assortative networks exhibit $\bar{k}_{nn}(k)$ functions increasing with k, which denotes that vertices are preferentially connected to other vertices with similar degree. Examples of assortative behavior are typically found in many social structures.
- Disassortative networks exhibit $\bar{k}_{nn}(k)$ functions decreasing with k, which implies that vertices are preferentially connected to other vertices with very different degree. Examples of disassortative behavior are typically found in several technological networks, as well as in communication and biological networks.

This measure provides a sharp evidence for the presence or absence of correlations since, in the case of uncorrelated networks, it is easy to demonstrate that this quantity should not depend on k. In fact, the uncorrelated ANND value is found to coincide with the heuristic parameter $\kappa = \langle k^2 \rangle / \langle k \rangle$, independently introduced to characterize the level of heterogeneity of networks.[12] For homogeneous networks $\kappa \sim \langle k \rangle$, whereas for scale-free (SF) networks with unbounded degree fluctuations it diverges in the thermodynamic limit. As a consequence, it comes to be a key parameter characterizing the properties of networks and the processes running on top of them.

Here, we deduce $\bar{k}_{nn}^{unc}(k)$ from the detailed balance and the normalization conditions. Summing Eq. 41 over k and recalling that $P^{unc}(k'|k)$ does not depend on this variable, we obtain that

$$P^{unc}(k'|k) = \frac{k'P(k')}{\langle k \rangle}, \tag{44}$$

from where we have

$$\bar{k}_{nn}^{unc}(k) = \frac{\langle k^2 \rangle}{\langle k \rangle}. \tag{45}$$

Therefore, a function $\bar{k}_{nn}(k)$ showing any explicit dependence on k signals the presence of degree correlations in the system.

As in the case of uncorrelated networks, it is also possible to derive some general exact results concerning the behavior of $\bar{k}_{nn}(k)$ in the case of SF networks with a degree distribution of the form $P(k) \sim k^{-\gamma}$ for $k \in [1, k_c]$. The cut-off value k_c is a consequence of the finiteness of the network and diverges in the thermodynamic limit.[56] The specific dependency of k_c on N depends, in general, on the details of the model. Let once again exploit the detailed balance and the normalization conditions. By multiplying by a k factor both terms of Eq. 41 and summing over k' and k up to k_c, we obtain

$$\langle k^2 \rangle = \sum_{k'} k'P(k') \sum_{k}^{k_c} kP(k \mid k') = \sum_{k'} k'P(k')\bar{k}_{nn}(k', k_c), \tag{46}$$

where we have made explicit the dependence on k_c. In scale-free networks with exponent $2 < \gamma < 3$ the second moment of the degree distribution diverges as $\langle k^2 \rangle \sim k_c^{3-\gamma}$, and therefore

$$\sum_{k'} k'P(k')\bar{k}_{nn}(k', k_c) \sim \frac{A}{3 - \gamma} k_c^{3-\gamma}, \tag{47}$$

where A is a constant pre-factor depending on the details of $P(k)$. As a consequence, the left hand side of this equation must bear divergences[g].

In the case of disassortative correlations, the divergence should just be contained in the k_c dependence of $\bar{k}_{nn}(k', k_c)$, since $\bar{k}_{nn}(k', k_c)$ is decreasing in k' and furthermore $k'P(k')$ is an integrable function.

When correlations are assortative, however, there may be singularities associated with the sum over k' depending on the rate of growth of the increasing $\bar{k}_{nn}(k', k_c)$. Nevertheless, it can be demonstrated that, even for strong growth rates, the divergence associated to the explicit k_c dependence is predominant.[56]

---

[g]For $\gamma = 3$ the arguments are still valid although more involved.

Therefore, one can conclude, just from the detailed balance and the normalization conditions, that in SF networks with $2 < \gamma \leq 3$ the function $\bar{k}_{nn}(k', k_c)$ must diverge when $k_c \to \infty$ in a nonzero measure set, regardless of the character and level of the correlations present in the network. This fact is, for instance, fundamental in determining the properties of epidemic spreading processes in correlated scale-free networks.[56]

From a practical point of view, when studying real SF networks, one can always take advantage of the fact that the divergence of the function ANND is independent of the underlying correlation structure, so that $\bar{k}_{nn}(k)$ can be always normalized by the uncorrelated value $\bar{k}_{nn}(k)_{unc} = \frac{\langle k^2 \rangle}{\langle k \rangle}$. This finite size correction makes comparable the ANND functions of different real networks.

As we have mentioned at the beginning of this section, it is also possible to obtain information on the nature of two vertices correlations by examining a single scalar quantity, the Pearson correlation coefficient of the degrees of the vertices at the end of edges.[41] The Pearson coefficient r can be defined as follows:

$$r = \frac{\langle kk' \rangle_e - \langle k \rangle_e^2}{\langle k^2 \rangle_e - \langle k \rangle_e^2},\tag{48}$$

where $\langle kk' \rangle_e$ is the average of the product the degrees at the end points of all edges and $\langle k^n \rangle_e$ is the average of the n-th power of the degree at the end of any edge[h]. These averages can be expressed in terms of the joint degree distribution as

$$\langle kk' \rangle_e = \sum_{kk'} kk' P(k, k'),\tag{49}$$

$$\langle k^n \rangle_e = \sum_{kk'} \frac{k^n + k'^n}{2} P(k, k').\tag{50}$$

Using the detailed balance condition Eq. 41, we obtain the following relation between the Pearson coefficient and the ANND function

$$r = \frac{\langle k \rangle \sum_k k^2 \bar{k}_{nn}(k) P(k) - \langle k^2 \rangle^2}{\langle k \rangle \langle k^3 \rangle - \langle k^2 \rangle^2}\tag{51}$$

---

[h]In the original definition,[41] r was defined in terms of the averages of the excess degree, that is, discounting the connection from the considered edge. It is easy to see, however, that both definitions yield the same result.

For uncorrelated networks, with $\bar{k}_{nn}^{unc}(k) = \langle k^2 \rangle / \langle k \rangle$, we obtain $r = 0$, while $r < 0$ ($r > 0$) is interpreted as a signature of dissasortative (assortative) two vertices correlations. While the Pearson coefficient can be useful to give a single value measure of the character of correlations, its efficiency suffers from some drawbacks as compared with the ANND function. On the one hand, it misses the possible hierarchical structure of correlations that is explicitly evident in the k dependence of the ANND. On the other hand, for SF networks it strongly depends on the size of the network. To see this, consider a dissasortative SF network with $2 < \gamma < 3$ and degree cut-off k_c. In this case, we have $\langle k^n \rangle \sim k_c^{n+1-\gamma}$. Since the network is dissasortative, $r < 0$ and we have $\langle k \rangle \sum_k k^2 \bar{k}_{nn}(k) P(k) < \langle k^2 \rangle^2$, so at leading order

$$|r| \sim \frac{\langle k^2 \rangle^2}{\langle k^3 \rangle} \sim k_c^{2-\gamma}, \qquad (52)$$

which tends to zero in the thermodynamic limit for $2 < \gamma \leq 3$. This indicates that one has to be very cautious when drawing conclusions about the nature of correlations in SF networks based only on the information provided by the Pearson coefficient.

To finish this section, we discuss another consideration that must be taken into account, and which refers to the distinction between the purely uncorrelated case and the maximally random case achievable when respecting the degree distribution. It turns out that completely uncorrelated networks are not always feasible due to architectural constraints. Given a certain degree distribution $P(k)$, finite size effects could condition in some cases the closure of the network to either the presence of multiple and self-connections or disassortative two vertices correlations.[84-86] Bounded degree distributions, in which $\langle k^2 \rangle$ is finite, present maximum degree values k_c below or around a structural cut-off k_s, so that physical networks can indeed be constructed as uncorrelated. However, when dealing with unbounded degree distributions and diverging fluctuations in the infinite network size limit (for instance, scale-free degree distributions with $2 < \gamma < 3$ as observed in many real systems), $k_c > k_s$ and then structural correlations are important and cannot be avoided. In that case, one can just consider the maximally random network with a given degree distribution $P(k)$. For bounded degree distributions with actual cut-offs below the structural one, the maximally random network will indeed correspond to the uncorrelated case. However, for unbounded degree distributions with divergent second moment and actual cut-off well above the structural one, the closure of the maximally random network forces the conservation of structural correlations. Whereas correlation measures provide information about the overall presence of correlations in the network, the comparison with the maximally random case discounts the structural effects, so that physical correlations can be detected.

3.3.2. *Three vertices correlations: Clustering*

Correlations among three vertices can be measured by means of the conditional probability $P(k', k'' \mid k)$ that a vertex of degree k is simultaneously connected to two vertices with degrees k' and k''. Only in the case of Markovian networks, this function can be expressed in terms of two vertices correlations through the relation $P(k', k'' \mid k) = P(k' \mid k)P(k'' \mid k)$.

As previously indicated, the conditional probabilities $P(k', k'' \mid k)$ or $P(k'' \mid k)$ are difficult to estimate directly from real data, so other assessments have been proposed. All of them are based in the concept of clustering, which refers to the tendency to form triangles (loops of length 3) in the neighborhood of any given vertex.

The clustering in a network quantifies the likelihood that vertex j is connected to vertex l, if vertices j and l are simultaneously connected to vertex i. Watts and Strogatz originally proposed a scalar local measure for clustering, which is known as the clustering coefficient.[6] It is computed for every vertex i as the ratio of the number of edges e_i existing between the k_i neighbors of i and the maximum possible value, i.e.:

$$c_i = \frac{2e_i}{k_i(k_i - 1)}. \tag{53}$$

The clustering coefficient of the whole network C is then defined as the average of all individual c_i's, $C = \sum_i c_i/N$. Watts and Strogatz also pointed out that real networks display a level of clustering typically much larger than the value for a classical random network of the same size, $C_{rand} = \langle k \rangle / N$.

The clustering coefficient has been redefined in a number of ways, for instance as a function of triples in the network (triples are defined as subgraphs which contain exactly three nodes) and reversing the order of average and division in Eq. 53:[49,57]

$$C_\triangle = \frac{3 \times \text{number fully connected triples}}{\text{number triples}}. \tag{54}$$

This definition corresponds to the concept of the fraction of transitive triples introduced in sociology long time ago.[7]

Although overall scalar measures are helpful as a first indication of clustering, it is always more informative to work with quantities which explicitly depend on the degree. As in the case of two vertices correlations, an uniparametric function $\bar{c}(k)^{50}$ can also be computed. In practice, the degree-dependent local clustering $\bar{c}(k)$ is calculated as the clustering coefficient averaged for each degree class k. Formally, it is defined as the probability that two vertices, neighbors of a vertex of degree k, are linked to each other. Hence, it can be written as a function of the three vertices correlations:

$$\bar{c}(k) = \sum_{k',k''} P(k',k'' \mid k) r_{k'k''}(k),$$ (55)

where $r_{k'k''}(k)$ is the probability that the vertices of degree k' and degree k'' are connected given that they both are neighbors of the same vertex of degree k. The corresponding scalar measure is the mean clustering coefficient

$$\bar{c} = \sum_{k} P(k)\bar{c}(k),$$ (56)

which is related to the clustering coefficient by[i]:

$$C = \frac{\bar{c}}{1 - P(0) - P(1)}.$$ (57)

For Markovian networks, $\bar{c}(k)$ can be expressed as a function of the two vertices degree correlations, giving the asymptotic expression:[58,59]

$$\bar{c}(k) = \frac{\langle k \rangle^3}{Nk^2 P^2(k)} \sum_{k',k''>1} \frac{(k''-1)(k'-1)P(k'',k')P(k'',k)P(k',k)}{k'k'' P(k')P(k'')}.$$ (58)

In the case of uncorrelated networks, $\bar{c}(k)$ is independent of k. Furthermore, all the measures collapse and reduce to C.[58,60,61]

$$\bar{c}(k) = C = C_\Delta = \frac{1}{N} \frac{(\langle k^2 \rangle - \langle k \rangle)^2}{\langle k \rangle^3}.$$ (59)

Therefore, a functional dependence of the local clustering on the degree can be attributed to the presence of a complex structure in the three vertex correlation pattern. Indeed, it has been observed that $\bar{c}(k)$ exhibits a power-law behavior $\bar{c}(k) \sim k^{-\alpha}$ for several real scale-free networks. Hence, $\bar{c}(k)$ has been proposed as a measure of hierarchical organization and modularity in complex networks.[62]

---

[i]Notice that we have implicitly assumed that $\bar{c}(0) = \bar{c}(1) = 0$ whereas in the definition of C we only consider an average over the set of vertices with degree $k > 1$. This fact explains the difference between both measures.

3.4. *Networks in the real world*

Degree correlations are ubiquitous in real networks, denoting the presence of structural organization and hierarchy. Usually, empirical networks show a highly clustered architecture and two vertices correlations are present as well, which demonstrates that nodes in networks do not mix randomly. What is more, among a number of theoretical possibilities, pair correlations commonly display one out of only two well-defined mixing patterns. As discussed, this observation has led to the segregation of most real networks into two universality classes, assortative and disassortative, depending on whether their ANND function is an increasing or a decreasing function of k, respectively.

Empirical networks are often classified in several loose general categories as well, and within a given class most networks are found to display the same type of correlations.[42] Indeed, among other specific features, many social networks are assortative,[41,63,64] such as, for instance, company director networks,[65] co-authorship and collaboration networks,[66–68] or the network of email address books.[69] On the contrary, most biological networks (protein-protein interaction network in the yeast cell,[70] metabolic networks in bacteria,[71] food webs[72]) or technological networks (the Internet at the Autonomous System level,[12] the network of hyperlinks between pages in the World Wide Web,[73] *etc.*) appear to be disassortative. In some cases, it is difficult, if not impossible, to classify real networks into single categories, especially for systems related to human action or when functionality is also taken into account. Since different sets of classification criteria can be defined, and although in some cases classifications are unquestionable, here we prefer to treat specific examples instead of whole categories in order to avoid any potential conflict. Next, we will examine the details concerning correlations of a number of well-known and representative real networks.

Protein interaction networks

Biological structures are among the most complex systems that can be represented as networks, and simplified models turn out to be very useful to understand how they organize and evolve. Cells themselves are very intricate systems comprising millions of molecules acting in a coherent manner as open systems exchanging matter, energy and information with the environment. Therefore, the cellular network, albeit one, is commonly reduced to three different sub-webs: the metabolome, or the ensemble of all metabolites and the reactions that they enter, the genome, or the set of all genes

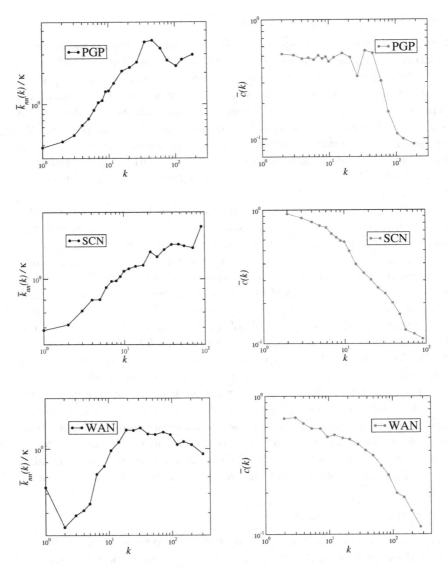

Fig. 11. Assortative real networks. The average nearest-neighbor degree is shown in the column on the left scaled by the heterogeneity parameter κ. The column on the right exhibits the clustering coefficient as a function of the vertex degree. PGP is the Pretty-Good-Privacy web of trust between users of digital communications, SCN stands for the scientific collaboration network of researchers co-authoring academic papers in the cond-mat e-Print archive, and WAN is the world-wide airport transportation network. For the data publicly available visit the site http://www.cosin.org.

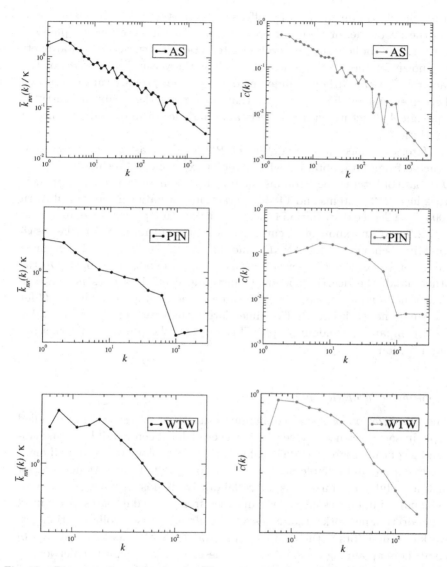

Fig. 12. Disassortative real networks. The average nearest-neighbor degree is shown in the column on the left scaled by the heterogeneity parameter κ. The column on the right exhibits the clustering coefficient as a function of the vertex degree. AS stands for the Internet map at the Autonomous System level, PIN is the protein interaction network of the yeast *S. Cerevisiae*, and WTW is the world trade web of commercial exchanges between countries in the world. For the data publicly available visit the site http://www.cosin.org.

in a cell which can interact by affecting each other's level of expression, and the proteome, or group of proteins and their interactions by physical contact. Metabolic webs and protein interactions networks (PINs) are better known for the most simple cells, such as the yeast *S. Cerevisiae* or the bacteria *E. Coli.* Although different data sets can provide varying results, there is enough evidence to ensure that these networks exhibit a nontrivial topological structure with a statistical abundance of hubs and presence of correlations.

Here, we inspect in more detail the PIN of the yeast *S. Cerevisiae* constructed from data, obtained with different experimental techniques, at the Database of Interacting Proteins (http://dip.doe-mbi.ucla.edu).[74] The network has 4713 proteins and 14846 interactions for data collected until April 2003. The degree distribution is heavy tailed, with a power-law of exponent $\gamma \simeq 2.5$ and an exponential cut-off. A signature of hierarchy is the disassortative behavior of its ANND function, as shown in Fig. 12. For most values of k the decay is power-law like with an exponent ~ 0.24. On the other hand, the degree-dependent clustering coefficient does not show a clear functional form. However, the value of the clustering coefficient C for the whole network is 0.09, five times larger than the corresponding value for a comparable random graph. This suggests the presence of structural organization.

Scientific collaboration network

The organization of social communities has been an extensively studied topic in social sciences. Recently, however, it has been possible to take advantage of the progress made in Information Technology to access and manage extensive and reliable data sets in various kind of social structures, for instance clubs, organizations, or collaborative teams. Among others, professional communities have been analyzed from large databases as complex collaboration networks. Examples are the already classic collaboration network of film actors,[68] the company directors network[65] and the network of co-authorship among academics.[66,67] These are in fact bipartite networks,[7] although the one mode projection is usually used so that members are tied through common participation in one or more films, boards of directors, or academic papers.

As an illustration, here we consider the scientific collaboration network (SCN) reconstructed from the submitted papers to the condensed matter physics section of the e-Print Archive (http://xxx.lanl.gov/archive/cond-mat) between 1995 and 1998. The network has 15179 scientists with an average number of collaborators $\langle k \rangle = 5.67$. The analysis of correlations confirms the commonly accepted expectations for social networks. The presence of assortative pair correlations is denoted by the increasing trend of the function $\bar{k}_{nn}(k)$ in Fig. 11, which indicates that researchers with a relatively large number of collaborators tend to be connected among them. The mean clustering coefficient is very high with a value of $\bar{c} = 0.64$. Furthermore, the degree-dependent local clustering follows a clear decay with increasing k, indicating the existence of some hierarchy[50] or modularity.[62]

3.4.1. *Pretty-good-privacy web of trust*

The web of trust[75] between users of the Pretty-Good-Privacy (PGP) encryption algorithm[76,77] is one of the largest reported non-bipartite graphs one can build from a social network emerging in the technological world. On the technical side, the PGP software encrypts files or email messages which may only be opened by the intended recipients. Moreover, it allows to protect also identities. The sender of a digital communication signs the outgoing document so that the recipients know for certain who the author is. The cryptographic system uses two keys associated to each user, a public key known to everyone and a private or secret key known only to the recipient of the message. The public and private keys are related in such a way that only the public key can be used to encrypt messages and only the corresponding private key can be used to decrypt them, being computationally infeasible to deduce one key from the other. When A wants to send a secure message to B, it must use B's public key to encrypt the message. B then uses its private key to decrypt it.

Provided that pairs of keys can be generated by everyone, users should verify that a given key belongs really to the person stated in the key. This requires authentication of the public key, which implies a signing procedure where a person signs the public key of another, meaning that she trusts the other person is who she claims to be. This procedure generates a web of peers that have signed public keys of another based on trust, the so-called web of trust of PGP.

The undirected web of trust (with an edge between peers who have mutually signed their keys) as it was on July 2001 (http://www.dtype.org) comprises 57243 public keys and its average degree is $\langle k \rangle = 2.16$. It shows a scale-free degree distribution with an exponent $\gamma = 2.6$ for small degrees $k < 40$, and a crossover towards another power law with a higher exponent,

~ 4, for large values of the degree. This indicates that, in contrast to many technological networks or social collaboration networks, the PGP is not a scale-free network but has a bounded degree distribution.

However, as for many other social networks, it shows assortative mixing and a large clustering coefficient $C = 0.4$.[75] In Fig. 11 we analyze the correlations of the PGP network as measured by the function $\bar{k}_{nn}(k)$. The growing trend confirms the assortative character of the connections between users. Remarkably, the function $\bar{k}_{nn}(k)$ has an approximately linear behavior, at least for not very large values of k. In Fig. 11, we also plot the clustering coefficient as a function of the degree, $\bar{c}(k)$. Despite the short range of values of k shown in the plot (due to the limited size of the network and the bounded nature of the degree distribution), we can observe that $\bar{c}(k)$ is a nearly independent function of the degree for most k values. This absence of structure is surprisingly in contrast to many other real networks in which $\bar{c}(k)$ has been shown to be a decreasing function of the degree.[62]

The internet at the autonomous system level

The Internet has become a paradigm in complex networks science. Its own organization as a networked system of physical connections between computers makes the graph abstraction a natural representation. However, its intricate ever-evolving structure forces to opt for coarse-grained descriptions so that it is usually examined at the level of routers (special devices that transfer the packets of information across the Internet's different networks) or at the level of Autonomous Systems (ASs) (which are defined as independently administered domains which autonomously determine internal communication and routing policies for Internet communications[12]). Several projects, CAIDA (http://www.caida.org/) and DIMES (http://www.netdimes.org/) among others, have been gathering and analyzing data on the Internet at different levels. In particular, measurements on the Internet structure and topology allow to recreate maps that display connectivity information.

Here, we review one of these Internet maps, which reconstructs the Internet topology at the AS level, from data collected by the *Oregon route-views* project (http://www.routeviews.org/). The map is dated May 2001 and comprises 11174 nodes with an average degree $\langle k \rangle = 4.2$. Statistical measures on this map provide evidence of the large-scale heterogeneity of the Internet, characterized by the small-world property and a scale-free degree distribution with exponent $\gamma \simeq 2.1$. It also clearly reveals its hierarchical

structure. More precisely, degree-degree correlations are strongly disassortative and exhibit a heavy tail that can be fitted by a power-law decay with
a characteristic exponent close to 0.55, as shown in Fig. 12. The clustering
coefficient $\bar{c}(k)$ for nodes of degree k is also displayed. The power-law behavior is not so sharp in this case, but nevertheless the curve also shows a
very clear heavy tail. The scalar clustering coefficient is $C = 0.3$.[48,50,78] All
these features rule out the possibility of a purely random graph structure
or a regular architecture.

The world airport network

The World Airport Network (WAN)[79] is a representative example of a large
transportation infrastructure which can be examined under the perspective
of complex networks theory. At the level of functionality, the WAN is also
a communication network bringing passengers from one side of the world
to another.

The database of the International Air Transportation Association
(http://www.iata.org) compiles information about direct flights between
world airports, and the number of available seats in each flight. For the
year 2002, a network with 3880 nodes and 18810 edges can be reconstructed
from the data. The topology of the network exhibits the small-world property and a scale-free degree distribution of exponent $\gamma \simeq 2$, which presents
an exponential cut-off induced by physical restrictions in the number of
connections that a single airport can handle.

Regarding correlations, the topological $\bar{k}_{nn}(k)$ in Fig. 11 surprisingly
shows assortative behavior for small degrees and a plateau for higher degrees, which denotes the absence of noticeable topological correlations for
large k's. This picture changes notably if the weighted character of the
network is taken into account. Then, the ANND function appears to be assortative in the whole k spectrum. With reference to clustering, low degree
vertices present a much higher interconnected neighborhood than hubs, as
can be seen in Fig. 11 showing a decaying $\bar{c}(k)$. That means that large
airports act as bridges on the international and intercontinental scale. The
weighted version follows the same trend with a much more limited decay.

The world trade web

The network of trade relationships between different countries in
the world can be classified as an economic system where the activity is governed by optimization criteria and competition and co-

operation forces. Publicly available import, export, and gross domestic product databases (http://www.intracen.org/menus/countries.htm, http://www.tswoam.co.uk/world) provide the information to analyze the international trade system as a complex network. Nodes in the world trade web (WTW)[80] represent countries and edges appear between them whenever a commercial channel exists. Despite its relatively small size ($N = 179$ and $\langle k \rangle \simeq 18$ in the undirected version) this socioeconomic structure displays the typical properties of complex networks, namely, the small-world property and scale-free degree distribution with $\gamma \simeq 2.6$ for high degrees.

Correlations also match clear patterns and reflect a discerning hierarchical organization, where countries that belong to influential areas connect to other influential areas through hubs. As can be observed in Fig. 12, the function $\bar{k}_{nn}(k)$ clearly depend on k, with a power law decay of exponent $\simeq 0.5$. This result means that the WTW is a disassortative network where highly connected countries tends to connect to poorly connected ones. There exists a high positive correlation between the number of trade channels of a country and its wealth (measured by the per capita Gross Domestic Product) so that, as expected, highly connected nodes correspond to rich countries and poorly connected nodes to poor ones. The socio-economic implication of disassortativity is then that poor countries do not trade to each other but they do that only with rich countries. Hierarchy is also reflected by the high level of local cohesiveness. Fig. 12 shows the clustering coefficient of the undirected WTW as a function of the vertex degree. As is distinctly seen, this function has a strong dependence on k, with a power law behavior of exponent $\simeq 0.7$. The clustering coefficient averaged over the whole network is $C = 0.65$, greater by a factor 2.7 than the value corresponding to a random network of the same size. Surprisingly, these results point to a high similarity between the WTW and other completely different types of networks, for instance the Internet.

3.5. Modeling correlations

All the empirical evidences reported in the previous section about the hierarchical architecture of real networks should be included in models aiming to help us to understand how these complex systems self-organize and evolve. Models that neglect correlations will inevitably fail to trustworthy recreate actual systems. In this section, we will review how disassortative correlations arise in the classical configuration model and in scale-free growing networks as a by-product. Then, we will go over recent efforts in the construction of models attending to correlations. Some of them are intended to reproduce specific correlation behaviors and others, more ambitious, are devoted to set up a general framework to study the origin of correlations in random networks.

3.5.1. *Disassortative correlations*

Models reproducing disassortative correlations can be divided into two main classes referring to static and dynamic algorithms. In the first category, the classical configuration model[81–83] provides correlations for scale-free degree distributions although, *a priori*, it was supposed to generate uncorrelated networks. In the second group, growing scale-free networks display disassortative correlations between the degrees of neighboring vertices, which spontaneously appear as a consequence of the asymmetry in the history of nodes introduced at different times.

3.5.2. *The configuration model*

The configuration model (CM) is a classical algorithm to construct random networks with a specific degree distribution $P(k)$ settled *a priori*. This is a static model where the total number of nodes in the network N remains constant. For each one of these nodes, a random number k_i is drawn from the probability distribution $P(k)$ and is assigned to it in the form of stubs or ends of edges emerging from that vertex. Several constraints apply. The first one states that no vertex can have a degree larger than $N - 1$. The second is that the sum $\sum_i k_i$ must be even and is imposed by the closure condition. The network is constructed by connecting pairs of these edge ends chosen uniformly at random. The result of this assembly is a random network with degrees distributed according to $P(k)$, by definition.

Given the random nature of the assignment of stubs, it was expected that the ensuing network was uncorrelated, and it is in fact the case if the degree distribution is bounded or multiple connections and tadpoles (self-connections) are allowed. On the other hand, the CM indeed generates disassortative correlations when fluctuations diverge in the infinite-network-size limit, for instance, when the expected degree distribution is scale-free with exponent $2 < \gamma \leq 3$, and no more than one edge is allowed between any two vertices.[47,84]

If the degree distribution has a finite second moment $\langle k^2 \rangle$, the fraction of multiple edges and tadpoles resulting from the construction process vanishes in the thermodynamic limit and, as a consequence, they can be neglected. For scale-free degree distributions with exponent $2 < \gamma \leq 3$, the weight of these multiple edges with respect to the overall number of edges is small but cannot be ignored since they are not evenly distributed among all the degree classes. In the thermodynamic limit, a finite fraction of multiple edges and tadpoles will remain among high degree vertices.[85] There are theoretical and technical reasons to try to avoid multiple edges in some instances, but imposing the restriction on the algorithm that multiple edges are prohibited originates the presence of disassortative correlations.[47,84]

The origin of this phenomenon can be traced back to be a cut-off effect,[85] with the maximum degree ruling the presence or absence of correlations in a random network with no multiple or self-connections. These facts have been taken into account in the construction of a procedure, the uncorrelated configuration model,[86] to generate uncorrelated scale-free networks with no multiple and self-connections.

3.5.3. *Growing models*

Real networks, as everything else in the world we experience, are far from being static. Their evolution is relevant, specially when the time scale of the occurrence of structural changes in the network is of the same magnitude of the characteristic time associated to processes taking place on top of them. Therefore, dynamic models are more appropriate to describe reality and they can further contribute to the understanding of the mechanisms that shape the topological properties of complex networks.

These dynamical models are typically devised as growing networks models, where nodes and edges are gradually added to the network and connected following specific attachment rules. This kind of theoretical construction has succeed in explaining the scale-free structure observed in real nets applying mechanism such as the preferential attachment rule.[87]

A number of authors have worked out analytic studies on this sort of networks. All of them are centered on solving the basic dynamical equations governing the network evolution and take the network size $N(t)$ as the natural time scale. Aside the degree distribution and other first order properties, degree correlations have also been examined.[58,88,89] Before going into further details, let us first briefly revise the standard procedure which assembles this sort of networks:

- At each time step, a new node with m edges is added to the network.
- Ends of the new edges are distributed among old vertices. Each

vertex i has a probability $\Pi(k_i)$ of getting new edges, where k_i is its degree.

In the original Barabási-Albert model,[87] the probability $\Pi(k_i)$ is proportional to k_i, and the system evolves into a steady power-law degree distribution with the form $P(k) \sim k^{-3}$. Many variations have been introduced. In particular, the preferential attachment probability has been generalized and allowed to grow more slowly or faster than linearly with the degree. Only in the linear case, the ensuing degree distribution is power-law, but its exponent can be modulated by introducing an additional constant factor in the attachment probability, *i.e.*, $\Pi(k_i) = k_i + A$. Then, a scale-free degree distribution of the form $P(k) \sim k^{3+A/m}$ is obtained,[90] which for the range of values $-m < A < \infty$ yields degree exponents $2 < \gamma < \infty$ Other ingredients can be incorporated in order to account for a power-law degree distribution of exponent $2 < \gamma < 3$, such as edge disappearance[91] or wiring processes.[92] Summarizing, the class of growing scale-free networks models is described by power-law degree distributions of the form $P(k) \sim k^\gamma$, with an average degree at time t given by $\langle k(t,t') \rangle \sim (t/t')^\beta$, for a node introduced at time t'. The exponents γ and β are related through $\gamma = 1 + 1/\beta$.

As the network grows, it can be proved that correlations between the degrees of neighboring vertices spontaneously appear. The first theoretical derivation of this result[93] was obtained by calculating the number of nodes of degree k attached to an ancestor node of degree k'. In the framework of the rate equation approach, this joint distribution does not factorize so that correlations exit. This characterization of degree correlations is indeed measuring $P(k,k')$. With respect to measures of the average nearest neighbors degree function, it is found that, in the large k limit,

$$\bar{k}_{nn}(k) \sim N^{(3-\gamma)/(\gamma-1)} k^{-(3-\gamma)} \tag{60}$$

for $\gamma < 3$. That is, two vertices correlations are disassortative and characterized by a power-law decay.[58,88] On the other hand, it can also be proved that for $\gamma = 3$, the ANND function converges to a constant value independent of k and proportional to $\ln N$, and therefore, the Barabási-Albert model lacks appreciable correlations.

3.5.4. *Assortativity generators*

Unlike disassortative correlations, which are inherent to the very construction of some general models, assortative correlations must be specifically forced. The special character of this type of mixing is also patent in the implications for issues such as percolation or network resilience. Extensive numerical simulations show that assortative networks percolate more easily than disassortative ones. Concerning resilience, simulations also prove that assortative networks display robustness through redundancy against targeting hubs, since high degree vertices tend to be clustered together in groups of high cohesiveness. On the contrary, such attacks are much more effective in disassortative networks, where hub connections are broadly distributed.

The basic model generating assortative networks[41,42] proposes a specific Monte Carlo sampling scheme equivalent to the Metropolis-Hasting method.[94] The degree distribution can be computed from the distribution of excess degrees $q(k_e)$[j], which on its turn must be calculated from a given edge distribution $e(k_e, k'_e)$ representing the fraction of edges in the network between nodes with excess degree k_e and nodes of excess degree k'_e:

$$q(k) = \sum_{k'} e(k', k) \tag{61}$$

$$P(k) = \frac{q(k-1)/k}{\sum_{k'} q(k'-1)/k'}, \tag{62}$$

where nodes of degree zero are not considered. Once the degree distribution is known, the classical configuration model[81–83] can be applied to assemble the network. The algorithm generating the assortative mixing works then in two repeated steps:

- Two edges are selected at random, named $(1,2)$ and $(3,4)$ after the vertices they connect. The excess degrees q_1, q_2, q_3, q_4 of those vertices are calculated.
- The two edges $(1,2)$ and $(3,4)$ are replaced by the new ones $(1,3)$ and $(2,4)$ with probability 1 if $e(q_1, q_3)e(q_2, q_4) \geq e(q_1, q_2)e(q_3, q_4)$. Otherwise, the swap is performed with probability $p = [e(q_1, q_3)e(q_2, q_4)]/[e(q_1, q_2)e(q_3, q_4)]$.

Finally, the correlation structure of the resulting network will depend on the choice of $e(k', k)$. A uniparametric assortative family can be obtained from

$$e(k', k) = q(k)q(k') + r\sigma_q^2 m(k, k'), \tag{63}$$

where σ_q is the standard deviation of the distribution $q(k)$, $m(k, k')$ is any symmetric matrix that has all rows and columns sums zero and is normalized, and the parameter r is the assortative coefficient.

---

[j]The excess degree is defined as $k_e = k - 1$.

3.5.5. *Modeling clustered networks*

When it was realized that correlations were unavoidable in an accurate characterization of real networks, most modeling efforts merely focused on the reproduction of two point correlations typified by the average nearest neighbors degree. This finds a justification in the fact that many models are assumed to observe the Markovian property, not only because analytic analysis simplifies but also because several real networks, such as the Internet at the Autonomous System level, indeed share this attribute.[55] These systems are those whose topology is completely defined by the degree distribution $P(k)$ and the first conditional probability $P(k \mid k')$, so that all higher-order correlations can be expressed as a function of these two. Some examples of these types of models will be discussed in the following subsection, and the analytic expression for the degree-dependent clustering coefficient will be provided there along with the ANND function. Nonetheless, all these Markovian models fail to maintain clustering in the thermodynamic limit. An independent modeling of clustering is thus required.

The simplest more general approach follows the philosophy of the configuration model, which gives maximally random networks with a given degree distribution $P(k)$. Instead of fixing $P(k)$, one could fix the function $P(k, k')$ so to construct a network with an expected two vertices degree correlations and otherwise maximally random. It can be demonstrated that the clustering of these networks again vanishes in the thermodynamic limit without exception. However, scale-free networks with divergent second moment deserve special attention once more. The decay of their clustering with the increase of the network size is so slow that relatively large networks with an appreciable high cohesiveness can be obtained.

Growing linear preferential attachment models also yield vanishing $\bar{c}(k)$ in the thermodynamic limit, from which new variations are needed in order to recreate the empirically observed values. As an illustrative example of the prescriptions that have been used to generate clustering in scale-free growing networks, one of the proposed models[95] reproduces a large clustering coefficient by adding nodes which connect to the two extremities of a randomly chosen network edge, thus forming a triangle. The resulting network has the power-law degree distribution of the Barabási-Albert model $P(k) \sim k^{-3}$, with $\langle k \rangle = 4$, and since each new vertex induces the creation of at least one triangle, the model generate networks with finite clustering coefficient. A generalization on this model[88] which allows to tune the average degree to $\langle k \rangle = 2m$, with m an even integer, considers new nodes connected to the ends of $m/2$ randomly selected edges. Two vertices and three vertices correlations can be calculated analytically through a rate equation formalism. The average nearest neighbors degree is again equal to the one obtained for the Barabási-Albert model, which indicates a lack of two vertices correlations. On the other hand, the clustering spectrum is here finite in the infinite size limit and scales as k^{-1},

$$\bar{c}(k) = \frac{2k - m}{k(k - 1)}, \qquad (64)$$

and the overall clustering coefficient for large m is

$$C(m) \simeq 2m^2 - 3m - 4/3 + 2m^2(2 - m) \ln \frac{m}{m - 1}. \qquad (65)$$

Bipartite representations[7] constitute a special case since they provide high levels of clustering by construction. In bipartite networks, two types of nodes are present, such as for instance actors and films in the collaboration network of cinematographic productions. Links associate nodes in one category with nodes in the second, in the previous example, actors with films. The one-mode projection only preserves one of the two kinds of nodes connected among them whenever they were linked to the same second type node in the original bipartite composition, say only actors are preserved in the one-mode projection and linked among them whenever they play in the same movie. It is clear that this construction will produce fully connected subsets of actors appearing in the same films, so that the number of triangles in the network, and so the clustering, will be very high. On the other hand, nothing can be said about the dependence of the clustering with the degree and each pattern must be evaluated separately. Indeed, most social networks are represented as the one-mode projection of originally bipartite graphs. Then, the high levels of clustering measured in those networks are strongly affected by the network construction.

3.5.6. *Random graphs with attributes*

Aside partial models, several works attempt to establish a general framework for understanding and modeling correlations. Most of them are based on breaking the similarity of nodes by the introduction of a new stochastic characterization where vertices may come in different types. All these models generate ensembles of random networks which are able to reproduce a wide range of asymptotic topological properties, including different classes of correlation behaviors.

3.5.7. *Hidden color models*

The idea of inhomogeneity in the characterization of vertices is at the heart of the transition from regular latices to random graphs, where vertices have no longer a predefined degree but a stochastic one described by a probabilistic distribution. A further sophistication leads to the so called inhomogeneous random graphs models, where vertices may come in different types and edges appear between the different classes with different probabilities. In this context, the first unifying theoretical doctrine is the hidden color formalism for the generation of colored degree-based sparse random networks.[96-98] Notice these graphs should not be confused with the *colored random graph*.[45]

Graphs with hidden colors are constructed on the basis of the classical configuration model and hence are also a static class of models. The key idea is to define a color space $l = \{1, \ldots, l_a, \ldots, L\}$ and to assign one of these colors to each vertex's edge end or stub. Then, the coloring of a vertex i is given by $k_{li} = (k_{1i}, \ldots, k_{Li})$, where the number of stubs k_{ai} of a given color a is got from the colored degree distribution p_l defining the relative frequencies of vertices with different colored degrees. Finally, the color preference matrix $T_{L \times L}$ controls the relative abundance of edges between color pairs. The resulting ensemble of stub-colored graphs is well-defined if the coloring is considered unobservable. Hence, the coloring can be seen as a set of hidden variables introduced with the purpose of inducing a nontrivial correlation structure in the resulting graphs.

This general framework allows the analytical calculation, in the thermodynamic limit, of global and local properties for a large class of models, which are seen to contrast to those of standard degree-driven random graph (DRG) models. Edge correlations are studied through the generating function formalism by counting the expected number of triangles or three-cycles, $n_\triangle$, wedges or three-chains, $n_\wedge$, edges or two-chains, $n_|$ and m-chains. While the result for $\langle n_\wedge \rangle$ and $\langle n_| \rangle$ is identical to that obtained for plain degree-driven models, $\langle n_\wedge \rangle = NE/2$ and $\langle n_| \rangle = N\langle l \rangle/2$ (where $\langle l \rangle = \sum_{a=1}^{L} \sum_l p_l l_a$), the non-colored number of triangles and k-chains are found to be different. For instance, in the case of triangles:

$$\langle n_\triangle \rangle_{HC} = \frac{(TE)^3}{6} \tag{66}$$

$$\langle n_\triangle \rangle_{DRG} = \frac{E^3}{6\langle l \rangle^3}, \tag{67}$$

where E is the matrix of second order combinatorial moments, $E \equiv E_{ab} =$

$\partial_a \partial_b \hat{p}_l(x = 1)$, with $\hat{p}_l$ the Laplace transform of p_l. Thus, for the degree-driven random graphs one has $\langle n_\triangle \rangle_{DRG} = \langle \wedge \rangle^3 / [6 \langle n_| \rangle^3]$, a relation which is absent in the hidden colors scenario.

The clustering coefficient C can also be computed from the count of the expected number of triangles and three-chains:

$$C_{HC} = \frac{(TE)^3}{NE} \tag{68}$$

$$C_{DGR} = \frac{(E)^2}{N \langle l \rangle^3}. \tag{69}$$

Although C_{HC} indeed scales as $\mathcal{O}(N^{-1})$, the finite quantity NC_{HC} has a nontrivial dependence on the color preference matrix T, an example of the increased correlation possibilities of hidden color models over DRG models.

3.5.8. Fitness or hidden variables models

A powerful and systematic subclass of the family of models described above is introduced as a class of correlated random networks with fitness or hidden variables.[58] Again, a hidden variable h, which can be defined in a discrete or a continuous space, plays the role of a tag assigned to the vertices, and completely determines the topological properties of the network through their probability distribution and the probability to connect pairs of vertices.

The procedure, which generates correlated undirected random networks without loops or multiple edges, is as follows:

- Each vertex i is assigned a variable h_i, independently drawn from a probability distribution $\rho(h)$.
- An undirected edge is created between a pair of vertices i and j following a connection probability $r(h_i, h_j)$, where $r(h, h') \geq 0$ is a symmetric function of h and h'.

The resulting networks are Markovian at the hidden variable level, which makes possible the calculation of analytical expressions for the most important structural properties, such as the degree distribution, the ANND function for two vertices correlations, and the clustering coefficient for three vertices correlations. The clue is in the conditional probability (the propagator) $g(k|h)$ that a vertex with initial hidden variable h ends up connected to other k vertices, which enables to write expressions in the degree-space as a function of distributions in the hidden variables space. For instance,

$$P(k) = \sum_h g(k|h) \rho(h) \tag{70}$$

$$\langle k \rangle = \sum_k k P(k) = \sum_h \bar{k}(h)\rho(h),\qquad(71)$$

where $\bar{k}(h) = \sum_k k g(k|h)$ is the average degree of nodes with hidden variable h. The generating function formalism can be applied to find an explicit expression for the propagator:

$$\ln \hat{g}(z|h) = N \sum_{h'} \rho(h') \ln[1 - (1 - z) r(h, h')].\qquad(72)$$

Even without solving this equation, one can find that:

$$\bar{k}(h) = N \sum_{h'} \rho(h') r(h, h')\qquad(73)$$

$$\langle k \rangle = N \sum_{h,h'} \rho(h) r(h, h') \rho(h'),\qquad(74)$$

and these results are valid for sparse and non-sparse networks.

Pair degree correlations can be calculated as

$$\bar{k}_{nn}(k) = 1 + \frac{1}{P(k)} \sum_h g(k|h)\rho(h)\bar{k}_{nn}(h)\qquad(75)$$

$$\bar{k}_{nn}(h) = \sum_{h'} \bar{k}(h') p(h'|h),\qquad(76)$$

where $\bar{k}_{nn}(h)$ is the ANND of a vertex of hidden variable h.

The degree dependent clustering is

$$\bar{c}(k) = \frac{1}{P(k)} \sum_h \rho(h) g(k|h) c_h, \quad k = 2, 3, \dots\qquad(77)$$

$$c_h = \sum_{h',h''} p(h'|h) r(h', h'') p(h''|h),\qquad(78)$$

with c_h the clustering coefficient of a vertex h.

Furthermore, this analysis provides a new algorithm for the construction of random networks with a correlation structure determined *a priori*:

- Assign to each vertex i an integer random variable $\tilde{k}_i$, $i = 1, \dots, N$, drawn from the theoretical probability distribution $P_t(k)$.
- For each pair of vertices i and j, draw an indirect edge with probability $r(\tilde{k}_i, \tilde{k}_j) = \langle k \rangle P_t(\tilde{k}_i, \tilde{k}_j)/NP_t(\tilde{k}_i)P_t(\tilde{k}_j)$.

In the large-k limit, the degree structure of the ensuing network will be distributed according to the probability $P_t(k)$, with correlations given by $P_t(k, k')$.

Despite its static character, another of the main achievements of this general approach concerns its application to the mapping of growing networks into a particular kind of hidden variables model, where the hidden variable associated to each vertex corresponds to its injection time. All known results for growing models can be recovered from the hidden variables formalism.

3.5.9. *Fitness and preferential attachment models*

The original fitness model[99] appeared as an attempt to loosen the preferential attachment rule in the Barabási-Albert model so that degree distributions with exponents different from 3 could be obtained.

The fitness associated to each vertex is defined as a stochastic parameter η_i picked out from a probability distribution $\rho(\eta)$. The fitness embodies properties, different from the degree, that may also influence the probability Π of node i of gaining new edges, which is computed as

$$\Pi(k_i, \eta_i) = \frac{\eta_i k_i}{\sum_j \eta_j k_j}. \tag{79}$$

Even if the distribution $\rho(\eta)$ is the simplest one, that is uniform in the interval $[0, 1]$, the model generates a network displaying a non-trivial degree distribution, and for some more complex alternatives the model also reproduces structural correlations.

Inspired by the idea of fitness, a new mechanism leading also to scale-free networks is obtained if the preferential attachment rule in terms of the degree is eliminated and only the fitness remain.[19] Since the fitness is a non-evolving quantity, the network can then be built as static. Although previous in time, this intrinsic fitness model is a particular example of the general class of models with hidden variables, where the fitness is distributed exponentially and nodes are joined whenever the sum of the fitness of the endpoints is larger than a given constant threshold ζ, so that $r(h, h')$ is the Heaviside step function $\Theta(x)$:

$$\rho(h) = e^{-h}, \ h \, \epsilon \, [0, \infty] \tag{80}$$

$$r(h, h') = \Theta(h + h' - \zeta). \tag{81}$$

Within the hidden variables formalism, analytical expressions can be computed for the main properties of the model.[58] Two point correlations are disassortative:

$$\bar{k}_{nn}(k) = 1 + \frac{N^2 e^{-\zeta}}{k} \left[1 + \zeta + \ln\left(\frac{k}{N}\right) \right] \Theta_k(Ne^{-\zeta}, N). \tag{82}$$

The clustering coefficient is

$$\bar{c}(k) = \Theta_k(Ne^{-\zeta}, Ne^{-\zeta/2}) \tag{83}$$

$$+ \frac{N^2 e^{-\zeta}}{k^2}\left[1 + \zeta + 2\ln\left(\frac{k}{N}\right)\right]\Theta_k(Ne^{-\zeta/2}, N), \tag{84}$$

which reflects the fact that the clustering is equal to its maximum value 1 for all vertices with $h < \zeta/2$. On the other hand, for $Ne^{-\zeta/2} \le k \le N$ it decreases as k^{-2} but modulated by a logarithmic correction term.

3.6. *Outlook*

In general, as we have shown in the previous sections, uncorrelated random graphs do not match real networks, which indeed in most cases show non-trivial topological correlations encoding the properties of the underlying hierarchical architecture or community structure. While uncorrelated random networks are greatly valuable to provide null hypotheses for network structures, correlated models can provide a more faithful image of reality. Moreover, any deep understanding of the ordering principles governing the formation and evolution of networks must take into account correlations, clustering and other topological attributes. Despite the intense research activity witnessed by the various results reported in this chapter, several directions have yet to be fully explored. The characterization and modeling of correlations in directed networks is surely at an early stage due to various technical complications both in the mathematical tools and the data gathering. The effect of correlations on networks physical properties has been analyzed only in a handful of systems. Finally, the origin and meaning of correlations spur also the question of which phenomena and dynamical aspects rule the development of these features. The physics of the dynamical processes occurring on networks (traffic flows, communication transmission etc.) has as well a role in determining specific correlation patterns. It is therefore important to start bridging the topological properties of networks with the dynamics acting on them, finding the interplay of these various elements and their interaction rules. In this book, a chapter is devoted to recent studies on weighted networks and the interaction among topological features and weighted quantities representing the interactions or traffic carried by the edges.

CHAPTER 4

The Architecture of Complex Weighted Networks:
Measurements and Models

Alain Barrat[1], Marc Barthélemy[2,3] and Alessandro Vespignani[3]

[1] *Laboratoire de Physique Théorique (UMR du CNRS 8627), Bâtiment 210,
Université de Paris-Sud, 91405 Orsay, France*

[2] *CEA-Centre d'Etudes de Bruyères-le-Châtel, Département de Physique
Théorique et Appliquée BP12, 91680 Bruyères-Le-Châtel, France*

[3] *Biocomplexity center and School of Informatics, Indiana University,
Bloomington 47406 IN, USA*

4.1. *Introduction*

Along with a complex topological structure, real networks display a large
heterogeneity in the capacity and intensity of the connections represented
by the weight of the link. For example, in ecology the diversity of the
predator-prey interaction is believed to be a critical ingredient of ecosystems stability[100,101] and in social systems, the weight of interactions is
very important in the characterization of the corresponding networks.[102]
Similarly, the Internet traffic[12] or the number of passengers in the airline
network[40,68,103,104] are crucial quantities in the study of these systems.

Empirical studies of weighted networks[40,105–108] have shown that they
may exhibit additional complex features for the weighted properties that
do not find an explanation just in terms of the underlying topological structure. In the present chapter we review the appropriate metrics and some
modeling strategies that enable us to provide a theoretical framework for
the statistical analysis and characterization of large complex weighted networks. In particular, we start by introducing the set of quantities aimed
at the statistical analyisis of large weighted networks and characterize the
heterogeneity and structural ordering induced in these systems by the intensity of connections. We show these measures at work by reporting the
results of the empirical analysis of several networks representing transporta-

tion infrastructures, social and biological systems. Finally, motivated by the finding of the empirical analysis, we review models of weighted networks which naturally produce topology-weight correlations and heavy-tailed distributions for the various quantities characterizing the network.

4.2. *Tools for the characterization of weighted networks*

We start by reviewing the mathematical tools and the generalization of several topological measures to the case of weighted networks. These quantities will be used in the ensuing analysis of real weighted networks.

4.2.1. *Weights*

The topological properties of a graph are encoded in its adjacency matrix a_{ij}, whose elements take the value 1 if an edge connects the vertex i to the vertex j and 0 otherwise (with $i, j = 1, ..., N$ where N is the size of the network). Weighted networks are similarly described by a matrix w_{ij} specifying the weight on the edge connecting the vertices i and j ($w_{ij} = 0$ if the nodes i and j are not connected). In the following we will consider only the case of symmetric positive weights $w_{ij} = w_{ji} \geq 0$.

4.2.2. *Degree and weight distributions*

The standard topological characterization of networks is obtained by the analysis of the probability distribution $P(k)$ that a vertex has degree k. Complex networks often exhibit a heterogeneous degree distribution, e.g. of a power-law form $P(k) \sim k^{-\gamma}$ with $2 \leq \gamma \leq 3$. Similarly, a first characterization of weights is obtained by the distribution $P(w)$ that any given edge has weight w. This distribution may a priori be homogeneous and characterized by a typical scale, or on the contrary carry a novel heterogeneity.

4.2.3. *Weighted degree: Strength*

Along with the degree of a node, a very significant measure of the network properties in terms of the actual weights is obtained by looking at the vertex *strength* s_i defined as:[40,109]

$$s_i = \sum_{j \in \mathcal{V}(i)} w_{ij} \tag{85}$$

where the sum runs over the set $\mathcal{V}(i)$ of neighbors of i. The strength of a node integrates the information both about its degree and the importance of the weights of its links and can be considered as the natural generalization of the degree. When the weights are independent from the topology, the strength typically grows linearly with the degree i.e. with the number of terms in the sum (85): $s \simeq \langle w \rangle k$ where $\langle w \rangle$ is the average weight. In the presence of correlations we obtain in general $s \simeq Ak^{\beta}$ with $\beta = 1$ and $A \neq \langle w \rangle$ or $\beta > 1$.

4.2.4. *Weighted clustering*

The topological clustering coefficient[6] measures the local group cohesiveness and is defined for any vertex i as the fraction of connected neighbors of i. It therefore does not take into account the fact that some neighbors are more important than others. In order to solve this incongruity, it is possible to introduce different definitions of clustering coefficient that explicitly consider the weights of the links and combines the topological information with the weight distribution of the network.[40,110] A convenient *weighted clustering coefficient* is defined as:[40]

$$c^w(i) = \frac{1}{s_i(k_i - 1)} \sum_{j,h} \frac{(w_{ij} + w_{ih})}{2} a_{ij} a_{ih} a_{jh}. \tag{86}$$

The quantity $c^w(i)$ is counting for each triple formed in the neighborhood of the vertex i the weight of the two participating edges of the vertex i. In this way we are not just considering the number of closed triangles in the neighborhood of a vertex but also their total relative weight with respect to the vertex strength. The factor $s_i(k_i - 1)$ is a normalization factor and ensures that $0 \leq c_i^w \leq 1$. Consistently, the c_i^w definition recovers the topological clustering coefficient in the case that $w_{ij} = const$. It is customary to define C^w and $C^w(k)$ as the weighted clustering coefficient averaged over all vertices of the network and over all vertices with degree k, respectively. In the case of a large randomized network (lack of correlations between weights and topology), it is easy to see that $C^w = C$ and $C^w(k) = C(k)$. In real weighted networks, however, we can face two opposite cases. If $C^w > C$, we are in presence of a network in which the interconnected triples are more likely formed by the edges with larger weights. On the contrary, $C^w < C$ signals a network in which the topological clustering is generated by edges with low weight (see Fig. 13). In this case it is obvious that the clustering has a minor effect in the organization of the network since the largest part of the interactions (traffic, frequency of the relations, etc.) is occurring on edges not belonging to interconnected triples. In order to obtain a more detailed knowledge of the structure of the network, the variations of $C^w(k)$ with respect to the degree class k can be analyzed, and compared with those of $C(k)$.

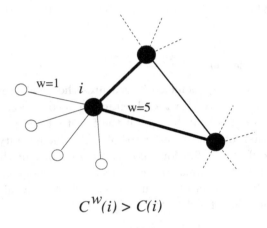

Fig. 13. The weighted clustering of a node i is larger than its topological counterpart if the weights of the links $i - j$ are concentrated on the cliques to which i participates.

4.2.5. Weighted assortativity: Affinity

Along with the weighted clustering coefficient, the *weighted average nearest neighbors degree* has been defined as[40]

$$k^w_{nn,i} = \frac{1}{s_i} \sum_{j=1}^{N} a_{ij} w_{ij} k_j. \tag{87}$$

This quantity is a simple generalization of the average nearest neighbors degree[48]

$$k_{nn,i} = \frac{1}{k_i} \sum_{j=1}^{N} a_{ij} k_j , \tag{88}$$

and performs a local weighted average of the nearest neighbor degree according to the normalized weight of the connecting edges, w_{ij}/s_i. This definition implies that $k^w_{nn,i} > k_{nn,i}$ if the edges with the larger weights are pointing to the neighbors with larger degree and $k_{nn,i}^w < k_{nn,i}$ in the opposite case (see Fig. 14). Thus, $k_{nn,i}^w$ measures the effective *affinity* to connect with high or low degree neighbors according to the magnitude of the actual interactions. As well, the behavior of the function $k_{nn}^w(k)$ (defined as the average of $k_{nn,i}^w$ over all vertices with degree k), marks the weighted assortative or disassortative properties[41] considering the actual interactions among the system's elements.

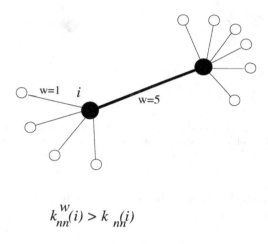

$$k_{nn}^w(i) > k_{nn}(i)$$

Fig. 14. Example of a node i with small average nearest neighbors degree but large *weighted* average nearest neighbors degree: i is mostly connected to low-degree nodes but the link with largest weight points towards a well-connected hub.

4.2.6. *Local heterogeneity*

The strength of a node i is the sum of the weights of all links to which i participates. The same strength can however be obtained with very different configurations: the weights w_{ij} may be either of the same order s_i/k_i or heterogeneously distributed among the links. For example, the most heterogeneous situation is obtained when one weight dominates over all the others. A simple way to measure this "disparity" is given by the quantity Y_2 introduced in other contexts[111,112]

$$Y_2(i) = \sum_{j \in \mathcal{V}(i)} \left[\frac{w_{ij}}{s_i} \right]^2 \tag{89}$$

If all weights are of the same order then $Y_2 \sim 1/k_i$ (for $k_i \gg 1$) and if a small number of weights dominate then Y_2 is of the order $1/m$ with m of order unity. This quantity was recently used for metabolic networks[108] in order to identify dominant reactions.

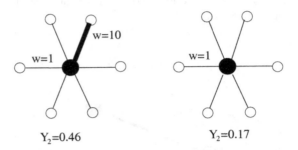

$$Y_2 = 0.46 \qquad\qquad Y_2 = 0.17$$

Fig. 15.   If there is a small number of important connections around i, the quantity Y_2 is of order $1/m$ with m of order unity. In contrast, if all the connections are of the same order, Y_2 is small and of order $1/k$.

A similar information is encoded in the local entropy, defined for nodes of degree larger than 2 as

$$f(i) = -\frac{1}{\ln k_i} \sum_{j \in \mathcal{V}(i)} \frac{w_{ij}}{s_i} \ln\left[\frac{w_{ij}}{s_i}\right] . \qquad (90)$$

This quantity indeed goes from 0 if the strength of i is fully concentrated on one link to the maximal value 1 for homogeneous weights: it can thus be used as a alternative or complement to the disparity Y_2 to investigate the local heterogeneity of the weights.

4.3. *Weighted networks: Empirical results*

Although most of the real-world networks can be considered as weighted, and although these weights usually carry important information for their understanding, rather few empirical datasets are actually available. We review some examples of transportation networks before describing a scientific collaboration network and some results concerning a network of biological nature.

4.3.1. *Transportation networks*

Transportation networks are important examples of weighted networks and emblematic of technological networks. The knowledge and description of these networks is critical in many instances. In the case of epidemics spreading for example, it is obviously important to be able to determine the human flows in order to model and understand the possible spread of a disease.[113,114]

As a first example, we consider the world-wide airport network (WAN).[40,103,104] In this network each node represents an airport, and two nodes are joined by a link if and only if there exists a direct airline connection between the corresponding airports. The weights of the links are given by the number of available seats on these direct connections. Data from the International Air Transportation Association (IATA)[k] database were analyzed by different groups. This database contains the world list of airports pairs connected by direct flights and the number of available seats on any given connection for the year 2002. The resulting air-transportation graph comprises $N = 3880$ vertices denoting airports and $E = 18810$ edges accounting for the presence of a direct flight connection. The average degree of the network is $\langle k \rangle = 2E/N = 9.70$, while the maximal degree is 318.

The second example is the network of inter-cities movement in the Italian island of Sardinia. The nodes are the 375 cities of this island and the weight w_{ij} of the link (i, j) represents the number of individuals going daily from i to j by any means (car, bus, etc.).

Finally, we briefly review the network of urban individual movements.[115] The nodes of this network are the different locations in a large city, corresponding to homes, offices, shops, etc... The weights of the links correspond to the number of individuals going from one location to another. The data are obtained from a large-scale individual-based urban traffic simulations built using the actual census, land-use and population-mobility data of the city of Portland, Oregon (USA). This dataset has been used in the modeling of disease propagation in urban social networks.[113]

4.3.2. *Airport network*

Topology
The topology of the WAN exhibits both small-world and strong heterogeneity as already observed in different dataset analyses.[103–105] In particular,

---

[k]http://www.iata.org.

A. Barrat, M. Barthélemy and A. Vespignani

the average shortest path length, measured as the average number of edges separating any two nodes in the network, has the value $\langle \ell \rangle = 4.37$, very small compared to the network size N. The degree distribution, displayed in Fig. 16, takes the form $P(k) = k^{-\gamma} f(k/k_x)$, where $\gamma \simeq 2.0$ and $f(k/k_x)$ is an exponential cut-off function that finds its origin in physical constraints on the maximum number of connections that a single airport can handle.[68,103,104] The airport connection graph is therefore a clear example of heterogeneous network showing scale-free properties on a definite range of degree values.

Strength distribution

The probability distribution $P(s)$ that a vertex has strength s is heavy tailed and the functional behavior exhibits similarities with the degree distribution $P(k)$ (see Fig. 16). This behavior is not unexpected since it is natural that the strength s_i increases with the vertex degree k_i, and thus the slow decaying tail of $P(s)$ stems directly from the very slow decay of the degree distribution.

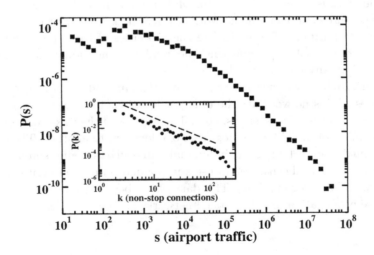

Fig. 16.   Degree and strength distributions for the world-wide airport network. The degree is the number of non-stop connections to other airports and the strength is the total number of passengers handled by any given airport. In this case, the degree distribution can be approximated by the power-law behavior $P(k) \sim k^{-\gamma}$ with $\gamma = 1.8 \pm 0.2$. The strength distribution has a heavy-tail extending over more than four orders of magnitude.

Topology-weight correlations

In Fig. 17 we report the relation between strength and degree obtained for both the real weighted network and its randomized version, generated by a random re-distribution of the actual weights on the existing topology of the network. This Figure clearly shows a very different behavior for the real data set and its randomized version. In particular, the power-law fit for the real data gives an "anomalous" exponent $\beta_{\text{WAN}} = 1.5 \pm 0.1$. This implies that the strength of vertices grows faster than their degree, i.e. the weight of edges belonging to highly connected vertices tends to have a value higher than the one corresponding to a random assignment of weights. This denotes a strong correlation between the weight and the topological properties in the WAN, where the larger is an airport, the more traffic it can handle.

The fingerprint of these correlations is also observed in the dependence of the weight w_{ij} on the degrees of the end point nodes k_i and k_j. For the WAN the behavior of the average weight as a function of the end points degrees can be well approximated by a power-law dependence $\langle w_{ij} \rangle \sim (k_i k_j)^\theta$ with an exponent $\theta = 0.5 \pm 0.1$.[40] This exponent can be related to the β exponent by noticing that $s(k) \sim k(k k_j)^\theta$, resulting in $\beta = 1 + \theta$, if the topological correlations between the degree of connected vertices can be neglected. We have checked that this is indeed the case of the WAN where the above scaling relation is well satisfied by the numerical values provided by the independent measurements of the exponents.

Clustering and assortativity properties

The compared analysis of topological and weighted quantities defined in Section 4.2 reveals a very rich and interesting picture.

i. $C(k)$ is monotonously decaying, as a consequence of the role of large airports that provide non-stop connections to very far destinations on an international and intercontinental scale. These destinations are usually not interconnected among them, giving rise to a low clustering coefficient for the hubs.

ii. We find, however, that $C^w/C \simeq 1.1$, indicating an accumulation of traffic on interconnected groups of vertices.

iii. The weighted clustering coefficient $C^w(k)$ has a much more limited variation in the whole spectrum of k and is systematically larger than $C(k)$, especially at large k. This implies that, for the high degree airports, a large part of the traffic corresponds to the triangles to which they participate.

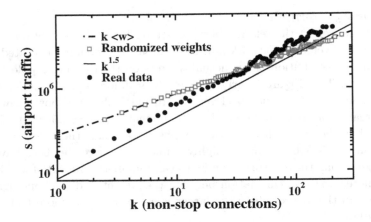

Fig. 17.   WAN: Average strength $s(k)$ as function of the degree k of nodes. In the world airport network real data follow a power-law behavior with exponent $\beta = 1.5 \pm 0.1$. This denotes very strong correlations between the traffic handled by an airport and the number of its connections.

iv. The topological $k_{nn}(k)$ shows an assortative behavior only at small degrees. For $k > 10$, $k_{nn}(k)$ approaches a constant value, a fact revealing an uncorrelated structure in which vertices with very different degrees have a very similar neighborhood. The analysis of the weighted $k_{nn}^w(k)$, however, exhibits a pronounced assortative behavior in the whole k spectrum, with $k_{nn}^w(k) > k_{nn}(k)$, providing a different picture in which high degree airports have a larger affinity for other large airports where the major part of the traffic is directed.

The combined analysis of $C^w(k)$ and $k_{nn}^w(k)$ shows that for the hubs, the links with large traffic are typically part of triangles and directed towards other hubs. This picture corresponds to a tendency to form interconnected groups with large traffic, and to a network in which high degree nodes form cliques with nodes with equal or higher degree, the so-called *rich-club* *phenomenon*.[116]

Disparity
The disparity in the case of the WAN shows a $1/k$ behavior for $k > 10$ which indicates that for hubs the traffic is rather homogeneously distributed among their different connections.

4.3.3. *Urban and inter-urban movement networks*

Intra-urban movements were analyzed by Chowell *et al*[115] in the specific case of the city of Portland, Oregon (USA). Using simulations combined with census data, Chowell *et al* were able to construct the network of human movements in this city. The nodes represent the different locations of the cities (offices, shops, homes, etc) while a link between two nodes i and j has a weight which represents the number of individuals going (daily) from location i to location j.

At a larger scale, the movements between cities were recently analyzed[117] in the specific case of the island of Sardinia (Italy). The nodes here represent the 375 different cities of Sardinia and the links have a weight which is the number of individuals going (daily) from one city to another.

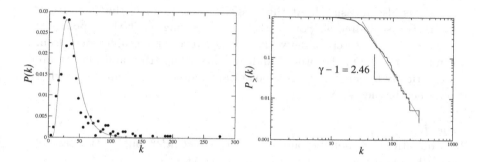

Fig. 18. The degree distribution for the Sardinian intercities network is skewed but, as shown on the right, there is no heavy tail.

Topology

While the intra-urban network is scale-free, with an exponent $\gamma \simeq 2.4$ (full day), the Sardinian network appears to have a peaked distribution of degrees, whose tail can be fitted with an exponent $\gamma \simeq 3.5$ larger than 3, which means that fluctuations are bounded. This result could probably be traced back to the spatial nature of this network.[118] Interestingly enough we will see in the following that even if the structure of the Sardinian network is relatively simple and trivial, traffic properties are complex.

Strength properties

The strengths are very broadly distributed in both cases with exponent $\gamma_s \simeq 2.0$ for the interurban traffic and $\gamma_s \simeq 2.7$ for the urban traffic.

The traffic-topology correlations as measured by the value of the exponent β informs us that in the inter-urban case the correlations are very large ($\beta \simeq 1.9$) while these correlations are much weaker with a linear dependence ($\beta \simeq 1.0$) at the inter-city level.

Clustering and assortativity properties

The clustering for the urban network is $C \simeq 0.06$ which is much larger than the value for the random graph with the same number of nodes and same average degree $C \sim 1/N \sim 1/180000$. This large clustering along with a hierarchical organization of the nodes is reflected in the quantity $C(k)$ which is a slowly decreasing function possibly as $1/k$. A different behavior is observed for the Sardinian interurban network with an even more slowly decreasing function but which order of magnitude is the same as the random graph with same distribution $P(k)$. For this network a slight disassortative behavior is also measured. At this stage, it thus appears that the urban network is a scale-free network with large clustering while the topological structure of the intercities network does not reveal large differences from a random graph. On the other hand, weighted clustering and affinity are systematically larger than their topological counterparts, similarly to what is obtained in the WAN.

Disparity

This quantity was not measured by Chowell *et al*[115] but in the case of inter-urban movements, it has been measured that

$$Y_2(k) \sim k^{-\theta} \tag{91}$$

with $\theta \simeq 0.4$ (see Fig. 19). This result shows that only a few connections carry a large traffic, a situation which is probably not optimal since it inevitably leads to road overload and traffic jam.

4.3.4. Transportation networks: Summary

We can summarize the results for the different transportations networks in Tab.1.

As we can see on this table, the topology of the graph does not seem to be a robust feature of these networks. In contrast it seems that broad traffic distribution and traffic-topology correlations are a common feature in these networks.

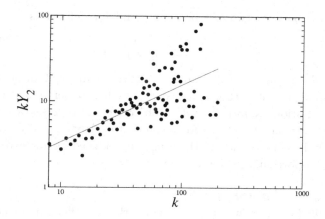

Fig. 19. This plot demonstrates that the disparity versus k is not $1/k$ in the case of the inter-cities network. The power law fit gives $Y_2 \sim k^{-\theta}$ with $\theta \approx 0.4$.

Table 1. Transportations networks at different scales and their properties.

Network	Degree distribution	Weight structure
Global scale: WAN	Scale-free ($\gamma \approx 2.0$)	Broad traffic Strong correlations ($\beta \approx 1.5$) Low disparity ($\theta = 1$)
Inter-cities scale	light tail	Broad traffic ($\gamma_s \approx 2.0$) Strong correlations ($\beta \approx 1.9$) High disparity ($\theta = 0.4$)
Intra-urban scale[115]	Scale-free ($\gamma \approx 2.4$)	Broad traffic ($\gamma_s \approx 2.7$) Weak correlations ($\beta \approx 1.0$)

4.3.5. *Social network: Example of the scientific collaboration network*

In the scientific collaboration network (SCN)[66,67,119] the nodes are identified with authors and the weight depends on the number of co-authored papers.[40,66,67] The network considered is made of scientists who have authored manuscripts submitted to the e-print archive relative to condensed matter physics (http://xxx.lanl.gov/archive/cond-mat) between 1995 and 1998. Scientists are identified with nodes and an edge exists between two scientists if they have co-authored at least one paper. The resulting connected network has $N = 12722$ nodes, with an average degree (i.e. average number of collaborators) $\langle k \rangle = 6.28$ and maximal degree 97. For the SCN, a convenient definition of the weight is necessary:[66,67] the intensity w_{ij} of the interaction between two collaborators i and j is defined as

$$w_{ij} = \sum_p \frac{\delta_i^p \delta_j^p}{n_p - 1} \tag{92}$$

where the index p runs over all papers, n_p is the number of authors of the paper p, and δ_i^p is 1 if author i has contributed to paper p, and 0 otherwise. This definition seems to be rather objective and representative of the scientific interaction: It is large for collaborators having many papers in common but the contribution to the weight introduced by any given paper is inversely proportional to the number of authors.

Degree and strength distributions
The topological properties of the SCN network and other similar networks of scientific collaborations have been intensively studied[66,67] and we report in Fig. 20 the degree distribution showing a definite heterogeneity.

Moreover, the strength, which gives the number of papers authored by a given scientist (excluding single-author publications), displays as well a heavy-tailed probability distribution, also shown in Fig. 20.

Topology-weight correlations
As for the WAN, we report in Fig. 21 the behavior obtained for both the real weighted network and its randomized version. The curves are very similar and well fitted by the uncorrelated approximation $s(k) = \langle w \rangle k$ in strong contrast with what is observed in the case of the WAN. This behaviour is confirmed by the study of w_{ij} as a function of k_i and k_j: in the SCN, $\langle w_{ij} \rangle$ is almost constant for over two decades confirming a general lack of correlations between the weights and the vertices degree.

Clustering and assortativity properties
We summarize the results[40] obtained for the SCN by comparing the regular topological quantities with the weighted ones introduced above.

   i. The SCN has a monotonously decaying spectrum $C(k)$. This implies that hubs present a much lower clustered neighborhood than low degree vertices which can be interpreted as the evidence that authors with few collaborators usually work within a well defined research group in which all the scientists collaborate together (high clustering). Authors with a large degree, however, collaborate with different groups and communities which on their turn do not have often collaborations, thus creating a lower clustering coefficient.

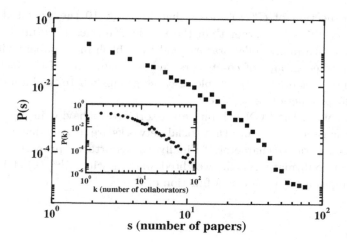

Fig. 20. Degree and strength distribution in the scientific collaboration network. The degree k corresponds to the number of co-authors of each scientist and the strength represent its total number of publications. The distributions are heavy-tailed even if it is not possible to distinguish a definite functional form.

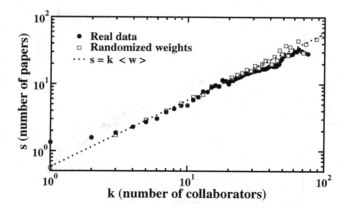

Fig. 21. Average strength $s(k)$ as function of the degree k of nodes. In the scientific collaboration network the real data are very similar to those obtained in a randomized weighted network. Only at very large k values it is possible to observe a slight departure from the expected linear behavior.

ii. The inspection of $C^w(k)$ shows that for $k \geq 10$ the weighted clustering coefficient is larger than the topological one. This implies that authors with many collaborators tend to publish more papers with interconnected groups of co-authors and is a signature of the fact that influential scientists form stable research groups where the largest part of their production is obtained.

iii. Furthermore, the SCN exhibits an assortative behavior in agreement with the general evidence that social networks are usually denoted by a strong assortative character.[41] Finally, the assortative properties find a clearcut confirmation in the weighted analysis with a $k_{nn}^w(k)$ strikingly growing as a power-law as a function of k.

Disparity

The disparity for the SCN is shown on Fig. 22 and displays a clear power law behavior $Y_2 \sim k^{-\theta}$ with $\theta \approx 0.77$. The fact that θ is not one indicates that the disparity is large which means that authors with a large number of collaborators do have "preferred" collaboration with whom they are publishing most of their papers.

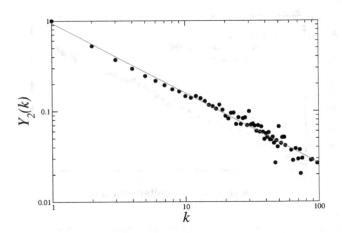

Fig. 22.   Disparity for the SCN. The line is the power law fit which gives $\theta \approx 0.77$. This value indicates that the number of papers an individual is co-authoring varies strongly from one co-author to another.

4.3.6. *Biological network: The case of the metabolic network*

The first studies of metabolic networks showed the existence of a very heterogeneous topology characterized by broad degree distributions with power-law functional forms.[120] While most of the metabolites participate to few reactions, some are thus involved in a large number of them. Moreover, the small-world character of such networks, together with a large clustering and a hierarchical structure, has been uncovered by various studies.[121,122]

More recently, a study of the weights associated to each link, i.e. the fluxes of the chemical reactions, has been carried out for the metabolic network of the bacterium *E. coli*.[108] The first important result is that the weights are very heterogeneous, with a power-law distribution of fluxes, rather independently of the external conditions. This means that the biochemical activity is actually dominated by a small number of reactions which carry large fluxes. Moreover, the study of the disparity $Y_2(k)$ showed a striking power-law behaviour $Y_2(k) \sim k^{-0.27}$, i.e. a much slower decay with k than if the weights were homogeneously distributed around the nodes. The distribution of the weights of the links around each node is thus quite heterogeneous: for each node, it is then possible to identify to which reaction it participates most, and to construct a "backbone" of important pathways in the network. The precise study of weighted clustering and affinity has however not yet been carried out.

4.4. *Modeling weighted networks*

4.4.1. *Coupling weight and topology*

A certain number of approaches to the modeling of weighted networks focus on growing topologies where weights are assigned statically, i.e. once for ever, with different rules related to the underlying topology[109,123–125] or assigned randomly.[126,127] These mechanisms, however, overlook the dynamical evolution of weights according to the topological variations, or, even in the case of evolving weights,[128] the corresponding feedback mechanism. We can illustrate this point in the case of the airline network. If a new airline connection is created between two airports (generally at least one of them being already large), it will generally provoke a modification of the existing traffic of both airports. In general, it will increase the traffic activity depending on the specific nature of the network and on the local dynamics. In the following, we review a model[40] that takes into account the coupled evolution in time of topology and weights: the evolution of topology is driven by the weights, which in turn are allowed to evolve dynamically during the growth of the system. This mimics the evolution and reinforcements of interactions in natural and infrastructure networks.

4.4.2. A simple model: Weight perturbation and "busy get busier" effects

The model dynamics starts from an initial seed of N_0 vertices connected by links with assigned weight w_0. At each time step, a new vertex n is added with m edges (with initial weight w_0). Each edge is attached to a previously existing vertex i chosen according to the probability

$$\Pi_{n \to i} = \frac{s_i}{\sum_j s_j}. \tag{93}$$

This rule of "busy get busier" relaxes the usual degree preferential attachment, focusing on a strength driven attachment in which new vertices connect more likely to vertices handling larger weights and which are more central in terms of the strength of interactions. This weight driven attachment eq.93 appears to be a plausible mechanism in many networks. In the Internet new routers connect to more central routers in terms of bandwidth and traffic handling capabilities and in the airport networks new connections are generally established to airports with a large passenger traffic. Even in the SCN this mechanism might play a role since an author with more co-authored papers is more visible and open to further collaborations.

The presence of the new edge (n, i) will introduce variations of the existing weights across the network. In particular, we consider the local rearrangements of weights between i and its neighbors $j \in \mathcal{V}(i)$ according to the simple rule

$$w_{ij} \to w_{ij} + \Delta w_{ij}, \tag{94}$$

where

$$\Delta w_{ij} = \delta \frac{w_{ij}}{s_i}. \tag{95}$$

This rule considers that the establishment of a new edge of weight w_0 with the vertex i induces a total increase of traffic δ that is proportionally distributed among the edges departing from the vertex according to their weights (see Fig. 23), yielding $s_i \to s_i + \delta + w_0$. At this stage, it is worth remarking that while we will essentially focus on the simplest model with $\delta = const$, different choices of Δw_{ij} with heterogeneous δ_i or depending on the specific properties of each vertex (w_{ij}, k_i, s_i) can be considered[129–131] (see 4.4.3). Finally, after the weights have been updated the growth process is iterated by introducing a new vertex with the corresponding rearrangement of weights.

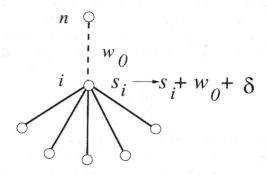

Fig. 23. Illustration of the construction rule. A new node n connects to a node i with probability proportional to $s_i / \sum_j s_j$. The weight of the new edge is w_0 and the total weight on the existing edges connected to i is modified by an amount equal to δ.

The model depends only on the dimensionless parameter δ (rescaled by w_0), that is the fraction of weight which is 'induced' by the new edge onto the others. According to the value of δ, different scenarios are possible. If the induced weight is $\delta \approx 1$ we mimic situations in which an appreciable fraction of traffic generated by the new connection will be dispatched in the already existing connections. This is plausible in the airport networks where the transit traffic is rather relevant in hubs. In the case of $\delta < 1$ we face situations such as the SCN where it is reasonable to consider that the birth of a new collaboration (co-authorship) is not triggering a more intense activity on previous collaborations. Finally, $\delta > 1$ is an extreme case in which a new edge generates a sort of multiplicative effect that is bursting the weight or traffic on neighbors.

The network's evolution can be inspected analytically by studying the time evolution of the average value of $s_i(t)$ and $k_i(t)$ of the i-th vertex at time t, and by relying on the continuous approximation that treats k, s and the time t as continuous variables.[8,11,40] The behavior of the strength and the degree are easily obtained and one has

$$s_i(t) = (2\delta + 1)k_i(t) - 2m\delta \qquad (96)$$

This proportionality relation $s \sim k$ implies $\beta = 1$ but the pre-factor is different from $\langle w \rangle$ ($\langle w \rangle = 1 + \delta$) which indicates the existence of correlations between topology and weights. This relation (96) is particularly relevant since it states that the weight-driven dynamics generates in eq.93 an effective degree preferential attachment that is parameter independent. This highlights an alternative microscopic mechanism accounting for the presence of the preferential attachment dynamics in growing networks.

The behavior of the various statistical distribution can be easily computed and one obtains in the large time limit $P(k) \sim k^{-\gamma}$ and $P(s) \sim s^{-\gamma}$ with

$$\gamma = \frac{4\delta + 3}{2\delta + 1}. \tag{97}$$

This result (see Fig. 24) shows that the obtained graph is a scale-free network described by an exponent $\gamma \in [2,3]$ that depends on the value of the parameter δ. In particular, when the addition of a new edge does not affect the existing weights ($\delta = 0$), the model is topologically equivalent to the Barabási-Albert model[15] and the value $\gamma = 3$ is recovered. For larger values of δ the distribution is progressively broader with $\gamma \to 2$ when $\delta \to \infty$. This indicates that the weight-driven growth generates scale-free networks with exponents varying in the range of values usually observed in the empirical analysis of networked structures.[8,11,12] Noticeably the exponents are nonuniversal and depend only on the parameter δ governing the microscopic dynamics of weights. The model therefore proposes a general mechanism for the occurrence of varying power-law behaviors without resorting on more complicate topological rules and variations of the basic preferential attachment mechanism.

Similarly to the previous quantities, it is possible to obtain analytical expressions for the evolution of weights and the relative statistical distribution.[40] The probability distribution $P(w)$ is in this case also a power-law $P(w) \sim w^{-\alpha}$ where $\alpha = 2 + \frac{1}{\delta}$ (see Fig. 24). The exponent α has large variations as a function of the parameter δ and $P(w)$ goes from a delta function for $\delta = 0$ to a very slow decaying power-law with $\alpha = 2$ if $\delta \to \infty$. This feature clearly shows that the weight distribution is extremely sensitive to changes in the microscopic dynamics ruling the network's growth.

It is interesting to measure, in the context of this simple model, the various weighted quantities defined in Section 4.2, that characterize the clustering and correlation properties.[129] For small δ, the average nearest neighbor degree $k_{nn}(k)$ is almost flat as in the BA model. A disassortative character emerges as δ increases and gives rise to a power law behavior of

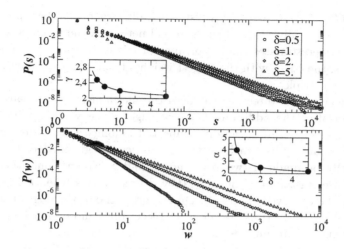

Fig. 24. Top: Probability distribution $P(s)$ for the model described in the text. Data are consistent with a power-law behavior $s^{-\gamma}$. Bottom: Probability distribution of the weights $P(w) \sim w^{-\alpha}$. In the insets we report the value of α obtained by data fitting (filled circles) and the analytic expressions $\gamma = (3 + 4\delta)/(1 + 2\delta)$ and $\alpha = 2 + 1/\delta$ (solid lines). The data are averaged over 200 networks of size $N = 10^5$.

$k_{nn}(k) \sim k^{-a}$. This is in fact a standard feature of growing networks built with preferential attachment mechanisms,[88] while the networks studied in Section 4.3 show an assortative behavior. We note that other real-world networks such as the Internet and the World-Wide-Web have instead a disassortative behavior, and that assortativity can be originated by various mechanisms such as community structure or geographical aspects which are not included in the model. On the other hand, the weighted average nearest neighbor degree displays for any δ a flat behavior, and this model reproduces the important feature that the weighted assortativity $k_{nn}^w(k)$ is significantly larger than $k_{nn}(k)$, as in real networks: the larger weights correspond to the links towards vertices with larger degrees.

Analogous properties are obtained for the clustering spectrum, as shown in Fig. 25. At small δ, the clustering coefficient of the network is small and $C(k)$ is flat. It is noteworthy that the simple mechanism driving weights reinforcement has also consequences on the clustering properties. In particular, values of the clustering coefficient closer to empirical values are obtained when δ is large enough (e.g. $C \approx 0.06 \gg 1/N$ for $\delta = 1$, $m = 2$, $N = 10^4$), and $C(k)$ takes a decreasing power-law like form. The weighted clustering C^w also increases and is systematically larger than the topological C, with an essentially flat $C^w(k)$: as in real networks, the usual clustering coefficient underestimates the importance of triples in the network since, for the hubs, the edges with the largest weights belong in great part to the interconnected triples.

This behaviour is directly related to the mechanism which rearranges the weights after the addition of a new edge. Since vertices with large strength and degree are generally connected among them, a new vertex has more probability to attach to the extremities of a given edge. Triangles will typically be made of two "old" nodes and a "young" one. therefore $C(k)$ increases faster for "younger" (low degree) nodes when δ increases generating the observed spectrum. On the other hand, the edges between "old" and "young" vertices are the most recent ones and do not have large weights. This feature implies that for low degree vertices c_i and c_i^w are rather close. In contrast, high degree vertices are connected to each other by edges with large weights, leading to a weighted clustering coefficient larger than the topological one.

Similarly to the data of real-networks analysed in 4.3, the comparison of weighted and topological correlations shows that the weights are typically concentrated on the links and cliques formed between large degree vertices. This confirms the importance of considering weighted correlations since topological correlations do not fully reveal the intrinsic coupling between topology and weights, that may lead to very different behavior of the correlation and clustering spectrum.

In summary, the networks generated by the model with strength driven preferential attachment and weight reinforcement display power-law behavior for the weight, degree and strength distributions with non-trivial exponents depending on the unique parameter defining the model's dynamics. These results suggest that the inclusion of weights in networks modeling naturally explains the diversity of scale-free behavior empirically observed in real networked structures. Strikingly, the weight-driven growth recovers an effective preferential attachment for the topological properties, providing a microscopic explanation for the ubiquitous presence of this mechanism.

4.4.3. *Local heterogeneities, nonlinearities and space-topology coupling*

The rules defining the model presented in the previous subsection are very simple and may therefore be easily modified to account for various effects.

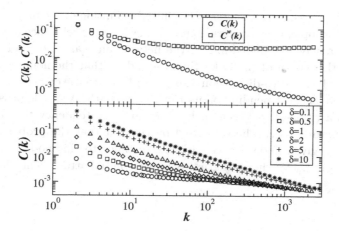

Fig. 25.   Top: Behaviour of $C(k)$ and $C^w(k)$ for $m = 2$, $\delta = 2$; bottom: $C(k)$ for various values of δ.

First of all, the nodes of a network need not have identical characteristics: during the growth, a newly arriving vertex may possess intrinsic properties which make it more (or less) attractive than others, so that its degree and strength grow faster (or slower). Such a feature allows to avoid treating all nodes as identical.[99] In a similar way, the model presented here can be modified by tagging each node i with a given redistribution ability δ_i taken randomly from a certain distribution characterizing the system's heterogeneity.[129] While the strength driven preferential attachment is not modified, the redistribution of weights reads $\Delta w_{ij} = \delta_i w_{ij}/s_i$. A large δ_i thus yields larger increases of the strength s_i and favors the attractivity of i. Assuming a bounded distribution of δ_i, the modified model can be self-consistently solved.[129] The resulting distributions of degree, strength and weights are still distributed according to a power-law with a logarithmic correction, and the clustering and correlation spectra are similar to the case of a uniform δ. A non-linear redistribution may as well be introduced for Δw_{ij}: the perturbation brought by a new incoming link may depend on the centrality of the corresponding node, as measured e.g. by its degree or strength. In this case, non-linear relations between s and k are obtained,[129] similarly to what has been observed in some real-world networks. Another generalization corresponding to directed networks has also been considered.[130]

Finally, the general character of the initial definition of the model allows to include a supplementary ingredient that has a strong relevance in various contexts, namely the embedding of the network in real space and a constraint on the length of the links. Suppose indeed that the nodes building the network lie in a two-dimensional space, and that to the creation of a link is associated a cost depending on its Euclidean length. A simple possibility to express a trade-off between such a cost and the tendency to establish connections to hubs can be expressed by the fact that the probability to connect to a given node decays with the distance to this node.[132,133] As proposed in Ref. 118, the strength driven preferential attachment (93) then becomes

$$\Pi_{n \to i} = \frac{s_i e^{-d_{ni}/r_c}}{\sum_j s_j e^{-d_{nj}/r_c}}, \tag{98}$$

where r_c is a typical scale and d_{ni} is the Euclidean distance between n and i. This rule of *strength driven preferential attachment with spatial selection*, generalizes the preferential attachment mechanism driven by the strength to spatial networks. Here, new vertices connect more likely to vertices which correspond to the best interplay between Euclidean distance and strength. The redistribution rules (94,95) are instead left unchanged.

If the ratio between the typical scale and the size of the system $\eta = r_c/L$ is large, the effect of distances is negligible and we recover the properties of the weighted model.[40] When η decreases, additional constraints appear and have important consequences on the structure of the network. In particular, a small η favors the creation of "regional" structures with hubs of smaller degree than the global hubs obtained at large η. On the other hand, the global traffic increases in the same way during the growth of the network, so that these regional hubs carry larger strengths than when global hubs are available. In short, the degree distribution is thus modified by a cut-off, and the relation between strength and degree becomes non-linear. Moreover, clustering is enhanced and the correlations and clustering spectra acquire shapes more similar to the case of the airport network.[118]

4.4.4. *Other models coupling traffic and topology*

The empirical evidences and the resulting modeling inspired by the coupling of topology and traffic has stimulated the development of several other models based on similar mechanisms as well as other dynamical rules. Here we provide a brief and necessarily incomplete overview of models for weighted networks recently proposed in the literature. A "minimal" model has been proposed:[134] the strength-driven preferential attachment is recovered by an attachment of each new node to the extremities of an edge chosen with probability proportional to its weight, and a reinforcement mechanism is present as well. As in a previous model,[135] this variation allows to obtain networks with large clustering coefficient, since a triangle is created at each time step. On the other hand, a slightly different version of the mechanism has been put forward[136,137] with a partial decoupling of the reinforcement of the weights from the topological growth. In these models, each new node is connected to old nodes with either degree or strength driven preferential attachment, and *already existing links* are reinforced with a probability depending on the strength of their extremities (i.e. in a "busy gets busier" way). Such mechanisms take into account the fact that traffic can grow and connections can be strengthened even on a static topology, and lead to broadly distributed degrees and strengths, with a non-linear relation $s \sim k^\beta$ ($\beta > 1$). Finally, a model mixing topological and strength preferential attachment, and adding a mechanism reinforcing the formation of triangles, together with a "busy gets busier" weight reinforcement,[138] shows similar properties as the original model.

4.5. *Outlook*

The analysis of the weighted quantities and the study of the correlations between weights and topology provide a complementary perspective on the structural organization of the network that might be undetected by quantities based only on topological information. The weighted quantities thus offer a quantitative and general approach to understand the complex architecture of real networks. On the other hand, while the abundance of large data sets on network topology has allowed the understanding of several basic properties of large scale networks and the ordering principle at their basis, the situation is still at an early stage for weighted networks. Data sets including reliable measures of the traffic or intensity on edges are still limited and in many cases refer only to limited network regions. Most important, any detailed understanding of the interplay between weights and topology needs a deeper insight on the basic forces determining the traffic or intensity values on the network's edges. For instance, in the Internet it is hardly possible to achieve a higher level of understanding without relating the weighted structure with the behavioral network of users that generate the traffic on the various physical and virtual networks. Analogously, traffic on transportation networks is related to the network of social and commercial relations of individuals. In other words, facing the problem of weighted networks readily spurs issues related to networks of networks and how to interface those. The study of weighted networks is therefore bringing the community at the forefront of network research defining the important questions to be faced in the near future of the field.

Acknowledgments

Acknowledgments. We thank IATA for making the airline commercial flight database available to us. We also thank M.E.J. Newman for conceding us the possibility of using the scientific collaboration network data (see http://www-personal.umich.edu/~mejn/collaboration/).

CHAPTER 5

Community Structure Identification

Leon Danon[1], Jordi Duch[2], Alex Arenas[2] and Albert Díaz-Guilera[1]

[1]*Departament de Fisica Fonamental, Universitat de Barcelona
Marti i Franques 1, 08086 Barcelona, Spain*

[2]*Departament d'Enginyeria Informàtica i Matemàtiques,
Universitat Rovira i Virgili, 43007 Tarragona, Spain*

5.1. *Introduction*

The study of complex networks has received an enormous amount of attention from the scientific community in recent years.[8–10,44,139,140] Physicists in particular have become interested in the study of networks describing the topologies of wide variety of systems, such as the world wide web, social and communication networks, biochemical networks and many more. Although several questions have been addressed, many important ones still resist complete resolution. One such problem is the analysis of modular structure found in many networks.[141] Distinct modules or communities within networks can loosely be defined as subsets of nodes which are more densely linked, when compared to the rest of the network. Such communities have been observed, using some of the methods we shall go on to describe, in many different contexts, including metabolic networks,[122,142] banking networks[143] and most notably social networks.[144] As a result, the problem of identification of communities has been the focus of many recent efforts.

Community detection in large networks is potentially very useful. Nodes belonging to a tight-knit community are more than likely to have other properties in common. In the world wide web, community analysis has uncovered thematic clusters.[145,146] In biochemical or neural networks, communities may be functional groups,[147] and separating the network into such groups could simplify the functional analysis considerably.

The problem of community detection is particularly tricky and has been the subject of discussion in various disciplines. A simpler version of this problem, the graph bi-partitioning problem (GBP) has been the topic of study in the realm of computer science for decades. Here one looks to separate the graph into two densely connected communities of equal size, which are connected with the minimum number of links. This is an NP complete problem,[148] however several methods have been proposed to reduce the complexity of the task.[149–151] In real complex networks we often have no idea how many communities we wish to discover, but in general it is more than two. This makes the process all the more costly. What is more, communities may also be hierarchical, that is communities may be further divided into sub-communities and so on.[152–154]

In this chapter we would like to present the recent advances made in the field of community identification in networks in a clear and simple fashion. To this end, the sections are organised as follows. In the next section we describe some ways to define communities in a network context. Following this, we present a method to evaluate the a particular partition of a network. Then, we go on to describe the various recent methods starting with link removal methods, going on to agglomerative methods, followed by methods optimising modularity and finally "other" methods. Some of the methods presented do not necessarily fit into just one of these classification, and there may be some overlap. In the final section, we compare the methods from a computational cost perspective and show how sensitive some of the methods are when applied to *ad hoc* networks with community structure.

5.2. *Definitions of communities*

Despite the large amount of study in this area, a consensus on what is the definition of community has not been reached. With a few exceptions, we will mostly be dealing with networks in which the links have no direction and are unweighted. In this case the definition of community must be purely topological.

Social networks has been the subject of interest for sociologists for decades.[7] The social science approach is largely (though by no means exclusively) concerned with the effect an individual player has on the network and vice versa. As a result, the local properties of networks take a more prominent role in social science research. Nonetheless, much of this knowledge is extremely useful. Some definitions[7] have been used and developed by methods we shall describe later. Here we present some of these.

Conceptually, the definitions can be separated into two main categories, self-referring and comparative definitions. Central to all such definitions is the concept of subgraph.

i. **Self referring definitions**

The basic community definition is *a clique*, defined as a subgroup of a graph containing more than two nodes where all the nodes are connected to each other by means of links in both directions. In other words, this is a fully connected subgraph. This is a particularly strong definition and rarely fulfilled in real sparse networks for larger groups. *n-cliques*, *n-clans* and *n-clubs* are similar definitions designed to relax the above constraint, while retaining its basic premise. The shortest path between all the nodes in a clique is unity. Allowing this distance to take higher values, one arrives at the definition of *n-cliques*, which are defined as a subgroups of the graph containing more than two nodes where the largest shortest path distance between any two nodes in the group is n. *n-clans* and *n-clubs* are subtle variations of *n-cliques*.

ii. **Comparative definitions**

Above, a community has been defined only in reference to itself. A somewhat different approach to this is to compare the number of internal links to the number of external links, coming from the intuitive notion that a community will be denser in terms of links than its surroundings. One such definition, an *LS set* is defined as a set of nodes in which each of its components has more links to other components within the same community. This is the same definition as the *strong definition of community* used by Radicchi *et al.*[155]

Again the above definition is quite restrictive, and in order to relax the constraints even further, Radicchi*et al* propose to use the *sum* of links. So a community in the *weak* sense is defined as a set of nodes whose total number of internal links is greater than the total number of links to the outside. This is the most intuitive of all definitions and is the one that is used most, although implicitly.

Self-referring definitions, while useful in characterising communities which are already known, are not the best choice while trying to find them. The Bron-Kerbosch algorithm[156] for finding cliques in a network is very costly, running in worst case time that scales exponentially with network size. Comparative definitions, on the other hand, lend themselves much more easily to the search for communities in large complex networks. In a way, comparing the internal structure of a community to the external structure gives rise to a measure of how good a particular partition is, as described in the next section.

5.3. *Evaluating community identification*

A question that has been raised in recent years is how to evaluate a given partition of a network into communities. A simple approach it is based on the intuitive idea that random networks do not exhibit community structure.[159] Let us imagine that we have an arbitrary network, and an arbitrary partition of that network into N_c communities. It is then possible to define a $N_c \times N_c$ size matrix $\mathbf{e}$ where the elements e_{ij} represent the fraction of total links starting at a node in partition i and ending at a node in partition j. Then, the sum of the any row (or column) of $\mathbf{e}$, $a_i = \sum_j e_{ij}$ corresponds to the fraction of links connected to i.

If the network does not exhibit community structure, or if the partitions are allocated without any regard to the underlying structure, the expected value of the fraction of links within partitions can be estimated. It is simply the probability that a link begins at a node in i, a_i, multiplied by the fraction of links that end at a node in i, a_i. So the expected number of intra-community links is just $a_i a_i$. On the other hand we know that the *real* fraction of links exclusively within a partition is e_{ii}. So, we can compare the two directly and sum over all the partitions in the graph.

$$Q = \sum_i (e_{ii} - a_i^2) \tag{99}$$

This is a measure known as *modularity*. Let us consider as an example a network comprised of two disconnected components. If we then have two partitions, corresponding exactly to the two components, modularity will have a value of 1. For particularly "bad" partitions, for example, when all the nodes are in a community of their own, the value of modularity can take negative values.

One might be tempted to think that random networks will exhibit very small values of modularity. As Guimerà *et al* show, this in general is not the case.[157] It is possible to find a partition which not only has a nonzero value of modularity for random networks of finite size, but that this value is quite high, for example a network of 128 nodes and 1024 links has a maximum modularity of 0.208. This suggests that these networks that seem to have no structure actually exhibit community structure due to fluctuations.

From here on we will look at different methods of community identification presented recently. First we consider methods based on link removal.

5.4. *Link removal methods*

Intuitively, the simplest way to partition a network is to cut some links until the network is no longer connected. Divisive methods do just that. However, cutting links haphazardly is unlikely to give useful results. So, several methods have been proposed to find the most appropriate links to remove, so that the disconnected components correspond to meaningful communities.

5.4.1. *Shortest path centrality*

This is one of the first methods presented, and remains one of the more elegant.[144] It is based on the idea of centrality, a measure of how central the node or link is in the network. Shortest path centrality is employed in this case, and is measured as the number of shortest paths between pairs of nodes that pass through a certain node or link. Intuitively, links which are most central are also the most "between", and as such, will act as bridges joining communities together in a connected whole. Removing these bridges should split the network into more densely connected communities, see Fig. 26.

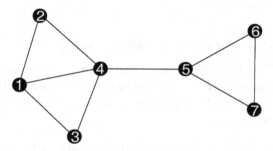

Fig. 26. Shortest path centrality (betweenness) is the number of shortest paths that go through a link or node. In this simple case, the link with the largest link centrality is that joining nodes 4 and 5.

The algorithm proceeds as follows:

i. Calculate shortest path centrality for all links.
ii. Remove link with the highest centrality.

iii. Recalculate all link centralizers.

iv. Repeat from step 2 until the network is split into two parts.

v. Proceed iteratively within each of the partitions until no links remain and the network is reduced to individual nodes, each in its own partition.

Should a particular link removal split the network, it necessarily does so into two components, since a link by definition connects two nodes. As the algorithm proceeds separating the network into ever smaller pieces, it is possible to construct a a dendrogram or *binary tree* to store the information of the entire process for later retrieval and analysis. Calculation of link betweenness is the most computer intensive part of the algorithm. Using the fastest methods developed independently by Newman[67] and Brandes[158] and for a network of size n with m links the speed of calculating all link betweenness-es still remains of $O(mn)$ for unweighted networks. Unfortunately, the calculation needs to be repeated each time since once any link is removed, the betweenness of all the other links is affected. In fact Girvan and Newman report that omitting step 3 leads to "wrong" community detection.[144] This algorithm is quite sensitive and is one of the few able to detect community structure at all levels. Its major drawback is the computational cost. It scales with the number of nodes n and number of links m as $O(m^2n)$, which limits the size of the graph one can treat with this method to around 10000 nodes (with current desktop computer technology and some patience).

5.5. *Current-flow and random walk centrality*

In an extension[159] of the method described above, the same authors present two other means to detect community structure. The basic method remains the same as above, with the difference being the way in which the link centrality is calculated.

i. *Resistor networks.* In this approach the network to be studied is considered to be a circuit, where links are assigned a unit resistance and a particular pair of nodes act as unit voltage source and sink. The current flows from source to sink along a number of paths, those with the lowest resistance (shortest path) carry the most current. So the *current-flow* betweenness of an link can be calculated using Kirchoff's laws by summing the value of the current flowing through that link over all pairs of nodes. This can be done in only in $O(n^4)$ time for sparse networks since

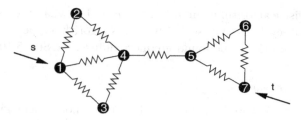

Fig. 27. Resistor networks and current flow centrality. The links in the network are considered as unit resistances. By choosing a pair of nodes to be a source of unit voltage *s* and sink *t*, one can can calculate the current flow through any link using Kirchoff's laws. Summing this value for every pair of nodes gives the total current flow betweenness of a link. In this case the biggest current flow is through link joining nodes 4 and 5.

the method is dependent on the inversion of an $N \times N$ matrix which takes $O(n^3)$ time in the worst case.

ii. *Random walks.* Here, the network is thought of as a substrate for signals that perform a random walk from a source vertex to a sink vertex. The link betweenness in this case is simply the rate of flow of random walkers through a particular link summed over all pairs of vertices. This measure of betweenness is numerically identical to current flow betweenness, although the derivation is different.

Although conceptually interesting, these approaches are computationally costly. As the authors themselves note, and we can see in Section 5.10, the shortest path betweenness outperforms these approaches in both speed and accuracy. Both the resistor network approach and the random walk approach ideas have been developed further by other authors (see Section 5.9.2 and Section 5.8.4).

5.5.1. *Information centrality*

Another divisive algorithm was presented by Fortunato *et al*[160] In this paper they employ the *network efficiency* measure, previously proposed by Latora and Marchiori[161] to quantify how efficient a particular network **G** is in the context of information exchange. Once a particular link is removed from **G**, its efficiency is reduced by a measurable amount C^I, or *information centrality*. The idea behind the algorithm is that the links responsible for the largest drop in network efficiency are those that act as bridges between communities. The algorithm proceeds in a similar way as the GN algorithm, that is, recursively calculating the links with highest C^I and removing them, until the entire hierarchy is unravelled. The algorithm is somewhat slower than other divisive algorithms running at $(O(n^4))$, but what it loses in speed it gains in accuracy. In comparison with the GN algorithm it performs better when the communities to be found are more diffuse, see Sec. 5.10.

5.5.2. *Link clustering*

This algorithm[155] is based on the idea that linked nodes belonging to the same community should have a larger number of 'common friends'. In other words links inside communities should be part of a large proportion of possible loops, and links pointing to outside of the community should be included in few or no loops. The algorithm proceeds as in 5.4.1, but instead of using the link centrality value, it works with the 'link-clustering coefficient' $C^{(g)}$, which represents the fraction of possible loops of order g that pass through a certain link. The algorithm is implemented for triangles ($g = 3$) or squares ($g = 4$). The system computes the $C^{(g)}$ values for all links, and cuts the one with the *minimum* value. These two steps are repeated recursively as long as all the partitions fulfill one of the community definitions (see Sec. 5.2). The algorithm is very fast, since calculating the clustering coefficient can be done with local information only. It is also interesting because it was the first algorithm which contained a definition of community to stop the analysis when a certain condition is fulfilled. This method is not appropriate for trees, sparse graphs and disassortative networks due to the small number of triangles and squares.

5.6. *Agglomerative methods*

Instead of starting with the network as a whole and looking for a way to split it into meaningful communities, one can look at the problem from a different perspective. One can start with all the nodes in the network being separate, and use some method to join up, or agglomerate, nodes which are likely to be in the same community.

5.6.1. *Hierarchical clustering*

Traditional methods for detecting communities in social networks have been based on "hierarchical clustering".[162,163] In general they proceed by calculating a similarity metric for each pair of vertices, representing how close the vertices are according to some property of the network. In the beginning, only vertices in the network are considered, with no links between them, and links are added one by one in order of their weights. Such methods have previously been very successful in small scale case studies, particularly when the complexity of the network under study is not great. Recently however, since this method is very fast and scales well with system size, it has been employed to study the temporal evolution of communities in large networks.[164] Hopcroft *et al* study the CiteSeer citation network, where papers in the CiteSeer database are considered as nodes, and citations are considered as links. As a weight metric they use a measure based on the number of citations which any two papers share. The sheer size of this network (around 250,000 papers) makes it intractable with most other methods, and demonstrates the ability of hierarchical clustering methods to deal with large data sets.

5.6.2. *L-shell method*

This method proposes a different take on agglomerative methods. The algorithm[165] consists of a shell of size l, starting at a node i is a subset of nodes, all within a shortest path distance of $d \leq l$ (L-shell) spreading outward from a starting node i. As the shell expands the *total emerging degree*, K_i^l, is measured which is simply the number of links pointing to vertices outside the expanding shell. When the ratio of the emerging degree at step l to that at step $l - i$, $\frac{K_i^l}{K_i^{l-1}}$, is lower than a cut-off value, the algorithm is stopped. Those nodes within a distance l of the starting vertex are grouped within one community, and all other nodes are said to be outside. This part of the algorithm may be applied when one is concerned with a single community and not the entire community structure, and for this purpose the algorithm is computationally inexpensive scaling linearly with the size of the community under scrutiny. To make the method more general the authors also propose one possible method to apply the algorithm globally. The above process for each node in the network is repeated and a *membership matrix* M is built with the information extracted in the following way: if the process starting at node i classes node j as being in the same community, the element m_{ij} is given the value of 1. Otherwise it is set to 0^l.

---

[l]The membership matrix is not necessarily symmetric: an L-shell starting at node i may class node j as being in the same community, but this does not imply that an L-shell starting at j will class i as being in the same community.

5.7. Methods based on maximising modularity

As described in Sec. 5.3, the modularity measure is one way to evaluate quantitatively a network partition. So, as many authors have asked themselves, why not optimise this value directly? The main problem is that the partition space of any graph (even relatively small ones) is huge, and one needs a guide to navigate this space and find maximum values. Here we outline the approaches that have tackled this problem.

5.7.1. Greedy algorithm

In the first attempt at optimising Q directly Newman takes a greedy optimisation (hill climbing) approach.[166] At the start of the algorithm, each node is placed into its own partition. One can then calculate the change in Q should any two partitions be joined. The algorithm proceeds by choosing the pair of partitions producing the largest change, and joining them. This process is repeated until a maximum value of Q is obtained. The algorithm is one of the fastest available, especially when applied using the data structure for sparse networks.[167] However, while also pretty good at identifying community structure, more recent approaches have achieved even more accuracy (see Sec. 5.10).

This method has been used to study the size distributions of communities. Due to the speed of the approach, large networks can be decomposed into meaningful communities and the distribution of the sizes can be plotted with enough statistics to be able to make conclusions. It has previously been noted that the distribution of community sizes seems to follow a power law.[152–154] However there seems to be some discussion about the exponent of these power laws. On the original analysis[141] on collaboration network,[66] the size distribution follows a power law with exponent -2. However, repeating this experiment we recover an exponent of around -1.5. The explanation of these exponents still remains an open problem.

5.7.2. Simulated annealing methods

Another approach to optimise the modularity measure Q is to employ simulated annealing methods.[168] This is done by using two modifications of the Monte Carlo sampling method with simulated annealing. The process begins with any initial partition of the nodes into communities. At each step, a node is chosen at random and moved to a different community, also chosen at random. If the change improves the modularity it is always ac-

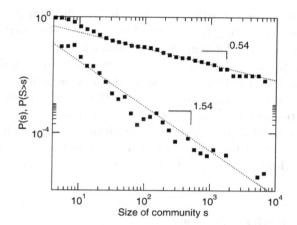

Fig. 28. The size distribution of community sizes in the ArXiv collaboration network. The cumulative distribution follows a power law over several decades with exponent −0.5. The non-cumulative distribution, although noisier seems to follow a power law with exponent with around −1.5 as expected.

cepted, otherwise it is accepted with a probability $\exp(\beta\Delta Q)^{\mathrm{m}}$. The authors try to improve the success of in two ways. Firstly, the algorithm is stopped periodically, or quenched, and ΔQ is calculated for moving each node to every community that is not its own. Finally, the move corresponding to the largest value of ΔQ is accepted. The second way to improve the efficiency is using a Basin-Hopping approach, where in each step a series of nodes is moved from one community to another, not just one. In this case, the acceptance criterion is calculated directly from the partition that results at the end of the move. The authors report that the second method is slower to run, but able to find high values of Q quickly. In case of large networks it requires less computer memory than the other presented, since it doesn't need extra data structures.

5.7.3. *Extremal optimisation*

In this approach,[169] an heuristic search procedure based on extremal optimisation[170] is used to find the network community configuration that has the best modularity value. The algorithm optimises the *local* modularity, a measure which represents the contribution of each node to the *global* modularity. To begin with, nodes are assigned one of two partitions at ran-

---

^{m}This is the Metropolis criterion.

dom. As it evolves, the algorithm improves the contribution of nodes with the worst local modularity, by moving them to the other partition, and therefore improving the global modularity until a maximum possible value is found. Then the links between the two partitions are removed, and the process is repeated recursively while the modularity keeps increasing.

Extra information is not needed to detect the optimal number of communities and the process stops when the partition modularity cannot be improved further. While not the fastest algorithm, scaling as $O(n^2 \log(n))$ (a good application of the greedy algorithm scaling with $O(n \log^2(n))$), it achieves the highest known modularity values for all networks studied, see Sec. 5.10.

5.8. Spectral analysis methods

The adjacency matrix of a network contains all the information about the networks topology. A graph of size N can be represented by a matrix A of size $N \times N$ whose element $A_{i,j}$ is zero if no link exists between nodes i and j, and greater than zero if a link exists, where the value of the non-zero element represents the weight of the link.

An alternative representation of an unweighted graph in matrix form is the Laplacian matrix[n]. If a link exists between nodes i and j, the element $L_{i,j} = -1$. The diagonal of the matrix $L_{i,i}$ contains the degree of node i, so that the sum of each row and column is equal to zero. Methods which take advantage of algebraic properties of these matrices have been proposed over several decades.

5.8.1. Spectral bisection

Since the sum of elements over each row or column of the Laplacian matrix is equal to zero, there necessarily exists an eigenvector with eigenvalue 0. If the network to be analysed is connected there is only one zero eigenvalue. However, for disconnected graphs with m separate components, the Laplacian matrix is block diagonal, and has m degenerate eigenvectors all corresponding to eigenvalue 0. If the division is not so clear, that is, there exist some links between the m components, the degeneration is no longer present, leaving one eigenvector with eigenvalue zero and $m - 1$ eigenvector with eigenvalue slightly greater from zero.[171] So it should be possible to find

---

[n]The name Laplacian is drawn from the fact that applying the discrete Laplacian operator on the network in question gives the Laplacian matrix.

the blocks, at least approximately by considering the eigenvalues slightly greater than zero and looking at the components of their eigenvectors. As the Laplacian matrix is symmetric, with orthogonal eigenvectors, the sums of the components of each eigenvector must vanish (apart from the first, trivial eigenvector, which has all equal components). The problem studied in classic papers[150,172] is a special case, where $m = 2$, the graph bisection problem. Here, the second eigenvector can provide a simple way to cut the graph in two. The components of the *second* eigenvector corresponding to nodes in one subgraph will be positive, and so must be negative for those components corresponding to the other.

Many improvements in both the time it takes for the algorithm to run as well as its precision have been described since.[173]

5.8.2. *Multi dimensional spectral analysis*

Taking further advantage of the properties of the Laplacian matrix, Donetti and Muñoz present a very nice approach.[174] The first few non-trivial eigenvectors can be extracted sequentially at minimum cost, using the Lanczos method, which can be applied to sparse matrices at minimum computational cost.[175] The individual eigenvector components, which represent nodes in the graph, can be thought of as coordinates in M-dimensional space, where M is the number of non-trivial eigenvectors considered. The idea is that if two nodes belong to the same community, they are close in this M-space. As the authors point out, there is more than one way to measure these distances.

Once separated in this space, the nodes can be clustered using hierarchical agglomerative methods, using both simple Euclidean distance and angular distance. The authors go on to show that the angular version in general performs much better. Once again, the authors employ different methods, both "single linkage" or "multiple linkage" clustering. They show that while faster, single linkage clustering performs worse than the multiple linkage version. The clustering is stopped at the highest value of modularity obtained (see Sec. 5.3), thus detecting the optimal configuration.

This algorithm is reasonably fast ($O(N^3)$ according to the authors), but needs *a priori* information on how many vectors need to be extracted to separate the communities properly. In terms of sensitivity, the algorithm performs well (see Sec. 5.10). In the comparison section, we use the aliases DMCS and DMCA for Single Angular and Complete Angular analyses respectively.

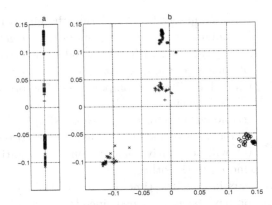

Fig. 29. (a) Components of the first non-trivial eigenvector for a *ad hoc* network with 4 communities (see Sec. 5.10). (b) All communities can be clearly identified when the components of more than one eigenvector are used as coordinates in M-dimensional space where M is the number of eigenvectors used. Here $M = 2$.

5.8.3. *Constrained optimisation*

This method,[176] is based on the spectral properties of the simple adjacency matrix as opposed to the Laplacian. The authors recast the costly problem of extracting eigenvectors of an $N \times N$ matrix into a constrained optimisation problem. In this way they are able to extract the eigenvectors much faster. As in the previous method[174] this gives information about the location of the different nodes ordered in different groups in an M-space (where M is once again, the number of eigenvectors extracted). To detect the groups that appear, they use a correlation of the average values of the eigenvectors to measure how close two nodes are in this space. Instead of providing a clear cut community structure, this method gives us an idea of how close any pair of nodes is in the context of communities.

To test the method they study both undirected and directed networks, using the appropriate optimisation function for each case, and test the algorithm on a word association network.[177] The network has over 10000 nodes and the method is able to give qualitatively good results.

5.8.4. *Approximate resistance networks*

In a development of the resistor network approach,[159] Wu *et al* present an approximate method, in order to reduce the computational time needed.[178] In this method, a pair of nodes is chosen at random to be a voltage source, $V_1 = 1$ and a sinks $V_2 = 0$. The authors then approximate the voltage of all other nodes in the network iteratively, avoiding the costly matrix inversion.[159] The accuracy of this approximation is dependent on how many times the iterative step is repeated. After obtaining the node voltages in this way, the values are ordered and large gaps in voltage values are identified. The graph is then split at a particular voltage gap, separating a number of nodes (within a tolerance limit), which must be previously known, from the rest of the network. This process is repeated, randomly choosing pairs of nodes to be voltage sources and sinks. Nodes are then bundled together into a community of the expected size using a simple majority rule over the realisations of the algorithm. Once one community is identified, the process can be restricted to choosing nodes from that community as voltage sources, and sinks from the rest of the network, improving the accuracy.

This method when employed to identify all communities in a graph is dependent on having a good idea of the sizes of communities one is looking for. In networks of larger size and complexity, this is generally not known, and the algorithm becomes more difficult to apply. However, the method can be employed to identify the community that any one nodes belongs to in linear time, similar to the approach of Bagrow and Bolt.[165]

5.9. *Other methods*

This section is dedicated to those methods that do not belong clearly to any of the previous classes.

5.9.1. *Clustering and curvature*

This is one of the first attempts at detecting thematic and functional communities based on clustering.[146] Eckmann and Moses use the concept of *curvature* of a node and relate it to clustering. Consider a node i; its neighbours will be separated by a geodesic distance of at most 2. If links exist between neighbours of node i, this distance is unity. The average distance between neighbours of any node, therefore, lies between 1 and 2. This value is directly related to clustering.[146] If one assumes that the distance from node i to any of its neighbours is unity, and take the distance between any of the neighbours to be the average, one can indeed think of the node to be in "curved" space, with the amount of curvature depending on the average distance between the nodes, see Fig. 30.

The method is based on the intuition that high curvature region of a network will belong to the same community. The authors show that finding connected components of high curvature give a good idea of community

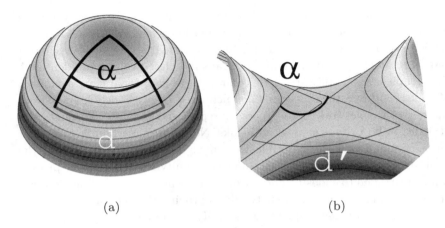

(a)   (b)

Fig. 30. How clustering is related to curvature.[146] For a node i, the shortest path distance between any of its neighbours will be either 1, if the neighbours are linked, or 2, if they are not. The average distance between the neighbours can give a measure of curvature. Positive curvature is depicted in (a) and negative curvature is depicted in (b). Both triangles have sides of length unity, and the angle between the two is the same, but the distances are different, $d < d'$.

structure. In a later effort, they go on to use the method to study communities in email dialogue.[179]

5.9.2. *Random walk based methods*

In a set of papers, Zhou and collaborators develop a methodology for community detection based on random walks.[180–182] Apart from a method for finding communities, Zhou also presents a definition of what a community is. Also worthy of note is that the method is applicable to both directed and undirected networks.

Instead of actually performing the random walk on the network, it is possible to calculate the average distance from node i to node j algebraically starting with the adjacency matrix°. From the information contained in the average distances *local* and *global attractors* of each node can be defined. The local attractor of node i is the closest node (smallest average distance) of its nearest neighbours, and the global attractor, the node closest to all

---

°Note that although the absolute distance from a node to one of its neighbours is necessarily 1, this is not generally true for a random walker, which could easily make a "mistake" and go where it is not supposed to.

other nodes in the network. From these two definitions, two different formal definitions of community are derived. A local community is defined as a subset of the network in question whose nodes satisfy the following three conditions:

- if node i belongs to the community, then its local attractor j also belongs to the same community.
- if node i is the local attractor of any other node k, k also belongs to the same community.
- any subset of the community in question is not a local community in its own right, ie. it is the smallest possible set.

The "global community" is defined in much the same way, although in this case local communities can form part of global communities.

Apart from the definition of community this method permits a formal definition of a central node for a community. So, that node which is its own global attractor is the central node.

In a more refined effort,[181] the author uses the average distance measure to define a *dissimilarity index* of any two nodes[P]. Using the dissimilarity index, the author describes an elaborate method of hierarchical agglomeration of nodes into communities.

Most recently Zhou and Lipowsky[147,182] present another method based on *biased random walks*. Instead of having the walkers performing purely random walks, the walker has a higher probability to jump from a node i to a node which shares the highest number of neighbours with i (essentially biasing the random walker to go down the link with the highest link clustering). This time Zhou presents an algorithm to detect communities similar to hierarchical clustering algorithms described

In a similar approach Latapy and Pons[183] also employ the intuitive idea that a random walker will get trapped for a longer time in a a densely connected community. They calculate a distance measure between two nodes, and apply an agglomerative method,[184] starting with all nodes in their own community, and joining them two by two. The main difference between this approach and the above is that at each step, the distances are recalculated. The two methods have very similar sensitivities, suggesting that recalculating the distances in each step is not crucial, see Sec. 5.10.

[P]For nodes i and j the dissimilarity index is simply the square of the difference between the distance from another node k to i and the distance from k to j summed over all nodes k.

5.9.3. *Q-potts model*

Another interesting approach[185] detects communities by mapping it to a spin system.[186] Here, each node is assigned a spin state between 1 and q, at random. The energy of the spin system is determined using a q-Potts Hamiltonian[q]. The idea is that in the ground state of the system, communities are identified as groups with equal spin values, see Fig. 31. To get to the ground state (or at least close to it) the system is allowed to evolve using a simple Monte-Carlo method with simulated annealing. At each step, the spin of a node selected at random is updated according to the Metropolis criterion depending on the change in the energy of the system. Every few steps, the Monte-Carlo "temperature" is reduced. The method has two parameters, q and γ. The value of q needs to be large enough to identify all the possible communities and γ is set to be the average link probability of the network. Appropriate values are discussed further in the paper.

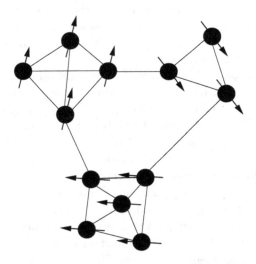

Fig. 31.   The q-Potts model as applied to a small network with communities. Each node is assigned one of q spins. As the Hamiltonian of the system is minimised, the spins in a tightly connected community take equal values, which are different to those of spins in other communities.

---

[q]The q-Potts model is essentially an Ising model with q states instead of just two.

One useful characteristic of this is that it permits the detection of communities which are "fuzzy", or clearly separate from the rest of the network. The method should be fast since one only needs only local information to calculate the Hamiltonian and update the spins. The sensitivity of the algorithm is also good, as we can see in the next section.

5.10. *Comparative evaluation*

In order for the reader to be able to compare the algorithms, both in terms of their speed and sensitivity, we would like to present a qualitative comparison for all the above community identification methods. This unfortunately is not possible for all the methods described, as they are very varied, both conceptually and in their applications.

For some of these methods we are able to estimate how the computational cost scales with network size n. Table 2 shows these values.

Table 2. We summarize how different approaches scale with number of nodes n and number of links m and k is the degree of any node. The alias show here is used in Figures 32 and 33.

Reference	Alias	Order
159	NG	$O(m^2 n)$
144	GN	$O(n^2 m)$
160	FLM	$O(n^4)$
155	RCCLP	$O(n^2)$
166	NF	$O(n \log^2 n)$
174	DMSA	$O(n^3)$
174	DMCA	$O(n^3)$
146	EM	$O(m\langle k^2\rangle)$
147	ZL	$O(n^3)$
185	RB	unknown
165	BB	$O(n^3)$
169	DA	$O(n^2 \log n)$
176	CSCC	$O(n^2)$
178	WH	$O(n + m)$

One method that has been employed in many cases is to see how the method performs when applied to *ad hoc* networks with well known, fixed community structure.[159]

The networks are generated with $n = 128$ nodes, split into four communities containing 32 nodes each. A pair of nodes both of which belong to the same community are linked with probability p_{in}, and a pair which belong to different communities are joined with probability p_{out}. The value of p_{out} is chosen so that the average number of links a node has to members of other community, z_{out} is controlled. The value of p_{in} is chosen to keep the total average node degree, z_{tot} constant. As z_{out} is increased from zero, the communities become more and more diffuse and harder to identify. Since the "real" community structure is well known in this case, it is possible to measure the number of nodes correctly classified by the method of community identification. The benchmark test, then, is to plot the fraction of correctly identified nodes as a function of z_{out}.

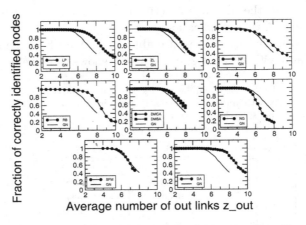

Fig. 32. Comparing algorithm sensitivity using *ad hoc* networks with predetermined community structure with $n = 128$, the network divided into four communities with 32 nodes each and total average degree of 16. The x-axis is the average number of connections to outside communities z_{out} and the y-axis is the fraction of nodes correctly identified by the method.

In Figure 32 we show the sensitivity of all methods we have been able to get gather. To summarise the large amount of information, in Figure 33 we plot the the fraction of correctly identified nodes for only three values of z_{out} (6, 7 and 8), for each method. From this we can see that most of the methods perform very well for $z_{out} = 6$ and even for $z_{out} = 7$ most can identify more than half the nodes correctly. For $z_{out} = 8$ there remain three methods able to identify more than half of the nodes correctly[r].

---

[r]It is important to note that there may be some differences in the way the authors calculated these values.

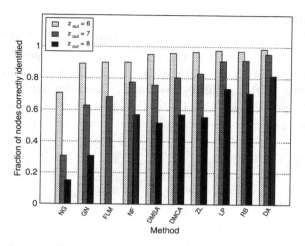

Fig. 33. The fraction of correctly identified nodes at three specific values of z_{out}, 6, 7 and 8 for all available methods. Here we can see that most of the methods are very good at finding the "correct" community structure for values of z_{out} up to 6. At $z_{out} = 7$ some methods begin to falter but most still identify more than half of the nodes correctly. At $z_{out} = 8$, only three methods are still able to identify the correct structure.

5.11. *Conclusion*

In this work we have attempted to give an overview of the modern approaches to community identification in complex networks. A large amount of knowledge has been collected in the field, and real progress has been made, both in the identification of communities and their characterisation. Some questions do remain open, and it is these that we would suggest for further study. Despite these efforts, computational cost involved in computing communities in complex network remain significant. At present, the fastest method for finding an unknown number of communities of unknown sizes has a cost which scales as $O(n \log^2 n)$ with network size. While this makes the analysis of extremely large networks feasible this algorithm does not guarantee that the partition found will be the best possible one. Other algorithms which give better partitions are more expensive. The challenge, then, is to come up with a method which is both fast and accurate.

Another major challenge is to understand the mechanisms which are responsible for the characteristic scale free distributions of community sizes observed. Such distributions often suggest an underlying optimisation is responsible, but this remains to be shown.

Acknowledgments

The authors are grateful to Luca Donetti, Haijun Zhou, Mark Newman, Santo Fortunato, Jörg Reichardt, Claudio Castellano, Matthieu Latapy and Jean-Pierre Eckmann for providing their data. This work has been supported by DGES of the Spanish Govenrment Grant No. BFM-2003-08258 and EC-FET Open Project COSIN no. IST-2001-33555. LD gratefully acknowledges the funding of Generalitat de Catalunya.

CHAPTER 6

Visualizing Large and Complex Networks

Marco Gaertler and Dorothea Wagner
Universität Karlsruhe (TH), Faculty of Informatics,
76128 Karlsruhe, Germany

6.1. *Introduction*

Due to the increasing importance of communication and the dissemination of information as well as the growing complexity and globalization in economy and society networked structures come to the fore of our perception. Understanding networks, how they arise and evolve is an exciting topic. Accordingly, the use of visualizations as means for the comprehension and analysis of networks is a increasingly relevant research field. Network visualizations are used already in many research fields, e.g. UML-diagrams in software engineering, diagrams of chemical pathways, genealogical tree and social networks. Already the size of such networks demands automatic methods to generate such drawings. If in addition such visualizations should support the comprehension of the according data and give an objective illustration of their structure, the systematic production becomes a very challenging issue.

First of all the representation, i.e. the way the nodes and edges or links of the network are described depends on the origin and properties of the networks data. The most common form to represent a network or graph consists in mapping the nodes to graphical marks like circles or rectangles and the edges to straight lines or curves connecting the corresponding end nodes. However, also representations based on an inclusion relation or incidence of node symbols are in some cases more adequate. Constraints for the drawing might concern the direction of the links, absolute or relative positions of the nodes or restrictions for the position of parts of the network. Moreover, certain additional criteria regard the readability or aesthetics of the drawing, e.g. the number of edge crossings, the variance of the edge lengths or the angular resolution.

Representation, constraints and criteria for the drawing induce the basic *graph layout problem* which is the algorithmic core problem of the visualization task. The layout problem consists in assigning appropriate positions to the network elements, i.e. the nodes and edges of the graph. For most criteria the corresponding layout problem is already NP-hard. Accordingly, it is very unlikely that a provably optimal layout with respect to any of those criteria an be generated by an efficient algorithm. As most networks we consider here are large, we have to resort to sophisticated, though heuristic, generic layout algorithms.

The basic problem "How to Draw a Graph?" has been studied in mathematics and computer science already in the sixties of the last century.[187,188] Meanwhile, "drawing graphs" is a research field by its own in computer science with a yearly international conference.[189] Further information is also available in various surveys and books.[190–194]

We give an overview of the state of the art in network visualization as far as algorithms for the layout problem are concerned. Additional features like the use of special graphical symbols, colors, transparency or other graphical means are mentioned by the way if relevant. Focus is on global algorithms to generate layouts of large networks. The advantages and shortcomings of different graph layout methods are discussed and examples are given how to support specific analytical aspects. Finally, case studies of layout algorithms tailored for the AS graph, i.e. the graph of autonomous systems in the Internet and for coauthor networks are presented.

6.2. *Global methods for visualizing large graphs*

The algorithmic core problem of network visualization is the *graph layout problem*. Given a set $\mathcal{E} = \{e_1, e_2, \ldots, e_n\}$ of *layout elements* and for each $e_i \in \mathcal{E}$ a set of χ_i *feasible positions*, a *layout* $L = (p_1, \ldots, p_n)$ is an assignment of positions $p_i \in \chi_i$ to the layout elements satisfying certain criteria. The most common graph layout problem consists in the construction of a well-balanced two-dimensional straight-line layout. Given an undirected graph $G = (V, E)$ the layout elements are the nodes $v_i \in V$ and for each $v_i \in V$ each position in $\mathbb{R}^2$ is feasible. Construct a layout L for G

such that the line segments representing the edges in E are all of equal length.

6.2.1. *Spring embedder based methods*

The *spring embedder*,[195] a classical approach to generate a well-balanced two-dimensional straight-line layout of a graph is based on a physical model where nodes are considered as physical objects and edges as connecting springs. If the system is let off it attains an equilibrium state in which all forces cancel each other. Such a model can be expressed formally and algorithms to simulate the system then typically try to move the objects iteratively into stable states. Formally, let $p_v = (x_v, y_v)$ denote a position of node $v \in V$ in position $p_v = (x_v, y_v)$ in $\mathbb{R}^2$, $\|p_v - p_u\|$ the length of the vector $p_v - p_u$, i.e. the Euclidean distance between positions p_v and p_u, $\overrightarrow{p_u p_v}$ the *unit length vector* $\frac{p_v - p_u}{\|p_v - p_u\|}$ from p_u to p_v.
Define *repelling forces*

$$f_{rep}(p_u, p_v) := \frac{c_{rep}}{\|p_v - p_u\|^2} \cdot \overrightarrow{p_u p_v} \quad \text{for all } u, v \in V, \{u, v\} \notin E,$$

between any pair of non-adjacent nodes, and a *spring force*

$$f_{spring}(p_u, p_v) := c_{spring} \cdot \log \frac{\|p_v - p_u\|}{l} \cdot \overrightarrow{p_v p_u} \quad \text{for all } \{u, v\} \in E.$$

Let c_{rep} be an appropriate repulsion constant, c_{spring} an appropriate spring constant and l the natural length of the spring.

The spring embedder algorithms starts with an arbitrary, e.g. random state of the springs and lets the system go. To obtain an equilibrium configuration, node v is moved at *time t* according to a *force vector* $F_v(t)$, where

$$F_v(t) := \sum_{u:\{u,v\} \notin E} f_{rep}(p_u, p_v) \quad + \sum_{u:\{u,v\} \in E} f_{spring}(p_u, p_v).$$

Thus the algorithm iteratively moves each node v by $\delta \cdot F_v(t)$; where δ is again an appropriate constant and the number of iterations K is fixed in advance.

Algorithm 1: Spring Embedder Algorithm

Input : $G = (V, E)$ connected graph and initial layout $p = (p_v)_{v \in V}$
Output: Layout p with low internal stress.

for $i=1$ **to** K **do**
    foreach $v \in V$ **do**
        set
        $F_v(t) := \sum_{u:\{u,v\} \notin E} f_{rep}(p_u, p_v) + \sum_{u:\{u,v\} \in E} f_{spring}(p_u, p_v);$
    foreach $v \in V$ **do**
        set $p_v := p_v + \delta \cdot F_v(t);$

Obviously, this algorithm is simple and easy to implement, and the results are surprisingly good. A disadvantage consists in the comparably high running time, i.e. in each iteration the calculation of f_{spring} is in $\mathcal{O}(|E|)$ and f_{rep} in $\mathcal{O}(|V|^2)$. There are a number of heuristics to speed up the layout computation and variants of the algorithm to improve its behavior.[196]

6.2.2. *Properties*

Layout techniques based on spring embedder produce very good results for homogeneous graphs, i.e., those that have small fluctuations in degree or clustering coefficient. Such an example is given in Fig. 34. There, the degree varies between two and six and the clustering coefficient ranges between zero and one. Further, this example demonstrates the good utilization of the available drawing area as wells as good angular resolution and small crossing number.

In the case of inhomogeneous graphs, e.g., graphs that contain large cliques or bipartite cliques and very sparse parts, the total resolution and readability can decrease. Fig. 35 gives such an example, where two rectangular grids are connected via a path where one intermediate node was replace by a large clique. Only a relatively small part of the available drawing area was used. Also, the length of the embedded edges, i.e. the distance of its end-nodes, varies significantly. While most of the edges of the grids are equally long, those of the clique are relatively short. The main reason for this 'strange' behavior, is the inhomogeneous distribution of repelling and attracting forces. The placement of a node in the grid mainly depends of

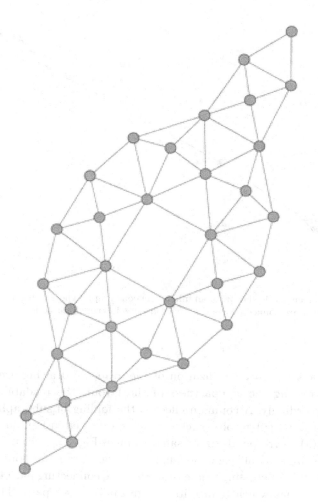

Fig. 34. Spring embedder layout of an almost planar, grid-like graph.

the repulsion from the other nodes, since it has at most four neighbors that could cause attraction. In contrast, a node in the clique also has a high number of attractive spring forces. Thus, the clique will always occupy a small area, while the distance between the two grids can be relatively large.

In order to overcome such drifting effects, one can introduce additional gravitational forces.[196] They act as global attractors for all nodes and are an

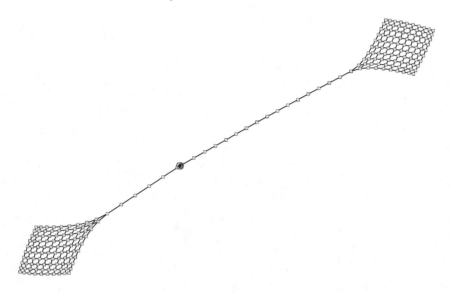

Fig. 35.   Spring embedder layout of an inhomogeneous graph. The graph consists of two large grids which are connected via a path where one intermediate node was replace by a large clique.

effective means to control utilization of the available drawing area. However, by increasing the compactness of the layout, the readability often decreases accordingly. A common effect is the folding of subgraphs or the overlap of 'distant' subgraphs. Such examples are given in Fig. 36. The left one (Fig. 36(a)) corresponds to the same graph as Fig. 35. The effects of the compactness are evident, e.g., the lengths of edges are more homogeneous while the number of crossings increases. Also, the connecting path has some bends and foldings which reduce its recognizability as a path. This effect is even more apparent in Fig. 36(b), there the connecting path (with its clique) was duplicated two times. Now, parts of the grids are folded and even a clique is placed 'inside' a grid.

Summarizing, spring embedder techniques produce very good results in the case of homogeneous graphs. The embedded edges are (almost) equally long. The angular resolution and the crossing number are not directly optimized, but are often sufficiently good. In the case of inhomogeneous graphs, drifting and other similar effects introduce unwanted artifacts. They can be partially prevented by additional forces, for example global attraction. Thus, certain layout properties, like the utilization of the available drawing

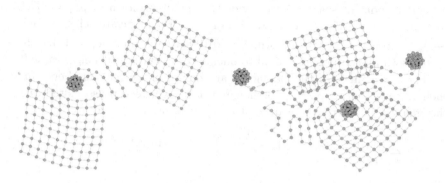

(a) Two grids with one connecting path containing a big clique.

(b) Two grids with three connecting path containing each a big clique.

Fig. 36.   Spring embedder layout of inhomogeneous graphs with area restriction and gravitational forces.

area or the total resolution, are improved while other quality aspects, like the readability and the recognizability of subgraphs, can decrease.

6.2.3. *Spectral layout*

Let $G = (V, E; \omega)$ be an undirected graph with positive edge weights, e.g. obtained from an edge strength in the underlying network. Consider the following minimization objective

$$\sum_{\{v,w\}\in E} \omega(e) \cdot \|p_v - p_w\|^2 = \sum_{\{v,w\}\in E} \omega(e) \cdot \big((x_v - x_w)^2 + (y_v - y_w)^2\big) \quad (100)$$

where $p_v = (x_v, y_v) \in \mathbb{R}^2$ is the location of vertex $v \in V$. Note that optimum solutions place all vertices in the same location. In *spectral graph layout*, first introduced by Hall,[197] these undesirable solutions are avoided not by fixing the location of select vertices, but by putting more uniform constraints on the location vector $p = (p_v)_v \in V$ as follows.

In matrix notation, this objective can be expressed as $p^T L(G)p$, where

$$L(G) = D(G) - A(G)$$

is called the *Laplacian matrix* of G, with $D(G)$ the diagonal matrix of vertex degrees and $A(G)$ the weighted adjacency matrix. To eliminate the dependency on the scale of p we divide this quadratic form by $p^T p = \|p\|^2$. Now observe that, if p is an eigenvector of $L(G)$, the associated eigenvalue is $\frac{p^T L(G)p}{p^T p}$, and that the trivial optima of eq.100 are multiples of $p = 1$, i.e. the vector with all components equal to one, and associated with eigenvalue 0.

The eigenvalues of the Laplacian are non-negative real numbers, and their eigenvectors are pairwise orthogonal. Two eigenvectors associated with the smallest non-zero eigenvalues of $L(G)$ therefore minimize

$$\sum_{\{v,w\} \in E} \omega(e) \cdot (x_v - x_w)^2 = \frac{x^T L(G) x}{x^T x} \qquad \text{subject to } \mathbf{0} \neq x \perp \mathbf{1}$$

and

$$\sum_{\{v,w\} \in E} \omega(e) \cdot (y_v - y_w)^2 = \frac{y^T L(G) y}{y^T y} \qquad \text{subject to } \mathbf{0} \neq y \perp \mathbf{1} \text{ and } y \perp x \, .$$

As a consequence of orthogonalization with $\mathbf{1}$, the resulting layouts are centered around the origin.

6.2.4. *Properties*

Symmetries are displayed well in spectral layouts, and structurally equivalent vertices (i.e. vertices with identical neighborhoods) are placed in the same location, if x and y are eigenvectors to different eigenvalues with multiplicity one. Otherwise, if x or y are eigenvectors to eigenvalues with larger multiplicity then structurally equivalent nodes can be placed in different positions. For example, the smallest non-zero eigenvalue of a star with n leaves has multiplicity $n - 1$. In Fig. 37, the spectral embedding of a star with five leaves is shown. The central node (rhombus) is placed close to the center, while only two of the five structurally equivalent nodes are placed in the same position (square and circle).

However, in many graphs the smallest and second smallest non-zero eigenvalues have multiplicity one. In these cases, even two nodes that share many neighbors are placed spatially close together. This effect is shown in Fig. 38. The graph consists of a tree where all nodes have been replaced by cliques of various sizes. In the spectral embedding (Fig. 38(b)), each clique occupies a very small area, because all nodes with the exception of at most two, are structurally equivalent and those that are not equivalent have only one additional neighbor. Further, the two cliques (in the middle of Fig. 38(a)) that are exclusively connected to the same clique are placed very close.

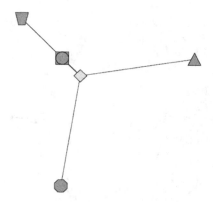

Fig. 37. Spectral embedding of a star with five leaves.

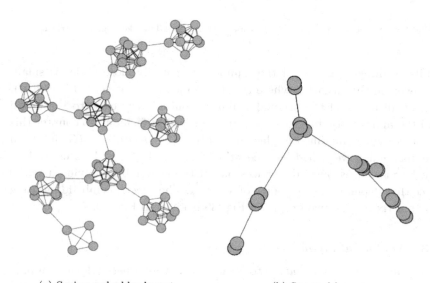

(a) Spring embedder layout.   (b) Spectral layout.

Fig. 38. Tree of cliques.

If a graph is not balanced, however, most vertices are clustered in the center of the drawing, and only some loosely connected vertices are placed far away. Such an example is given in Fig. 39. In the case where no tree-like annex is present (Fig. 39(a)), the graph is well distributed over the

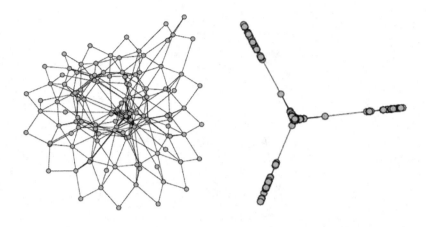

(a) Without any tree-like annexes.   (b) With three tree-like annexes.

Fig. 39.   Spectral embedding of a graph with a power-law like degree distribution.

available drawing area and the number of spatially close nodes is small. However, in the situation where tree-like annexes are present (Fig. 39(b)), almost all nodes of the original graph are placed very close to the origin and the annexes are placed around it in a star-like fashion. To counter this effect, a slightly modified Laplacian $L_\rho(G) = (1 - \rho)D(G) - A(G)$ in which the diagonal is weakened by a constant factor ρ, $0 \leq \rho \leq 1$, is used. This can be viewed as pushing vertices out of the center by applying a radial force that depends on the degree of a vertex. The spectral embedding using this matrix for the two graphs in Fig. 39 is given in Fig. 40.

6.3. *Analytical layouts*

The goal of *analytic layouts* is to create a layout of a network that emphasizes certain analytic aspects, e.g., a group structure or the distribution of a measurement. Since there is a large variety of analytic measurements, it is very difficult to establish general paradigms for analytic layouts. However, two main styles have been identified: First, techniques that use a traditional layout paradigm, like force-directed layouts, and include the analytic properties as side-constraints. In this way, the analytic input restricts the original degree of freedom. Second, methods that use the analytic properties to determine a global shape of the network and then try to fit the

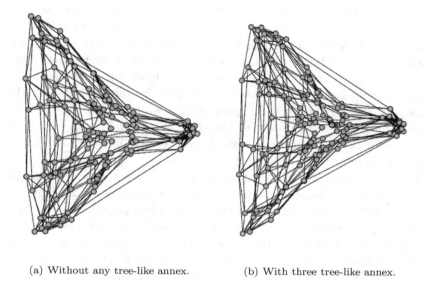

(a) Without any tree-like annex. (b) With three tree-like annex.

Fig. 40. Spectral embedding of the graphs shown in Fig. 39 using modified Laplacian matrix with $\rho = 0.5$.

network within this shape while optimizing readability. In the following, we present one example for a node measurement and three further examples which emphasize group structure.

6.3.1. *Centrality and status layouts*

Many research fields, especially social network analysis, focus on measurements expressing the importance of nodes or edges. Such measurements are usually called *centralities* for undirected networks and *statuses* for directed ones. The names correspond to the intuition, i.e., a node is very important if it has a central position in an undirected network or a large rank in a directed network. Therefor, a visualization which reflects this intuitive notation is desirable. Furthermore, the layout should show the information in an efficiently conveyable way as well as accurately represent the manifested information. Several layout techniques have been derived from intuition. In most approaches certain aspects of the layout are fixed by the centrality or status and the remaining degrees of freedom are optimized to meet the above goals as well as providing a readable visualization.

In the case of centralities, a radial layout is preferred where the distance of a node to the virtual center of the layout corresponds to its centrality. Thus, the only degree of freedom for placing the nodes is the angular position on a circle. The approaches mainly differ in their calculation of the position on these circles. As an example, some algorithms try to minimize the crossing number (of edges), while others minimize the total edge length. These methods work very well for sparse graphs, which are usually observed when dealing with social analyses. The achievable readability significantly decreases for dense networks. A typical result obtainable by radial layout techniques is presented in Fig. 41(a).

In the case of statuses, a rank or layered layout is the best choice. In such a layout, the coordinates in one dimension are already fixed by the status measurement. Usually this is the y-axis, thus a large status implies a position in the upper part of the visualization. Similar to radial layouts, the approaches mainly differ in their calculation of the x-coordinates. Again distinct aesthetic criteria such as crossing number, total edge length, or angular resolution can be optimized in order to maximize readability. In contrast to radial layouts, the general ease of perception of status layouts can be significantly lowered by local accumulation of nodes. Clumsy layouts can be often prevented by discretizing the remaining axis. This guarantees a minimum distance between every node pair. Converting 'continuous' x-coordinates into discrete ones is a straight forward approach, however, the improvements achieved thereby might not to be recognizable. More suitable techniques are based on eigenvectors or linear programming. Fig. 41(b) shows a portion of the WWW network, where PageRank was used as status. The y-axis represents the PageRank value (left side corresponds to small value and the right side corresponds to large values). The x-coordinates are discrete and calculated with an eigenvector heuristic.

Brandes et al.[200] gave a more complete view on topic of radial and layered layouts. The discussion also treats further aspects that are important in social network analysis which naturally carry over to general network analysis.

6.3.2. *Clustered layouts*

The first example that emphasizes group structure is a clustered layout. Given a graph $G = (V, E)$ and a partition $C = (C_1, \ldots, C_k)$ of the node set V, the goal is to find a layout such that first, nodes within the same cluster C_i are spatially close, and second, nodes in different clusters are spa-

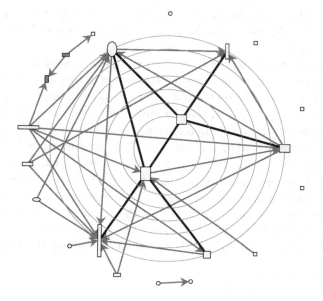

(a) Example of a centrality layout according to the method introduced in Ref. 198.

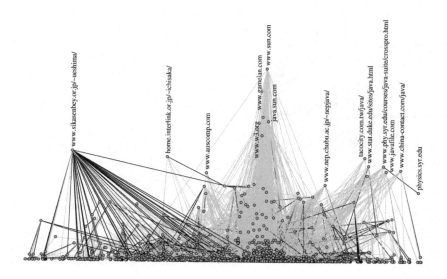

(b) PageRank layout for a portion of the WWW according to Brandes et al.[199]

Fig. 41.   Centrality and status visualizations.

tially separated, and finally, the lengths of the edges reflect their role, i.e., edges connecting different clusters are longer than those within a cluster, but not too long.

Traditionally, this is solved by using a two-phase approach. In the first phase the graph is collapsed according to the clustering, i.e., all the nodes within a cluster are represented with a super-node and the adjacencies between nodes are carried over to their super-nodes. In this way, we obtain a reduced version of the graph. In addition, weights are introduced to reflect the number of nodes within a super-node and the number of adjacencies between super-nodes. The first phase finishes after calculating a suitable layout for the reduced graph respecting the weight. For example, a layout where each super-node occupies an area that is proportional to its weight. Then, in the second phase, this layout of the reduced graph is converted into a layout for the whole graph. Usually, this is accomplished by running a layout algorithm for each cluster and then combining the two layouts properly.

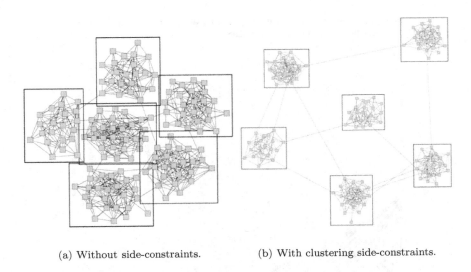

(a) Without side-constraints.   (b) With clustering side-constraints.

Fig. 42.   Force-directed layouts for a clustered network.

Fig. 42 shows an example comparing a standard force-directed approach with one that includes the clustering properties as side-constraints. It is apparent that the unrestricted methods cannot meet our goal in the sense that nodes in different clusters are sometimes closer than nodes within the same cluster. Moreover the edge length is rather uniform. In contrast, the version respecting constraints fulfills our goal very well.

A more complete view of this topic can be found in specific reviews.[201]

6.3.3. *Case studies*

As already mentioned, analytic layouts are very specialized, not only with respect to the analytic properties, but also with respect to the corresponding network. Concluding, we present two different techniques that have been primarily developed to graphically represent the Autonomous System network.

Autonomous systems

The Autonomous Systems network is an abstracted version of the physical Internet, where an Autonomous System (AS) is defined as the independently administered domain which autonomously determines internal communication and routing policies for Internet communications.[12] It possesses an implicit hierarchical structure, i.e., the ASes can be categorized as backbones, national, regional, and local providers as well as customer. Since it is not know if one can extract the real hierarchy, many heuristics and graph-theoretical concepts have been used as a replacement. Especially the concept of a nested hierarchical decomposition is frequently used, being a chain $H = (V_0 \subset V_1 \subset \cdots \subset V_k \subset V_{k+1})$ of pairwise nested subsets of the node set. Conventionally, the set V_0 contains all nodes and V_{k+1} is empty. In the following we focus on the k-core decomposition.[202,203]

Fig. 43 shows the result of standard force-directed methods applied to the AS network. Allowing nodes to overlap each other (Fig. 43(a)) causes almost all nodes to end up in a very small central area. This can be prevented by prohibiting nodes to overlap each other (Fig. 43(b)). Although the utilization of the drawing area improves, the structure is not recognizable.

Baur et al. have presented a new technique for an analytic layout based on a nested hierarchical decomposition.[204] Their main idea was to incrementally calculate a layout based on the given decomposition. The algorithm starts with a suitable layout for the inner-most non-empty node set V_k. Then the current layout is recursively extended by including the additional nodes in next bigger set. The extension step is realized in such a way as to respect both aesthetic criteria as well as the neighborhood of a node.

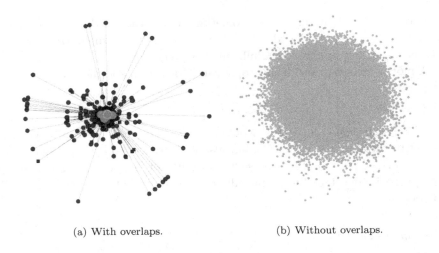

(a) With overlaps.   (b) Without overlaps.

Fig. 43.   Force based layouts of the AS network.

An example of the results is given in Fig. 44. Since the decomposition has a
large impact on the overall quality of the layout, one can choose to explicitly include this information in the layout, i.e., either as a 3D-visualization
(Fig. 44(a)) or a 2D side-view of the 3D-visualization (see Fig. 44(d)).
Beside the esthetically pleasing nature of the layout, there are a several
properties of the decomposition reflected in the visualization. First, the areas of the shells, i.e., nodes that included in the same subset, liker $V_i \setminus V_{i+1}$,
reflect the ratio $|V_i \setminus V_{i+1}|/|V_k|$. Second, the visualization emphasizes that
most edges have one end-node in a very low-level shell and other in a very
high-level shell. Baur et.al. also evaluated their techniques using different
snapshots over time. The visualizations confirmed that the lower shells had
the largest growth rate. Moreover, all tested instances had similar characteristics in their visualizations, thus verifying the usability of the layout technique as well as the stability of the network. Furthermore, Baur
et.al. showed that the real and the generated instances of the AS network
have distinguishable layouts, which suggests a graphical means to evaluate
generators.

Another approach[205] introduced by Alvarez-Hamelin *et al* follows the
second paradigm for analytic visualizations, i.e., using the analytic properties to determine the global shape of the network and then trying to fit
the network within this shape while optimizing readability. As mentioned
above, the AS network has a skew distribution of importance, i.e., a diminu-

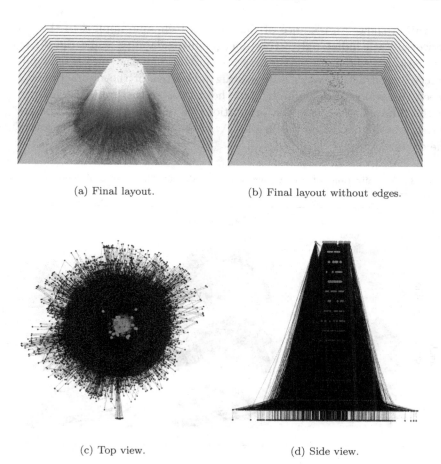

(a) Final layout.　　　　　　(b) Final layout without edges.

(c) Top view.　　　　　　(d) Side view.

Fig. 44.　Hierarchical layout of the AS network produced with the method of Baur et al.[204]

tive number of very important nodes and many nodes of low importance. Surprisingly, the majority of the edges connect these extreme groups. In order to take these facts into account, the authors employ a half annulus as the general underlying shape. Nodes of equal importance are placed within certain annular segments which in turn are positioned in increasing order of this importance. Additional features like scaling functions or transparency allow for visualizations of large networks while maintaining the overall readability as well as emphasizing analytic properties.

Tab. 3 shows an instance of the annulus technique applied to the AS network. Each individual picture offers high readability, while the direct comparison of different scaling functions provides an easy means of simultaneously extracting various interesting properties of the interaction between the importance hierarchy and the network structure. For example, in the 'linear-linear' view the proportions of the sizes of the groups are clearly obtainable, while the 'log-log' view emphasizes the distribution of the edges.

Table 3. Visualizations of the AS network (1st March, 2005) using different scaling options.[205]

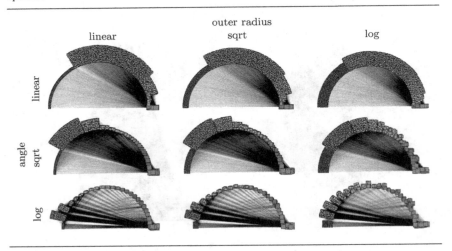

CHAPTER 7

Modeling the Webgraph: How Far We Are

Debora Donato, Luigi Laura, Stefano Leonardi and Stefano Millozzi

Dipartimento di Informatica e Sistemistica,
Universitá di Roma "La Sapienza", Via Salaria 113, 00198 Roma, Italy
E-mail: {donato, laura, leon, millozzi}@dis.uniroma1.it

7.1. *Introduction*

An extensive study of "the Web as a graph" appeared, in 1999, in the work of Kleinberg *et al*; here the authors, for the first time, explicitly focused on the directed graph induced by the hyperlink structure of the World Wide Web. Several previously appeared results, together with new ones, were listed in an homogeneous framework and from then on the term *Webgraph* addresses the graph whose nodes are the (static) html pages and edges are the (directed) hyperlinks among them.

Since then, the study of the Webgraph has been the subject of a large interest in the scientific community for several important reasons. The information provided by the Webgraph is for instance at the basis of link analysis algorithms for ranking Web documents, PageRank[206] and HITS[207] to mention the most popular such examples. In all these algorithms the insertion of a hyperlink between two documents is seen as the endorsement of authority from the first to the second document. The study of the Web is also attracting the attention of different scientific communities, from mathematical to life and social sciences, in the attempt to understand the laws that rule its structure and evolution.

To basic step to unearth the topological structure of the Webgraph is to collect the hyperlinked structure of large crawls spanning a good share of the whole Web. A first line of research has then focused on performing meaningful measures to draw relevant conclusions on the statistical and topological properties of the Webgraph. This approach assumes that large samples of the Web will faithfully reproduce its properties, and this assumption has been comforted by the work of Dill *et al*,[208] that showed that regardless which criterion is used to sample the Web, all the samples exhibit the same properties.

A second important research line has concentrated on the development of models of the evolution of the Webgraph, able to simulate the emerging of global properties from the microscopic activity of link creation. Developing a realistic and accurate stochastic graph model for the Webgraph is also relevant for many practical purposes:

- Devising web applications, since many problems that are computationally difficult for general graphs could be considerably easier on graphs arising from specific stochastic processes.
- Testing web applications on synthetic benchmarks of small dimension.
- Detecting peculiar regions of the Webgraph, i.e., local subsets that have different statistical properties with respect to the whole structure.
- Predicting the evolution of new phenomena in the Web.
- Dealing more efficiently with large scale computations (e.g., by recognizing the possibility of compressing a graph generated according to such model[209,210]).

The study of the topological structure of networks of several billion edges also poses new computational problems. We expect this branch of applied algorithmic to grow fast in the next years[211,212] due to the increasing number of applications dealing with the mining of massive data. A third line of research has then focused on the development of computational tools to manipulate graphs and perform web-related measures at very large scale.

This chapter is organised as follows: in the following section we recall some basic definitions. In Section 7.3 the analysis of the WebBase sample is presented. In Section 7.4 we illustrate the results of a comparison study over several random Webgraph models. Section 7.5 deals with the computational issues of generating and measuring massive webgraphs in secondary memory. We conclude (Section 7.6) with final remarks and comments.

7.2. *Preliminaries*

Basic graph terminology. A *graph* (also addressed as *undirected graph*) consists of a finite nonempty set of *nodes* (also called *vertices*) V together with a collection of pairs of distinct nodes, called *edges* or *arcs*.

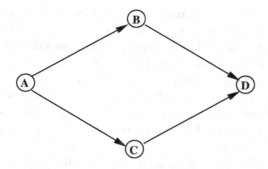

Fig. 45. A simple directed graph.

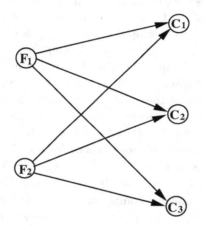

Fig. 46. A $(2, 3)$-bipartite clique.

A *directed graph* or *digraph* consists of a finite nonempty set of *nodes* (vertices) V together with a collection of pairs of **ordered** distinct nodes, called *edges* or *arcs*.

The *degree* of a vertex is the number of edges incident to it. In a directed graph the *in-degree* (*out-degree*) of a node is the number of incoming (outgoing) edges. For example, if we refer to the simple digraph shown in Fig. 45, the in-degree of vertex D is 2 (it is linked from B and C) while its out-degree is 0 (it has no outgoing edges).

A *bipartite core* is made of two sets of nodes; all the nodes in the first set (the *fan* set) point to each node of the second one (the *center* set). An example is shown in Fig. 46: we have on the left side the set of the fan nodes (labeled F_1 and F_2), all of them pointing to all center nodes on the right side (labeled C_1, C_2 and C_3). A *walk* is an alternating sequence of vertices and edges $v_0, e_1, v_1, e_2, \ldots, v_{n-1}, e_{n-1}, v_n$ such that each edge is incident with the two nodes immediately preceding and following it. A walk is a *path* if all the nodes are distinct. A walk is *closed* if $v_0 = v_n$ and it is *open* otherwise. A closed walk is a *cycle* if all the vertices are distinct, except v_0 and v_n, and $n \geq 3$ ($n \geq 2$ in a digraph). An *acyclic* graph is one that contains no cycles. In a digraph the analogous definitions of directed walk and directed path hold if we replace edge with directed edge and we consider the orientation.

A *connected component* of an undirected graph G is a subset of nodes S such that for every pair of vertices $u, v \in S$, u is reachable from v (i.e. it exists the path starting from u and ending in v). A graph is *connected* if, for every pair of vertices $u, v \in V$, u is reachable from v. An acyclic connected graph is a *tree*, and an acyclic graph is a *forest* (i.e. is made of many trees).

A set of nodes S is a *strongly connected component* (SCC) of a digraph if and only if, for every couple of nodes $A, B \in S$, there exists a directed path from A to B and from B to A and the set is maximal. The number of nodes of S is the *size* of the SCC. For example, in the graph shown in Fig. 47 there are 3 distinct strongly connected components: vertices A_1, A_2 and A_3 all can reach each other: they form a strongly connected component (SCC) of size 3. The same holds for vertices B_1, B_2, B_3 and B_4, that are a size 4 SCC, and for the vertices C_1 and C_2 (size 2 SCC). A set of nodes S is a *weakly connected component (WCC)* in a directed graph G, if and only if the set S is a connected component of the undirected graph G that is obtained by removing the orientation of the edges in G.

For a subset of nodes $S \subseteq V$ we define the *subgraph induced* by S to be the graph $G_S = (S, E_S)$, where E_S is the set of edges between the nodes in S. A *traversal* of a graph explores the edges of the graph until all vertices are visited. A traversal starts from a vertex, say u, explores the whole portion of the graph that is reachable from u, and then continues with a vertex not yet visited. A forest is naturally associated to a visit by considering all edges that lead to the discovery of a new vertex. A *Breadth First Search (BFS)* is a traversal which, when visiting a new vertex, stores the adjacent vertices not yet visited in a queue. That is, it explores the local neighborhood before going any deeper. A *Depth First Search (DFS)* is a traversal which, when visiting a new vertex, stores the adjacent vertices not yet visited in a stack. That is, it always tries to go as deeply as possible.

Good introduction to graph theory are the classical work of Harary[213] and the more recent book of Diestel.[3]

Power law distribution. A discrete random variable X follows a *power law* distribution if the probability of taking value i is $P[X = i] \propto 1/i^\gamma$, for a constant $\gamma \geq 0$. The value γ is the exponent of the power law. An interesting review on power law distributions has been written by Mitzenmacher.[214]

Scale-free networks. If the degree distribution of the nodes in a network follows a power law, the ratio of very connected nodes to the number of nodes in the rest of the network remains constant as the network changes in size; these networks are also called *scale-free*.

Crawlers, spiders and robots. A *crawl* of the Web is a set of webpages together with their links. The programs that collect web pages are usually referred to as *crawlers, spiders or robots*. Roughly, a crawler starts from an initial set of URLs S and, at each iteration, it extracts one URL u from S, visits it and adds to S the (not yet visited) URLs that are linked by u. A crawler is one essential component of modern search engines. As the size of the Web grows the engineering of a crawler is an increasingly difficult task.[215,216]

External and semi-external memory algorithms. Modern computer systems have a hierarchical memory architecture that comprises CPU registers, cache (several levels), main memory, buffers and secondary storage devices. Traditional analysis of algorithms assumes one level of memory, i.e. computations are performed in main memory. In many problems the amount of data to be processed is far too massive to fit main memory, and the analysis of algorithms under the assumption of a single level of memory can be meaningless, because the I/O performance is the main bottleneck. Usually the analysis considers only two memory levels, i.e. one fast (main memory) and one slow (secondary memory). With *external memory algorithms* we denote the ones that are explicitly designed to perform "well" in a hierarchical memory system. When we deal with graph algorithms, we call *semi-external* algorithms the ones that are allowed to store in main memory only a limited amount of bytes for each node.[217,218]

7.3. *WebBase*

In this section we present the results of our experiments, conducted on a $200M$ nodes crawl collected from the WebBase project at Stanford[219] in 2001. The repository makes several crawls available to researchers. The sample we study in our work contains only link information, i.e. no information about URLs is available. We compare these results with the ones, presented in the literature, concerning other samples of the Webgraph. Note

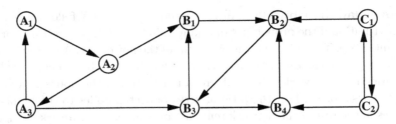

Fig. 47.   An example of strongly connected component (B) in a graph.

that there are no recent estimates about the size of the Web, but a study made by Cyvellance[220] showed that in July 2000 the Web reached 2.1 billion webpages, and the number is growing at a rate of 7 million pages each days. This means that the WebBase sample, when it was collected, contained about one tenth of the Web.

7.3.1. *In-degree and out-degree*

Since the very first analysis, the Webgraph has shown the ubiquitous presence of power law distributions, a typical signature of scale-free properties. Barabási and Albert[15] and Kumar *et al*[221] suggested that the in-degree of the Webgraph follows a *power law* distribution. Later experiments by Broder *et al*[222] on a crawl of 200M pages from 1999 by Altavista confirmed it as a basic property: the probability that the in-degree of a vertex is i is distributed as $Pr_u[\text{in-degree}(u) = i] \propto 1/i^\gamma$, for $\gamma \approx 2.1$. The out-degree of a vertex was also shown to be distributed according to a power law with exponent roughly equal to 2.7 with the exception of the initial segment of the distribution. The average number of incoming links observed in the several samples of the webgraph is about equal to 7 times the number of vertices.

The in-degree distribution, shown in Fig. 48, follows a power law with $\gamma = 2.1$. This confirms the observations done on the crawl of 1997 from Alexa,[221] the crawl of 1999 from Altavista[222] and the notredame.edu domain.[15]

We note a *bump* between the values 1.000 and 10,000, that has also been observed in other analysis[222] and it is probably due to a huge clique created by a single *spammer*. Since our sample contains only structural information and not URLs, we can't propose or deny possible explanations for this phenomenon.

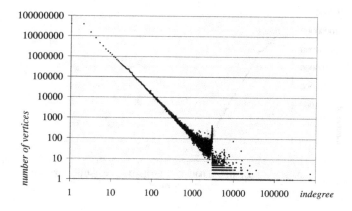

Fig. 48.   In-degree distribution of the WebBase crawl.

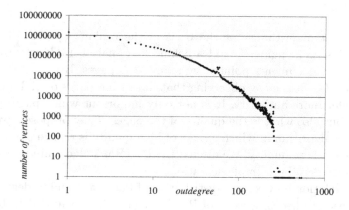

Fig. 49.   Out-degree distribution of the WebBase crawl.

In Figure 49 it is shown the out-degree distribution of the WebBase crawl. While the in-degree distribution is fitted with a power law, the out-degree is not, even for the final segment of the distribution. A deviation from a power law for the initial segment of the distribution was already observed in the Altavista crawl.[222] A possible explanation of this phenomenon is that writing a scale-free series of hyperlinks is seriously limited by the patience of webmasters.

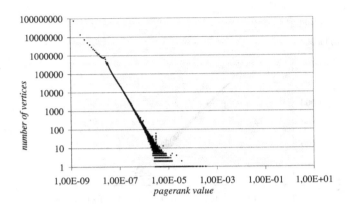

Fig. 50.   PageRank distribution of the WebBase crawl.

7.3.2. *PageRank*

The *PageRank* algorithm is at the basis of the ranking operated by the Google Web search engine. The idea behind link analysis ranking is to give higher rank to documents pointed by many Web pages. Brin and Page[206] extend this idea further by observing that links from pages of high quality should confer more authority. It is not only important which pages point to a page, but also what is the quality of the pages. They propose a weight propagation algorithm in which a page of high quality is a page pointed by many pages of high quality. We discuss the PageRank algorithm in Section 7.5, where we detail our implementation.

The correlation between the distribution of PageRank and in-degree has recently been studied in a work of Pandurangan, Raghavan and Upfal.[223] They show by analyzing a sample of 100,000 pages of the brown.edu domain that PageRank is distributed with a power law of exponent 2.1. This exactly matches the in-degree distribution, but very surprisingly it is observed very little correlation between these quantities, i.e., pages with high in-degree may have low PageRank.[224]

We computed the PageRank distribution on the WebBase crawl. Here, we confirm the observation of Pandurangan *et al* by showing this quantity distributed according to a power law with exponent $\gamma = 2.109$. We also computed the statistical correlation between PageRank and in-degree. We obtained a value of 0.3097, on a range of variation in $[-1, 1]$ from negative to positive correlation. This result confirms the weak correlation between PageRank and in-degree values.

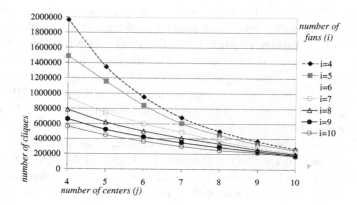

Fig. 51.   Number of bipartite cores in the Web Base crawl.

7.3.3. *Bipartite cliques*

A surprising number of specific topological structures such as bipartite cliques of relatively small size has been observed[221] with the aim of tracing the emergence of hidden *cyber-communities*. A bipartite clique is interpreted as a core of such a community, formed by a set of fans, each one pointing to a set of centers/authorities, and a set of centers, each pointed by all the fans. Over 100,000 such communities have been recognized[221] on a snapshot of 200M taken by Alexa in 1997.

In Fig. 51 is shown the distribution of the number of bipartite cliques (i,j), with $i,j = 1,\ldots,10$. The shape of the plot follows the one presented by Kumar *et al* for the 200M crawl by Alexa. However, we detect a much larger number of bipartite cliques. For instance the number of cliques of size $(4,j)$ differs from the crawl from Alexa for more than one order of magnitude. A possible (and quite natural) explanation is that the number of cyber-communities has consistently increased from 1997 to 2001. We also recall that the longevity of cyber-communities' websites is bigger as compared to other websites.[221] A second possible explanation is that our algorithm for finding disjoint bipartite cliques, which is detailed in Section 7.5, is more efficient than the one implemented in Ref. 221.

7.3.4. *Strongly connected components*

Broder *et al*[222] identified a very large strongly connected component of about 28% of the entire crawl, and showed a picture of the whole Web as divided into five distinct regions: SCC, IN, OUT, TENDRILS and DIS-CONNECTED. The SCC set is the set of all the nodes in the single largest strongly connected component; in the IN (OUT) region we find all the nodes that can reach the SCC set (are reached from the SCC). TENDRILS are either nodes that leave the IN without entering the SCC or enter the OUT without leaving the SCC. In Tab.4 we report the relative size of the 5 regions. We can still observe in the WebBase crawl a large SCC, however the biggest component is the OUT region, and both IN and TENDRILS have a reduced relative size if compared to the Altavista crawl. We also observe a huge difference between the size of the largest SCC, which consists of about 48 millions nodes, and the size of the second largest SCC that is less than 10 thousands nodes.

Table 4.   Size of regions in both Altavista and WebBase crawl.

	SCC	IN	OUT	TENDR.	DISC.
Altavista (1999)[222]	28%	21%	21%	22%	9%
WebBase (2001)	33%	11%	39%	13%	4%

In Fig. 52 it is shown the global SCC distribution of the Webbase sample and of its different regions (except the SCC region, that is a single SCC). All distributions follow a power law whose exponent is 2.07, very close to the value observed for both the in-degree and the PageRank distributions.

7.4. *Stochastic models of the webgraph*

As we said in the introduction, the topological properties observed in the Webgraph, such as the ones seen in the previous section, cannot be found in the traditional random graph model of Erdős and Rényi (ER).[14] Kleinberg *et al*,[225] that first explicitly considered the Web as a graph, listed a number of *desiderata* for a Webgraph model:

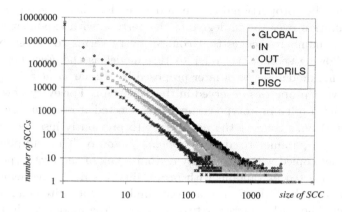

Fig. 52.   SCC distribution of the Web Base crawl.

i. It should have a short and fairly natural description.
ii. It should be rooted in a plausible macro-level process for the creation of content of the Web.
iii. It should not require some a priori static set of "topics".
iv. It should reflect many of the structural phenomena observed in the Web.

Several models appeared recently in the literature. A first comparison study has been presented by Laura *et al*,[226] and the authors showed that three models, the Evolving, the Copying and the Multi-Layer were outstanding. These models show some common traits: they are *evolving*, in the sense that nodes (webpages) are added to the graph one after the other; they have "natural" laws that rule the choice of which page to link to, as we see in the following; they reflect many of the structural phenomena of the Webgraph. In the following sections we start by addressing the main features of the Evolving, the Copying and the more recent PageRank models; then we detail a "revised" version of the Multi-Layer model,[226] and we conclude showing the results of our experimental comparison of these models.

7.4.1. *Models of the webgraph*

Barabási and Albert[15] started the study of evolving networks by presenting a model in which at every discrete time step a new vertex is inserted in the graph. The new vertex connects to a constant number of previously inserted vertices chosen according to the *preferential attachment* rule, i.e.

with probability proportional to the in-degree. This model shows a power law distribution over the in-degree of the vertices with exponent roughly 2 when the number of edges that connect every vertex to the graph is 7. In the following sections we refer to this model as the *Evolving* model. The Copying model has been later proposed by Kumar *et al*[227] to explain other relevant properties observed in the Webgraph. For every new vertex entering the graph a prototype vertex p it is selected at random. A constant number d of links connect the new vertex to previously inserted vertices. The model is parameterized on a *copying factor* α. The end-point of a link is either copied with probability α from a link of the prototype vertex p, or it is selected at random with probability $1 - \alpha$. The copying event aims to model the formation of a large number of bipartite cliques in the Webgraph. The authors present two versions of the models with different growth factor: the *linear* model in which the graph grows by some absolute amount (usually one node) at every step and an *exponential* model in which the graph grows by an amount that is a function of its actual size. In our experimental study we consider the *linear* version, and we refer to it simply as the *Copying* model. The model has been analytically studied and showed to yield power law distributions on both the in-degree and the number of disjoint bipartite cliques for specific values of α. In particular, the in-degree is distributed with a power law with exponent 2.1 when $\alpha = 0.8$.

More recently Pandurangan *et al*[223] proposed a model that complements the Evolving model by choosing the endpoint of a link with probability proportional to the in-degree and to the PageRank of a vertex. There are two parameters $\alpha, \beta \in [0, 1]$ such that $\alpha + \beta \leq 1$. With probability α a node is chosen as the end-point of the the lth edge with probability proportional to its in-degree (preferential attachment), with probability β it is chosen with probability proportional to its PageRank value, and with probability $1 - \alpha - \beta$ at random (uniform probability). The authors show by computer simulation that with an appropriate tuning of the parameters the generated graphs capture the distributional properties of both PageRank and in-degree. We refer to this model as the PageRank model.

7.4.2. *A multi-layer model*

An interesting point of view on the structure of the Webgraph has been presented in the work of Dill *et al*[208] Here the authors explain how the Web shows a fractal structure in many different ways. The Webgraph can be viewed as the outcome of a number of similar and independent stochastic processes. At various scales we have that there are "cohesive collections" of web pages (for example pages on a site, or pages about a topic) and these collections are structurally similar to the whole Web. The central regions of such collections are called "Thematically Unified Clusters" (TUCs) and they provide a navigational backbone of the Web. In a different work, Pennock *et al*[228] argue that the Web is the sum of stochastic independent processes that share a common (fractal) structure, but this structure sometimes can vary. Indeed they provide examples where the distributions exhibit large deviation from power laws. Motivated by the above works, Laura *et al*[226] proposed a *Multi-Layer* model of the Webgraph in which every new page that enters into the graph (i) is assigned to a number of regions (layers) it belongs to and (ii) it is allowed to link only to vertices of these regions. Inside each region, the links are chosen according to a combination of the Evolving and Copying model. This model showed some nice properties such as a distribution of the in-degree with a power law of exponent 2.1 for a wide range of variation of the parameters.

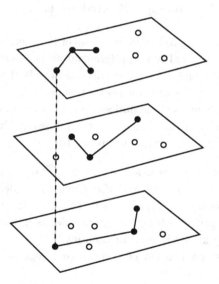

Fig. 53. A Multi-Layer view of a graph. The leftmost node is active on the top and bottom layer, and not active in the middle layer. Note that, on each layer, links are between active (black) nodes.

In the following we detail the *Multi-Layer* model. The model evolves at discrete time steps. The graph will be formed by the union of L regions, also denoted as *layers*. At each time step t a new page x enters the graph and it is assigned to a fixed number l of regions; then the page connects to a total number of d pages that belong to its regions.

Let $X_i(t)$ be the number of pages assigned to region i at time t. Let $L(x)$ be the set of regions which the page x belongs to.

We repeat l times the following random choice:

- $L(x) = L(x) \cup \{i\}$, where region i is chosen in $L/L(x)$ with probability proportional to $X_i(t)$ with a suitable normalization factor.

The stochastic process above clearly defines a Zipf's distribution over the size of the population of the regions, i.e., the value $X_i(t)$.

The d edges are evenly distributed (up to 1) between the l regions. Let $c = \lfloor d/l \rfloor$ and α be the copying factor. Consider each region i to which vertex x is assigned. Vertex x will be connected by c or $c+1$ edges to other vertices of region i. Denote by $\mathcal{X}$ the set of $X_i(t)$ vertices assigned to region i not later than time t. The layer i graph, denoted by $G_i(t)$, is formed by the vertices of $\mathcal{X}$ and by the edges inserted not later than time t between edges of $\mathcal{X}$.

So once we assign pages to layers, every layer is generated independently (in particular, when we deal with preferential attachment, only the edges that connect vertices in the same layer are considered). This completely defines the extra-layer behaviour (how nodes belong to layer). We considered several intra-layer behaviors (how nodes are connected in a single layer): in particular, in the next section we measure the following Multi-Layer models where the single layer is generated according to:

- LCE: this is the original Multi-Layer model;[226] every layer is an hybrid between the *Evolving* model and the *Copying* model: a link is either copied from a prototype vertex (as in the Copying model) or chosen according to the preferential attachment rule, as in the Evolving model.
- LE: the *Evolving* model is used in each layer.
- LC: each layer is generated according to the *Copying* model.

7.4.3. *Large scale simulation*

In this section we present the experimental results on the four stochastic graph models we discussed in the previous sections: the Evolving, Copying, PageRank and Multi-Layer models.

We will compare these models on the following measures:

   i. In-degree;
   ii. bipartite cliques;
  iii. size of the largest SCC;
  iv. PageRank distribution;
   v. PageRank/In-degree correlation;
  vi. In-degree/Average In-degree of predecessors correlation;

All the synthetic models we study do not contain cycles. We then *rewired*: we add a number of edges whose endpoints are chosen at random. In particular, we introduce random edges for a number equal to 50%, 100% and 200% of the number of vertices in the graph.

All simulation have been carried on graphs of 1 Ml vertices and average degree of each vertex equal to 7. We consider the variant of the Copying Linear model with a copying factor $\alpha = 0.8$, the value for which the In-degree distribution meets a power law with slope 2.1, the one observed in the real Web. The Copying Linear model with copying factor smaller than $\alpha = 0.5$ does not follow a power law distribution.

In the following we summarize our main experimental findings.

All simulated models, with the exception of the copying model, do no exhibit any clique. This can be explained from an intuitive point of view because it is very unlikely that, after pruning, two nodes with a small in-degree share a subset of predecessors.

We also observed that in all models the largest SCC spans almost the whole graph when the number of edges that are added to the graph is about 200% of the number of vertices. PageRank and In-degree are positively correlated in all models. Moreover, PageRank always follows a power law distribution with slope similar to that of the In-degree.

The in-degree of a vertex and the average in-degree of its predecessors are weakly correlated in all models with the exception of Multi-Layer-LC. In this version the in-degree distribution does not follow a power law.

Multi-Layer-LCE and Multi-Layer-LE present several feature that can also be found in real samples of the Web. In-degree and PageRank follow a power law with slope 2.1 for a wide range of the parameters, such as the copying factor and the number of layers. Differently from the real Web the graphs generated according to this model do not contain small cliques and have In-degree and PageRank highly correlated.

We emphasize that the prominent aspect of the Multi-Layer model is a relatively independence from the generating model used in each single layer (and its parameters): we see that many versions of the Multi-Layer exhibit properties resembling the ones of real samples of the Web. It seems therefore that summing up various stochastic processes creates a graph whose characteristics do not depends strongly on the underlying processes. This can confirm on an experimental base the observation[208] that the Web is the sum of independent stochastic processes.

The most remarkable observation for all these stochastic models is that, differently from the Erdős-Rényi model,[14] we do not observe any threshold phenomenon in the emerging of a large SCC. This can be explained with the presence in the graph of a number of vertices of high degree that form the skeleton of the strongly connected component. Similar conclusions are also formally obtained for undirected graphs by Bollobas and Riordan.[229] In a classical random graph, it is observed the emerging of a giant connected component when the number of edges grows over a threshold that is slightly more than linear in the number of vertices. We observe that the size of the largest SCC increases smoothly with the number of edges that are rewired up to span a big part of the graph. We also observe that the number of SCCs decreases smoothly with the increase of the percentage of rewired edges. This can be observed in Fig. 54 for the Evolving model on a graph of 10M vertices.

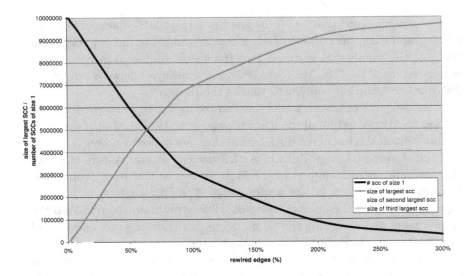

Fig. 54.   Number and size of SCCs − (Evolving Network Model)

Table 5.   Properties of models and data sets.

Model	N. of edges	γ	# Cliques (4,3)	Max scc size	Max scc percent	π	Correlation indeg - PR
Evolving	0	2	0	1	0.0001	2.2	0.935804612
	0.5M	2	0	404907	40.4907	2.2	0.941112952
	1M	2	0	692714	69.2714	2.2	0.948764657
	2M	2	0	910955	91.0955	2.2	0.84754201
Copying	0	2.1	2673	1	0.0001	2.1	0.650691063
	0.5M	2.1	2661	647942	64.7942	2.2	0.738855883
	1M	2.1	2647	824165	82.4165	2.3	0.764060435
	2M	2.1	2628	947255	94.7255	2.4	0.798681635
PageRank	0	3	0	1	0.0001	2.1	0.1977538252
	0.5M	3	0	814.552	81.4552	2.1	0.2392437130
	1M	3	0	908605	90.8605	2.1	0.2917959368
	2M	3	0	971854	97.1854	2.1	0.3299212975
multiLayer Copying (LC)	0M	No	0	1	0.0001	2.1	0.141732415
	0.5M	No	0	397645	39.7645	2.2	0.317389402
	1M	No	0	680906	68.0906	2.2	0.501913657
	2M	No	0	901211	90.1211	2.23	0.708833201
multiLayer Copy+Evol (LCB)	0	2.1	0	1	0.0001	2.1	0.345893784
	0.5M	2.1	0	298801	29.8801	2.1	0.390800789
	1M	2.1	0	620923	62.0923	2.05	0.531627042
	2M	2.1	0	883783	88.3783	2	0.692679365
multiLayer Evolving (LB)	0	2.1	0	1	0.0001	2.1	0.679171342
	0.5M	2.1	0	657848	65.7848	2.1	0.67020433
	1M	2.1	0	829717	82.9717	2.1	0.69044359
	2M	2.1	0	948958	94.8958	2.1	0.745121517
WebBase crawl	-	2.1	2949486	44713193	32.9	2.1	0.3076062794

7.5. *Algorithmic techniques for generating and measuring webgraphs*

In this section we detail a complete methodology for handling massive webgraphs. As a first step we need to identify the distinctive components of the Webgraph. For this we need to be able to perform traversals of the Webgraph. The traditional graph algorithms are designed to work in main memory, so they present a drastic slump in performance as soon as the amount of data exceeds the available main memory space. The link structure of the Web graph takes several gigabytes of disk space, making it prohibitive to use traditional graph algorithms. Therefore, we examine alternative approaches that use external memory. We implement *semi-external* algorithms, that use only a small constant amount of memory for each node of the graph, as opposed to *fully-external* ones, that use an amount of main memory that is independent of the graph size.

We implemented the following algorithms.

- External versions of Breadth and Depth First search, based on random accesses to the disk, in order to avoid maintaining the data in main memory.
- The traditional traversal algorithms that work in main memory.
- Semi-external random graph generators that create webgraphs according to the random models described in Section 7.4 (Copying, Evolving, Multi-Layer and PageRank).
- A semi-external PageRank.
- A semi-external algorithm for computing bipartite cores.
- A semi-external graph traversal for determining vertex reachability using only 2 bits per node.
- A semi-external Breadth First Search that computes blocks of reachable nodes and splits them up in layers. In a second step, these layers are sorted to produce the standard traversal result.
- A semi-external Depth First Search (DFS) that needs 12 bytes plus one bit for each node in the graph. This traversal has been developed following the standard approach.[230]
- A semi-external algorithm for computing all SCCs of the graph, based on the semi-external DFS.
- An algorithm for computing the largest SCC of the Webgraph. The algorithm adopts a heuristic approach that exploits structural properties of the Webgraph to compute the biggest SCC, using a simple reachability algorithm. As a result of the algorithm we obtain the bow-tie regions of the Webgraph, and we are able to compute all the remaining SCCs of the graph efficiently using the semi-external DFS algorithm.

Remarkable performance improvements are achieved using the semi-external algorithms — vertex reachability and DFS — and exploiting the Webgraph structure. All the algorithm listed above are publicly available, together with other routines, in a software library.[231]

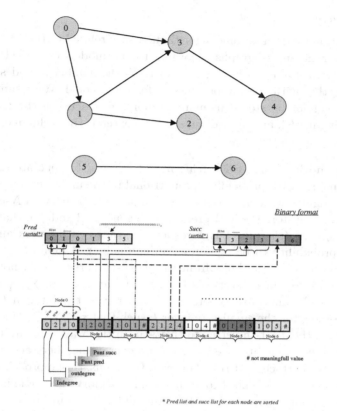

Fig. 55.   An example graph and its representation in the .ips format

7.5.1. *Data representation and multifiles*

The first problem when dealing with massive data in secondary memory is the size limit of a single file[s]. All our routines operate on a *multifile*, that is, we store a single graph into more than one file. More precisely, we use one .info file, that contains information about the nodes, one or more .prec files that contain information about the predecessors of each node, and one or more .succ files that contain information about the successors of each node. We refer to all these files related to a single graph as the .ips multifile. Fig. 55 shows a simple graph together with its representation.[231]

---

[s]This limit can be changed but we preferred, for portability reasons, to use a multifile format.

7.5.2. *Generating webgraphs*

In this section we discuss some algorithmic issues related to the generation of massive random webgraphs according to the models described above. The input for a random graph generator is N, the number of nodes of the graph, together with specific parameters for each model. We assume that the graph cannot be stored in main memory. We focus on the Evolving and Copying model, and later discuss how to extends the techniques to the other models presented.

Evolving model. For the Evolving model we need to generate the endpoint of an edge with probability proportional to the in-degree of a vertex[t]
    The straightforward approach is to keep in main memory an N-element array i where we store the in-degree for each generated node, so that $i[k] = indegree(v_k) + 1$ (the plus 1 is necessary to give to each vertex an initial non-zero probability to be chosen as an end-point). Assume that we are currently generating the links from the $g + 1$-th vertex; we denote by I the total in-degree of the vertices $v_1 \ldots v_g$ plus g, i.e. $I = \sum_{j=1}^{g} i[j]$. We randomly (and uniformly) generate a number r in the interval $(1 \ldots I)$; then, we search for the smallest integer k such that $r \leq \sum_{j=1}^{k} i[j]$: we add the link from the $g + 1$-th vertex to the k-th. In this way, using an uniform random number generator we are able to generate numbers according to the preferential attachment rule. For massive graphs, this approach has two main drawbacks: i.) We need to keep in main memory the whole in-degree array to speed up operations; ii.) It can be difficult to quickly identify the integer k.
    To overcome both problems the idea is to partition the set of vertices in a certain number of blocks, let's say B. We use a B-element array S to keep the sum of the in-degrees of all the vertices in the block. Then we alternate the following 2 phases:

Phase I. We store in main memory tuples corresponding to pending edges, i.e. edges that have been decided but not yet stored. Tuple $t = \langle g+1, k', r - \sum_{j=1}^{k'-1} S[j] \rangle$ associated with vertex $g + 1$, maintains the block number k' and the relative position of the endpoint within the block. We also group together the tuples referring to a specific block. We switch to phase II when a sufficiently large number of tuples has been generated.

---

[t]The problem of generating efficiently random discrete variables according to general distributions has been intensively studied.[232,233]

Phase II. In this phase we generate the edges and we update the information on disk. This is done by considering, in order, all the tuples that refer to a single block when this is moved to main memory. For every tuple, we find the pointed node and we update the information stored in i. The list of successors is also stored as the graph is generated.

In the real implementation we use multiple levels of blocks, instead of only one, in order to speed up the process of finding the endpoint of an edge. An alternative is the use of additional data structures to speed up the process of identifying the position of the node inside the block, like dyadic range-sums.

Copying model. The Copying model is parameterized with a copying factor α. As we recalled in Section 7.4, every new vertex u inserted in the graph by the Copying model is connected with d edges to previously existing vertices. A random prototype vertex p is also selected. The endpoint of the lth outgoing edge of vertex u, $l = 1, \ldots, d$, is either copied with probability α from the endpoint of the lth outgoing link of vertex p, or chosen uniformly at random among the existing nodes with probability $1 - \alpha$.

A natural strategy would be to generate the graph with a batch process that, alternately, i) generates edges and writes them to disk and ii) reads from disk the edges that need to be "copied". This clearly requires two accesses to disk for every newly generated vertex.

Instead we generate for every node $1 + 2 \cdot d$ random integers: one for the choice of the prototype vertex, d for the endpoints chosen at random, and d for the values of α drawn for the d edges. We store the seed of the random number generator at fixed steps, say every x generated nodes.

When we need to copy an edge from a prototype vertex p, we step back to the last time when the seed has been saved before vertex p has been generated, and let the computation progress until the outgoing edges of p are recomputed; for an appropriate choice of x, this sequence of computations is still faster than accessing the disk. Observe that p might also have copied some of its edges. In this case we recursively refer to the prototype vertex of p. We store the generated edges in a memory buffer and write it to disk when complete.

PageRank model. The PageRank model is a generalization of the Evolving model, and therefore the only difference in the algorithm sketched above is that we have to store (in main memory) also the preassigned PageRank values for each node.

Multi-Layer model. The Multi-Layer model presents more difficulties, and we implemented it by generating each layer by itself and then merging the result. This required the use of an additional array for each layer to keep track of the correspondence between vertices in the single layer and in the "whole" graph.

7.5.3. *Traversal with two bits for each node*

We now describe an algorithm for computing all the vertices reachable by a single node, or by a set of nodes. The algorithm does not use a standard graph traversal algorithm such as BFS or DFS. Instead it operates on the principle that the order in which the vertices are visited is not important. For each vertex u in the graph, it maintains only two bits of information:

i. The first bit *reached*[u] is true if u has already been reached, and false otherwise.
ii. The second bit *completed*[u] is true if the adjacency list of u has been visited, that is, all adjacent vertices are marked as reached.

At the beginning, no vertex is completed, and only the nodes in the start set are reached. The files of the .ips multifile representation of the graph are sequentially scanned, and the nodes, together with their adjacency lists, are brought to main memory one by one. When we consider a node u that is reached but not completed, then all its successors are marked as reached. At this point the node u is marked as completed. If the node u is not reached, no processing is performed and we just move on to the next node. After a number of scans over the graph, all nodes that are *reached* are also *completed*. At this point the graph traversal is completed.

To reduce the number of scans over the graph, we scan the files by loading in main memory a whole block of nodes (with their adjacency lists). The algorithm makes multiple passes over this block of nodes so as to extend as much as possible the traversal of the graph, that is, until all the nodes in this block that are reached and have their adjacency list stored in main memory are also completed.

The reachability traversal is a powerful and efficient tool that enables us to perform many different measurements on the Webgraph.

7.5.4. *Semi-external breadth first search*

The semi-external memory BFS is performed by executing a layered graph traversal. The BFS algorithm discovers vertices of the graph at increasing distance from the root. When at layer i, the algorithm performs a complete scan of the graph so as to find all successors of the vertices at layer i that have not been reached so far (This information is stored into a bit vector available in main memory). These vertices will form the $(i + 1)$-th layer of the graph. We also label the vertices according to the layer they belong to, in order to produce a BFS numbering of the graph. The efficiency of this procedure for the Web graph relies on the fact that most of the vertices of the graph can be found within few hops from the CORE.

7.5.5. *Semi-external depth first search*

Unfortunately, so far there are no efficient external-memory algorithms to compute DFS trees for general directed graphs. We therefore apply a recently proposed heuristic for semi-external DFS.[230] It maintains a tentative forest which is updated by bringing in from external memory a set non-tree edges (edges that are not part of the current DFS tentative forest) so as to reduce the number of cross edges (edges between two vertices that are not in ancestor-descendant relation in the tentative forest). The basic idea must be complemented with several implementation hacks in order to lead to a good algorithm.[230]

In our implementation, the algorithm maintains at most three integer arrays and three boolean arrays of size N, where N is the number of nodes in the graph. With four bytes per integer and one bit for each boolean, this means that the program has an internal memory requirement of $\left(12 + \frac{3}{8}\right) N$ bytes. The standard DFS needs to store $16dN$ bytes, where d is the average degree. This can be reduced if one does not store both endpoints for every edge. Still, under memory limitations, standard DFS starts paging at a point when the semi-external approach still performs efficiently.

7.5.6. *Computation of the SCCs*

It is well known[234] that the computation of all SCCs of a graph can be reduced to the execution of two DFS visits, one on the graph, and one on its transpose.[235] Due to memory limitations, even a semi-external DFS is prohibitive for Web graphs of the size we consider. We tackle this problem by removing the CORE of the Web graph before proceeding with the computation of all SCCs. We can then apply the semi-external DFS.

The question is how to identify the CORE efficiently. Using the graph traversal algorithm described in section 7.5.3, there is a simple way for determining the SCC that contains a given node u. Compute the set of vertices reachable from a forward and a backward visit starting from u, and then return the intersection of the two. This simple method suggests a heuristic strategy for determining the largest SCC of a graph with a bow tie structure: i) select uniformly at random a starting set of nodes S; ii) for each node u in S compute the SCC that contains u and return the largest one. For a graph that includes a CORE of about a quarter of the all pages, using a starting set of just 20 nodes, the probability of not finding the CORE is only $(3/4)^{20} \approx 0,3\%$.

7.5.7. *Computation of the bow-tie regions*

The computation of the largest SCC returns the CORE of the bow-tie graph. Starting from the CORE we can now compute the remaining components of the bow-tie structure.

The IN Component: The nodes of the IN component can be found by performing a backward traversal, using the CORE as the starting set. The nodes returned are the union of the CORE and IN. The IN component can be obtained by deleting the CORE nodes from this set. This operation is performed with a simple XOR logic operation between boolean vectors.

The OUT Component: The nodes of the OUT component can be found by performing a forward traversal, using the CORE as the start set. The nodes returned are the union of the CORE and OUT. The OUT component can be obtained by deleting the CORE nodes from this set, using an XOR operation as before.

TENDRILS and TUBES: The TENDRILS are sets of nodes, not belonging to the CORE, that are either reachable by nodes in IN, or that can reach nodes in OUT. The TUBES are subsets of the TENDRILS that are reachable by nodes in IN, and that can reach nodes in OUT. They form paths that lead from IN to OUT without passing through the CORE. The computation of these two sets is accomplished in three steps

i. In the first step, we identify the set TENDRILS_IN which consists of all the nodes that are reachable by IN and belong neither to the CORE, nor to the OUT set. In order to determine TENDRILS_IN, we perform a forward visit from IN, where all the nodes in the CORE are marked as *completed*, and the nodes in IN are marked as *reached*. From the set computed in this way, we discard the nodes that belong to IN or OUT. The OUT nodes are reachable through the TUBES, but they should not be considered in the TENDRILS_IN set.

ii. In the second step, symmetric to the first one, we identify the set TEN-DRILS_OUT which consists of all the nodes that point to the OUT and don't belong neither to the CORE nor to IN.

iii. In the last step, we compute the TENDRILS and TUBES:

$$\text{TENDRILS} = \text{TENDRILS\_IN} \cup \text{TENDRILS\_OUT}$$
$$\text{TUBES} = \text{TENDRILS\_IN} \cap \text{TENDRILS\_OUT}$$

DISC: The DISC consists of all the remaining nodes. These are sets of nodes that are not attached in any way to the central bow-tie structure.

7.5.8. *Disjoint bipartite cliques*

In the work of Kumar *et al*[221] an algorithm for enumerating disjoint bipartite cliques (i, j) of size at most 10 has been presented, with i being the fan vertices on the left side and j being the center vertices on the right side. The algorithm they proposed is composed of a pruning phase that consistently reduces the size of the graph in order to store it into main memory. A second phase enumerates all bipartite cliques of the graph. A final phase selects a set of bipartite cliques that form the solution. Every time a new clique is selected, all intersecting cliques are discarded. Two cliques are intersecting if they have a common fan or a common center. A vertex can then appear as a fan in a first clique and as a center in a second clique. Before detailing our algorithm we prove that the problem of enumerating disjoint bipartite cliques, as defined below, is NP-complete.

ENUMERATING BIPARTITE CORES (EBC). Given a directed graph $G = (V, E)$, a pair of integer i, j and an integer k, does G contain at least k disjoint bipartite cores $K_{i,j}$?

Theorem 1: EBC is NP-complete.

Proof: It is easy to see that EBC $\in NP$, since a nondeterministic algorithm need only to guess k different bipartite cores and then check in polynomial time if they are disjoint or not. We recall the problem,[236] EX-ACT COVER BY 3-SETS (X3C): given a finite set X with $|X| = 3q$ and a collection C of 3-element subset of X, does C contain an *exact cover* for X, that is, a sub-collection $C' \subseteq C$ such that every element of X occurs in exactly one member of C'? Given an instance I_{X3C} of X3C we transform it in an instance I_{EBC} of EBC in the following way:

- For each element $x \in X$ we create a node v_x in the graph.

- For each subset $s \in C$ we create a node v_s in the graph.
- We create a directed edge from node v_s to node v_x if the collection s includes the element x.
- We set $k = q$, $i = 1$ and $j = 3$.

If we solve this instance I_{EBC}, i.e. if there are k disjoint bipartite cliques, then we solve the corresponding instance I_{X3C}: the set of the nodes v_s, that belong to the bipartite cliques solution of I_{EBC}, form an exact cover of the set X; for each node v_x there is only one v_s that points to it, because we have disjoint cliques, and all the nodes v_x are pointed because we asked for $k = q$ cliques.   □

In the following, we describe our semi-external heuristic algorithm for computing disjoint bipartite cliques. The algorithm searches bipartite cliques of a specific size (i, j).

Two n-bit arrays Fan and $Center$, stored into main memory, indicate with $Fan(v) = 1$ and $Center(v) = 1$ whether fan v or center v has been removed from the graph. We denote by $I(v)$ and $O(v)$ the list of predecessors and successors of vertex v. Furthermore, let $\tilde{I}(v)$ be the set of predecessors of vertex v with $Fan(\cdot) = 0$, and let $\tilde{O}(v)$ the set of successors of vertex v with $Center(\cdot) = 0$. Finally, let $T[i]$ be the first i vertices of an ordered set T.

We first outline the idea underlying the algorithm. Consider a fan vertex v with at least j successors with $Center(\cdot) = 0$, and enumerate all size j subsets of $\tilde{O}(v)$. Let S be one such subset of j vertices. If $|\cap_{u \in S} I(u)| \geq i$ then we have detected an (i, j) clique. We remove the fan and the center vertices of this clique from the graph. If the graph is not entirely stored into main memory, the algorithm has to access the disk for every retrieval of the list of predecessors of a vertex of $O(v)$. Once the exploration of a vertex has been completed, the algorithm moves to consider another fan vertex.

In our semi-external implementation, the graph is stored on secondary memory in a number of blocks. Every block b, $b = 1, ..., \lceil N/B \rceil$, contains the list of successors and the list of predecessors of B vertices of the graph. Denote by $b(v)$ the block containing vertex v, and by $B(b)$ the vertices of block b. We start by analyzing the fan vertices from the first block and proceed until the last block. The block currently under examination is moved to main memory. Once the last block has been examined, the exploration continues from the first block.

We start the analysis of a vertex v when block $b(v)$ is moved to main memory for the first time. We start considering all subsets S of $\tilde{O}(v)$ formed by vertices of block $b(v)$. However, we also have to consider those subsets of

$\tilde{O}(v)$ containing vertices of other blocks, for which the list of predecessors is not available in main memory. For this purpose, consider the next block b' that will be examined that contains a vertex of $\tilde{O}(v)$. We store $\tilde{O}(v)$ and the lists of predecessors of the vertices of $\tilde{O}(v) \cap B(b)$ into an auxiliary file $A(b')$ associated with block b'. We actually buffer the accesses to the auxiliary files. Once the buffer of block b reaches a given size, this is moved to the corresponding auxiliary file $A(b)$. In the following we abuse notation by denoting with $A(b)$ also the set of fan vertices v whose exploration will continue with block b.

When a block b is moved to main memory, we first seek to continue the exploration from the vertices of $A(b)$. If the exploration of a vertex v in $A(b)$ cannot be completed within block b, the list of predecessors of the vertices of $\tilde{O}(v)$ in blocks from $b(v)$ to block b are stored into the auxiliary file of the next block b' containing a vertex of $\tilde{O}(v)$. We then move to analyze the vertices $B(b)$ of the block. We keep on doing the process till all fan and center vertices have been removed from the graph. It is rather simple to see that every block is moved to main memory at most twice.

The core algorithm is preceded by two pruning phases. The first phase removes vertices of high degree,[221] since the objective is to detect cores of hidden communities. In a second phase, we remove vertices that cannot be selected as fans or centers of an (i, j) clique.

Phase I. Remove all fans v with $|O(v)| \geq 50$ and all centers v with $|I(v)| \geq 50$.

Phase II. Pruning Remove all fans v with $|\tilde{O}(v)| < i$ and all centers with $|\tilde{I}(v)| < j$.

When a fan or a center is removed in Phase II, the in-degree or the out-degree of a vertex is also reduced and this can lead to further removal of vertices. Phase II is carried on for few passes till only few vertices are removed. Phases I and II can be easily executed in a streaming fashion.[221] After the pruning phase, the graph of about 200M vertices is reduced to about 120M vertices. About 65M of the 80M vertices that are pruned belong to the border of the graph, i.e. they have indegree 1 and outdegree 0.

We then describe the algorithm to detect disjoint bipartite cliques.

Phase III.

1. While there is a fan vertex v with $Fan(v) = 0$
2. Move to main memory the next block b to be examined.
3. For every vertex $v \in A(b) \cup B(b)$ such that $|\tilde{O}(v)| \geq j$

3.1 For every subset S of size j of $\tilde{O}(v)$, with the list of predecessors of vertices in S stored either in the auxiliary file $A(b)$ or in block b:

3.2 If $|T = \cap_{u \in S} \tilde{I}(u)| \geq i$ then

    3.2.1 output clique $(T[i], S)$

    3.2.2 set $Fan(\cdot) = 1$ for all vertices of $T[i]$

    3.2.3 set $Center(\cdot) = 1$ for all vertices of S

We maintain 2 bit information $Fan(\cdot)$ and $Center(\cdot)$ for every vertex, and store two *long long* pointers to the list of successors and the list of predecessors of every vertex. Every vertex in the list of adjacent vertices requires 1 long. The graph after the pruning has average out/in 8.75. Therefore, on the average, we need about $.25N + B(2 \times 8 + 17.5 \times 4)$ bytes for a graph of N vertices and block size B. For a graph of 50M vertices this results in a block size of 1.68M vertices. We performed our experiments with a block size of 1M vertices. We observed the time performance to converge to a linear function for graphs larger than this size.

7.5.9. *PageRank*

The computation of PageRank can be expressed in matrix notation as follows. Let N be the number of vertices of the graph and let $n(j)$ be the out-degree of vertex j. Denote by M the square matrix whose entry M_{ij} has value $1/n(j)$ if there is a link from vertex j to vertex i. Denote by $\left[\frac{1}{N}\right]_{N \times N}$ the square matrix of size $N \times N$ with entries $\frac{1}{N}$. Vector *Rank* stores the value of PageRank computed for the N vertices. A matrix M' is then derived by adding transition edges of probability $(1 - c)/N$ between every pair of nodes to include the possibility of jumping to a random vertex of the graph:

$$M' = cM + (1 - c) \times \left[\frac{1}{N}\right]_{N \times N}$$

A single iteration of the PageRank algorithm is

$$M' \times Rank = cM \times Rank + (1 - c) \times \left[\frac{1}{N}\right]_{N \times 1}$$

We implement an external memory algorithm.[237] The algorithm uses a list of successors *Links*, and two arrays *Source* and *Dest* that store the vector Rank at iteration i and $i + 1$. The computation proceeds until either the error $r = ||Source - Dest||$ drops below a fixed value τ or the number of iterations exceeds a prescribed value.

Arrays *Source* and *Dest* are partitioned and stored into $\beta = \lceil N/B \rceil$ blocks, each holding the information on B vertices. *Links* is also partitioned into β blocks, where $Links_l$, $l = 0, ..., \beta - 1$, contains for every vertex of the graph only those successors directed to vertices in block l, i.e. in the range $[lB, (l + 1)B - 1]$. We bring to main memory one block of *Dest* per time. Say we have the ith block of *Dest* in main memory. To compute the new PageRank values for all the nodes of the ith block we read, in a streaming fashion, both arrays *Source* and $Links_i$. From array *Source* we read previous PageRank values, while from $Links_i$ we have the list of successors (and the out-degree) for each node of the graph to vertices of block i, and these are, from the above PageRank formula, exactly all the information required.

The main memory occupation is limited to one float for each node in the block, and, in our experiments, 256MB allowed us to keep the whole *Dest* in memory for a 50M vertices graph. Only a small buffer area is required to store *Source* and *Links*, since they are read in a streaming fashion.

7.6. *Summary and outlook*

In this chapter we presented an overview of the Webgraph. We first detailed its known properties, then we discussed and compared several random graph generators that try to model it. We examined also the algorithmic aspects of this research, and we detailed several algorithms to generate and measure massive webgraphs. It should be clear that we made only a first step in modeling the Webgraph: several aspects are missing and, among them, we mention that no model captures the out-degree distribution observed in samples, and the nature of the "rewiring" process is still obscure. Probably the most important aspect not considered is that, despite its dynamic nature, the Webgraph has been studied so far from a static point of view: snapshots of it have been analyzed but it is still missing the projection of its properties against a temporal axis. A first step towards this direction has been presented;[238] here, each edge is labeled with the dates of its first and last appearance in the Web. This new data, of course, pose several challenges; among them we cite (i) the problem of efficiently representing dynamic graphs in secondary memory, (ii) whether it is possible to adapt the Webgraph compression techniques to it and (iii) if it is possible to design algorithms able to deal explicitly with the time labels without the need of generating multiple snapshots from it.

CHAPTER 8

The Large Scale Structure of the Internet

Alain Barrat[1], Luca Dall'Asta[1], Ignacio Alvarez-Hamelin[1] and
Alessandro Vespignani[2]

[1]*Laboratoire de Physique Théorique (UMR du CNRS 8627), Bâtiment 210,
Université de Paris-Sud, 91405 Orsay, France*
[2]*School of Informatics, Indiana University, Bloomington 47406 IN, USA*

8.1. *Introduction*

The Internet is a prototypical example of info-structure that has grown
following a self-organized dynamics. Even though governments are waking
up to the reality that the Internet is a critical infrastructure that has dramatically changed our way to access information, exploit social relations,
and run commerce, nobody has ever run the Internet growth or drawn a
blueprint for its development. The dynamics of Internet is indeed defined
by the interplay between cooperation (the network has to work efficiently)
and competition (providers wish to earn money). These evolutionary principles have shaped an intrinsically heterogeneous system ruled by different
administrative policies whose complicate structure cannot be found in any
repository or "official" map. For these reasons, in the last years, several
research groups have started to deploy technologies and infrastructures in
order to obtain a more global picture of the Internet. Several studies aiming
at tracking and visualizing the Internet large scale topology and/or performance are now providing Internet maps at different resolution scales. These
projects typically collect data on Internet nodes (routers, domains, etc.)
and links in order to create a graph-like representation of large parts of the
Internet. The obtained Internet graphs exhibit most of the features characterizing large scale complex networks and in the present chapter we provide
a review of the results obtained in the characterization of their structure.
We also present a critical discussion of the eventual experimental biases

that might lead to erroneous conclusions on the actual topological properties of the Internet network. Finally we discuss some novel measurements aimed at uncovering the hierarchical and ordering principles underlying the Internet structure.

8.2. *Internet maps*

Internet mapping projects focus essentially on two levels of topological description. First, by inferring router adjacencies it has been possible to measure the Internet Router (IR) level graph. The second mapping effort concerns the Autonomous System (AS) level graph of the Internet referring to autonomously administered *domains* that to a first approximation identify Internet Service Providers and Organizations. Therefore, Internet maps are usually viewed as undirected graphs in which vertices represent routers or ASes and edges (links) represent the physical connections between them. Although these two graph representations are related, it is clear that they describe the Internet at rather different scales. In fact, the collection of ASes and the inter-domain routing system define a coarse-grained picture of the Internet in which each AS groups many routers together and links are the aggregation of all the individual connections between the routers of the corresponding ASes.

In order to obtain Internet connectivity information at the AS level it is possible to inspect routing tables and paths stored in each router (passive measurements) or to directly explore the network with a software probe (active measurements). In the following we consider data from large scale Internet mapping projects using different strategies.

Mercator[239] was one of the first attempts to map Internet at the router level. It exploits the *source routing* IP option to explore the whole Internet from only one source. This IP option allows to use some routers as sources, potentially providing as many sources as there are routers with source routing capabilities. At the time of the Mercator project, it was possible to use approximately 8% of the routers for source routing; because of security reasons however, most of them are no more available. Therefore, only one such map has ever been obtained through this technique. Based on another strategy, the *Oregon route-views*[240] project (RV) provides maps of the AS graph with a passive measurement strategy based on the knowledge of the routing tables of several Border Gateway Protocol (BGP) peers. On the other hand, another active measurement approach has been implemented by the skitter project at CAIDA.[241] This project deployed several strategically placed probing monitors using a path probing software. All the data are then centrally collected and merged in order to obtain Internet maps that maximize the estimate of cross-connectivity. The fourth set we consider is provided by the Distributed Internet Measurements and Simulations (DIMES) project.[242,243] This recently launched project proposes to use a distributed measurement infrastructure, based on the deployment of thousands of light weight measurement agents around the globe. At the moment, more than 3,000 agents are collecting data through tools such as `traceroute` and `ping`. The CAIDA and DIMES projects collect data both at the AS and IR level while the RV project yields only AS maps. It is interesting to note that, due to the different locations of the various probing sources, the projects give substantially different maps of the Internet. For example, it is possible[243] to compare the data of RV and DIMES obtained from March to June 2005, showing that many ASes are not discovered through active measurements because they block `traceroute`-like probing; on the other hand, DIMES obtains for many ASes a larger degree than RV; in particular, the degree of small ASes is often much larger in DIMES than in RV maps. This points to the relevance of comparisons between various mapping projects and strategies, and of the study of the temporal evolution of the various maps.

The starting point for the study of large scale Internet maps is the analysis of the most basic set of standard network metrics. The degree of a vertex, and the shortest path lengths to other vertices, in the IR (AS) level graphs, have an immediate physical interpretation, quantifying how well a router (AS) is connected, and its minimum distance to other routers (ASes), in terms of router (AS) hops. The betweenness of a vertex gives a measure of the amount of traffic that goes through it, if the shortest path length is used as the metric defining the optimal path between pairs of vertices[u]. The betweenness, sometimes refereed to as "load",[18] is thus a measure of the *centrality* of a vertex in the network. Furthermore, the clustering coefficient is a measure of the level of local interconnectivity among neighboring routers (ASes). For instance, a high clustering coefficient indicates a well interconnected local community of routers (ASes), very likely within the same administrative domain or geographical region.

In Tab.6 we report the main characteristics of the analyzed maps at both the IR and AS granularity. The average values reported readily give some

---

[u]This is not always the case, since policy agreements can indeed impose non-optimal paths in the routing tables.

Table 6. Main characteristics of the various Internet maps: number N of vertices, average ($\langle d \rangle$) and maximal (d_{max}) degree, ratio $\kappa = \langle d^2 \rangle / \langle d \rangle$, average shortest path $\langle \ell \rangle$ between pairs of vertices, and average clustering coefficient $\langle c \rangle$.

Name	Date	Size N	$\langle d \rangle$	d_{max}	κ	$\langle \ell \rangle$	$\langle c \rangle$
AS RV	2005/04	18119	3.54771	1382	2369.82	3.92	0.083
AS CAIDA	2005/04	8542	5.96851	1171	521.751	3.18	0.222
AS Dimes	2005/04	20455	6.03862	2800	1556.24	3.35	0.236
IR Mercator	2001	228297	2.79635	1314	36838.6	9.5	0.013
IR CAIDA	2003	192243	6.33085	841	8884.23	5.6	0.08
IP Dimes	2005	328011	8.2142	1453	10954	5.5	0.066

indications on the Internet overall structure. The average degree of the three maps is very small if compared with the network sizes; they are therefore very *sparse* graphs. Despite this small average degree, however, the average shortest path length $\langle \ell \rangle$ is also very small. This feature points towards the so-called *small-world* property. To be more precise, the small-world property refers to networks in which $\langle \ell \rangle$ scales logarithmically, or slower, with the number of vertices N (see Chapter 1). In Fig. 56 we show the so-called *hop plot* $M(\ell)$, defined in the early investigations of the statistical properties of the Internet:[78]

$$M(\ell) = N \sum_{\ell'=0}^{\ell} P(\ell'). \qquad (101)$$

where $P(\ell)$ is the probability distribution of finding two vertices separated by a distance ℓ. The hop plot is therefore defined as the average number of vertices within a distance less than or equal to ℓ from any given vertex, and in this sense is a sort of measure of the average local *mass* of the graph. At $\ell = 0$ we find the starting vertex, and thus $M(0) = 1$. At $\ell = 1$ we find the starting vertex plus its nearest neighbors. When ℓ is equal to the diameter D of the network, $M(D) = N$. In the case of a small world the hop plot should exhibit an exponential growth as opposite to the power law behavior obtained in regular grids. For both the IR and AS maps, Fig. 56 shows the expected exponential growth followed by the saturation to N. The datasets from CAIDA and DIMES evidence stronger small world properties compared to Mercator, that is consistent with a considerable improvement in the sampling accuracy for recent mappings. The small-world phenomenon appears to characterize several infrastructure networks where the small av-

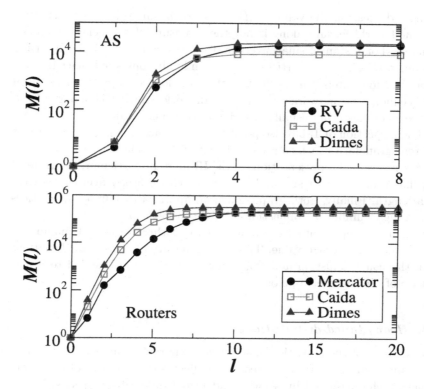

Fig. 56. Hop plots for Internet maps at the AS (top) and IR (bottom) levels. $M(\ell)$ is the average number of vertices at distance less than or equal to ℓ of any vertex. Data at AS level are complete (i.e. we computed the distance between each possible vertex pairs in the graphs), while maps at the router level have been sampled by collecting the shortest paths to all vertices from a set of $\mathcal{O}(10^3)$ sources chosen at random. For the maps from CAIDA and DIMES projects, at the AS (IR) level, more than 90% of vertex pairs are at a distance ℓ of 4 (7) steps or less. Differently, in the maps from RV (AS-level) and Mercator (IR-level), a similar proportion of vertices is reached for slightly larger distances ($\ell = 5$ and 9 respectively).

erage distance is crucially important to speed up communications.[244] For instance, if the Internet had the shape of a regular two-dimensional grid, its characteristic distance would scale as $\langle \ell \rangle \sim N^{1/2}$; with the present Internet size, each data packet would pass through 10^2 or more routers, drastically depleting the Internet communication capabilities. The small-world property is therefore implicitly enforced in the network architecture which incorporates hubs and backbones which connect different regional networks, strongly decreasing the value of $\langle \ell \rangle$. It is worth remarking, however, that the small-world feature alone is not the signature of a special organizing principle. For instance, small average distances can be achieved by using random graphs in which vertices are just randomly connected (see Chapters 2 and 3). More interesting is the fact that, in close analogy to many social and technological networks,[6,245] the small-world effect goes along with a high level of clustering usually associated to regular grids.

The inspection of Tab.6 also points out differences among the metrics at different granularities which are consistent with the fact that the AS maps are coarse-grained representations of the IR map. In particular, the IR level map has a much larger size and is sparser, with a larger average shortest path length. Finally, both graphs have an appreciable number of vertices with a high number of connections (hubs): we observe that the maximum degree in the representative graphs is two to three orders of magnitude larger that the average value. This is a signature of statistical deviations from the usual Gaussian and Poissonian statistics, that has led to a new picture of the Internet topology.

8.3. *Heavy tailed distributions*

The analysis of the statistical distributions characterizing the basic quantities analyzed in the previous sections indicates the presence of a network structure characterized by skewed and heavy tailed distributions.[78] This fact opened a new burst of activity and it corresponds to a new picture of the Internet structure in which the usual Poissonian statistical assumptions are not valid. In Fig. 57 we show the degree distribution at the AS and IR level obtained in the various projects. In all data samples the distribution is highly variable in the sense that degrees vary over a range close to three orders of magnitude. This behavior is very different from the case of bell-shaped, exponentially decaying distributions. The AS level degree distribution is stable along the years (not shown) and only the cut-off, fixed by the maximum degree of the system, is increasing due to the overall Internet growth. At the AS level, the decaying with the degree d appears to be well approximated by a linear behavior on the double logarithmic scale. More precisely, the distribution can be fitted by the power-law form $P(d) \simeq a d^{-\gamma}$ with exponent $\gamma \simeq 2.1$ and an opportune normalization constant a. In the IR case, the degree distributions are smoothed by a cut-off regime consistent with a finite size scaling of the form $P(d) = d^{-\gamma} f(d/d_c)$, where $f(x)$ has the asymptotic behavior $f(x) = $ const. for $x \ll 1$ and $f(x) \ll 1$ for

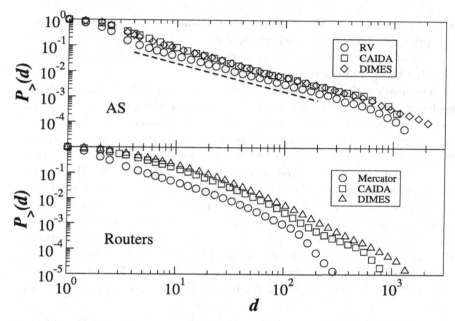

Fig. 57. Cumulative degree distributions of the various AS and IR maps. The degrees span three orders of magnitude. The dashed line corresponds to a power-law $d^{-1.1}$, i.e. to $d^{-2.1}$ for the corresponding degree distribution.

$x \gg 1$. Here d_c is the degree above which the distribution decays faster than a power law. Deviations from the power law behavior at large connectivities are also clearly observed[246] for the larger IP level maps[v], and other heavy-tail fit may also be used, such as Weibull or log-normal distributions. The presence of truncated power laws must not be considered a surprise, since it finds a natural place in the context of scale-free phenomena. Actually, bounded scale-free distributions (*i.e.* power-law distributions with a cut-off) are implicitly present in every real world system because of finite-size effects or physical constraints. Truncated power laws are observed also in other real networks[68] and different mechanisms have been proposed to explain the cut-off for large connectivities. In particular, the exponential

---

[v]Merging active explorations from different sources yields an IP map. Then, to obtain the final IR map one has to identify the various IP addresses belonging to each router. This association is not straightforward because there is no obvious correlations between the different addresses of a router's interfaces.[239]

cut-off, $f(x) = \exp(-x)$ can be explained in terms of a finite degree capacity of the network elements[68] or incomplete information.[247] This is likely what is happening at the IR level, where the finite capacity constraint (maximum number of router interfaces) is, in our opinion, the dominant mechanism affecting the tail of the degree distribution.

The heavy-tailed behavior implies that there is a statistically significant probability that a vertex has a very large number of connections compared to the average degree $\langle d \rangle$. In addition, the implicit divergence of $\langle d^2 \rangle$ is signaling the extreme heterogeneity of the connectivity pattern, since it implies that statistical fluctuations are unbounded, and tells us that the average degree is not the typical degree value in the system. The heavy tailed nature of the degree distribution has also important consequences in the dynamics of processes taking place on top of these networks. Indeed, recent studies about network resilience to removal of vertices[248] and virus spreading[249] have shown that the relevant parameter is the ratio $\kappa = \langle d^2 \rangle / \langle d \rangle$ between the first two moments of the degree distribution. If $\kappa \gg 1$ then the network manifests some properties that are not observed for networks with exponentially decaying degree distributions. For instance, we can randomly remove practically all the vertices in the network and a giant connected component[250] will still exist. In the AS and IR maps, we observe wide degree distributions with factors κ, which, being determined effectively by the tail of the distribution, take on quite large values.

Empirical evidence for the heavy-tailed behavior of the degree distribution has been collected both at the IR and AS level in several studies.[48,50,132,239,246,251,253,254,256–259] In addition, the heavy-tailed or scale-free behavior does not show up only in the degree distribution. For instance, additional evidence can be observed in the betweenness distribution $P_b(b)$ (i.e. the probability that any given vertex is traversed by b shortest paths between pairs of vertices) that shows heavy tails with scale-free behavior.[12] The heavy-tail behavior is especially evident from the heterogeneity parameter κ and the wide variations of the degree range, as reported in Tab.6.

It is important to stress at this point that the change in perspective offered by the presence of scale-free distributions has an impact that goes far beyond the discussion concerning truncations and finite size effects or the exact form of the fitting function. The really crucial issue is that the observation of heavy-tailed, highly variable distributions provides new experimental input for a radical change of the Internet representation and modeling.

8.4. *Sampling biases and the scale-free nature of the Internet*

As we have seen in the previous sections, mapping the Internet generally consists in sampling the network from a limited set of sources by using `traceroute`-like probes. This methodology, akin to the merging of different spanning trees to a set of destinations, has been argued to introduce uncontrolled sampling biases that might produce statistical properties of the sampled graph which sharply differ from the original ones. Indeed, while `traceroute`-driven strategies are very flexible and can be feasible for extensive use, the obtained maps are undoubtedly incomplete. Along with technical problems such as the instability of paths between routers and interface resolutions,[260] typical mapping projects are run from relatively small sets of sources whose combined views are missing a considerable number of edges and vertices.[256,258,261] In particular, the various spanning trees are specially missing the lateral connectivity of targets and sample more frequently nodes and links which are closer to each source, introducing spurious effects that might seriously compromise the statistical accuracy of the sampled graph. This question has spurred several works aimed at critically examining the statistical properties observed in Internet maps, and in particular the heavy-tail behavior mentioned previously.

The first systematic study of biases and the eventual impact on the observed statistical properties of the Internet shows[262] that biases can seriously affect the estimation of degree distributions. In particular, power-law like distributions can be observed for subgraphs of Erdös-Rényi random graphs when the subgraph is the product of a `traceroute` exploration with relatively few sources and destinations. The authors discuss the origin of these biases and the effect of the distance between source and target in the mapping process. In a different perspective, Petermann and De Los Rios have studied a `traceroute`-like procedure on various examples of scale-free graphs,[263] showing that, in the case of a single source, power-law distributions with underestimated exponents are obtained. Finally, Guillaume and Latapy[264] report a study in which shortest-paths explorations of synthetic graphs are obtained from different vantage points, focusing on the comparison between properties of the resulting sampled graph and those of the original network. In a recent work,[265] Clauset and Moore have given analytical foundations to the previous numerical work. They have modeled the single source probing to all possible destinations using differential equations. For an Erdös-Renyi random graph with average degree $\langle d \rangle$, they have shown that the connectivity distribution of the obtained spanning tree displays a power-law behavior d^{-1}, with an exponential cut-off setting in at a characteristic degree $d_c \sim \langle d \rangle$.

All these works explicitly warn that the evidence obtained from the analysis of the Internet sampled graphs might be insufficient to draw conclusions on the topology of the actual Internet network. On the other hand, the reliability of the graphs depends on the number of probing stations and targeted routers used to infer the physical connectivity.[266] For instance, the *Oregon route-views* collects and merges the connectivity inferred from the BGP routing tables of 20 to 50 operational routers. The CAIDA skitter project is using 23 probing stations, and the DIMES distributed measurement infrastructure amounts to almost 5,000 measuring agents. In this perspective it is therefore very important to address the role of the number of sources and targets in the evaluation of the statistical accuracy of the sampled graph and the reliability of the inferred topological properties of the underlying network. This issue may be tackled through a mean-field statistical analysis and extensive numerical study in different networks models of shortest path routed sampling, considered as the first approximation to `traceroute`-sampling.[267,268] This approach allows to derive analytically an approximate expression to obtain the average discovery probability of an edge i, j as

$$\langle \pi_{i,j} \rangle \simeq 1 - \exp\left(-\epsilon \widetilde{b}_{ij}\right), \tag{102}$$

where $\widetilde{b}_{ij} = N^{-1} b_{ij}$ is the rescaled edge betweenness, and $\epsilon = N_S N_T / N$ is the density of probes imposed to the system (N_S, N_T and N are respectively the number of sources and targets, and the total number of nodes in the original network). A similar expression can be obtained for the discovery probability of vertices, leading in the large N limit to the average

$$\langle \pi_i \rangle \simeq 1 - (1 - \rho_S - \rho_T) \exp\left(-\epsilon \widetilde{b}_i\right), \tag{103}$$

where $\widetilde{b}_i = N^{-1} b_i$ is the rescaled node betweenness, and $\rho_S = N_S / N$ and $\rho_T = N_T / N$ are the density of sources and targets, respectively. Analogous expressions can also be obtained for the discovery redundancy (the number of probes discovering a given node) and the average effective degree observed for each node, depending on its actual degree. The exploration process thus statistically focuses on high betweenness vertices, thus providing a very accurate sampling of the distribution tail. In graphs with heavy-tails, such as scale-free networks, the degree and betweenness are indeed usually strongly correlated, so that the main topological features are easily discriminated since the relevant statistical information is encapsulated in the degree distribution tail which is fairly well captured. Quite surprisingly, the sampling of homogeneous graphs appears more cumbersome than those of heavy-tailed graphs. Dramatic effects such as the existence of apparent power-laws, however, are found only in very peculiar cases. In general, exploration strategies provide sampled distributions with enough signatures to distinguish at the statistical level between graphs with different topologies. This result appears to be very relevant in the discussion of real data from Internet mapping projects. Indeed, data indicate the presence of heavy-tailed degree distributions both at the router and AS level, consistently across several different experiments. The present discussion indicates that it is very unlikely that this feature is just an artifact of the mapping strategies. The upper degree cut-off at the router and AS level runs up to more than 10^2 and 10^3, respectively. A homogeneous graph should have an average degree comparable to the measured cut-off, which is hardly conceivable in a realistic perspective (for instance, it would require that nine routers out of ten would have more than 100 links to other routers). In addition, the major part of mapping projects are multi-source, a feature that readily washes out the presence of spurious power-law behavior. Moreover, heterogeneous networks with heavy-tailed degree distributions are sampled with particular accuracy for the large degree part, generally at all probing levels. This makes very plausible, and a natural consequence, that the heavy-tail behavior observed in real mapping experiments is a genuine feature of the Internet.

8.5. *Hierarchies and correlations*

The primary known structural difference in the Internet is the distinction between *stub* and *transit* domains (or ASes).[12] Transit ASes correspond to large backbones, providing national or international connectivity, or to regional providers serving large metropolitan areas. Stub ASes, on the other hand, correspond to campus networks and local area networks. The purpose of transit ASes is to provide connectivity to stubs, minimizing the necessity of direct stub-stub connections. For this reason, transit ASes are well interconnected among them, and link stub ASes in their geographical neighborhood. The primary characteristic of this domain hierarchy is that traffic paths between vertices in the same domain stay entirely within that domain. For instance, stub ASes handle all the traffic that originates and

terminates inside the AS boundaries, while a routing path between two
vertices in different stub ASes goes generally through one or more transit
ASes. This traffic division can be schematically represented as a hierarchical structure, roughly partitioned into international connections, national
connections, regional networks, and local area networks. Vertices providing access to international connections or national backbones are of course
on top level of this hierarchy, since they make possible the communication
between regional and local area networks.

The study of the inherent structural organization of the AS level has led
to several hierarchical representations of the Internet. These pictures mainly
provide a decomposition of the structural organization of the Internet by
defining a certain number of hierarchical levels or *tiers*, usually corresponding to different connectivity classes.[269,270] The availability of large Internet
maps has however stimulated the analysis of hierarchies and correlations
through more stringent mathematical characterizations. Indeed, the hierarchical ordering introduces correlations in the network topology and it is an
important issue to understand how these features manifest at the statistical level. In order to quantify the presence of hierarchies in Internet maps
we consider two metrics based on the clustering coefficient and the nearest
neighbor average degree. These two quantities, studied as a function of the
vertex degree,[48,62,255] provide a wealth of information on the structural and
hierarchical ordering of networks (see Chapter 3). The *clustering coefficient*
measures the local group cohesiveness and is defined for any vertex j as
the fraction of connected neighbors of j: $c_j = 2 \cdot n_{\text{link}}/(d_j(d_j - 1))$, where
n_{link} is the number of links between the d_j neighbors of j. The study of
the clustering spectrum $c(d)$ of vertices of degree d allows e.g. to uncover
hierarchies in which low degree vertices belong generally to well interconnected communities (high clustering coefficient), while hubs connect many
vertices that are not directly connected (small clustering coefficient). Analogously, the *average degree of nearest neighbors* $d_{nn}(d)$ of vertices of degree
d is defined as:

$$d_{nn}(d) = \frac{1}{n_d} \sum_{j/d_j=d} \frac{1}{d_j} \sum_{i \in V(j)} d_i \quad , \tag{104}$$

where $V(j)$ is the set of neighbors of vertex j and n_d the number of vertices
of degree d. When correlations are present, two main classes of possible correlations have been identified: *assortative* behavior if $d_{nn}(d)$ increases with
d, which indicates that large degree vertices are preferentially connected

with other large degree vertices, and *disassortative* if $d_{nn}(d)$ decreases with d.[41] In Fig. 58 we report the clustering and correlation spectrum for the Internet maps at the AS and IR level. In the case of ASes, the clustering spec-

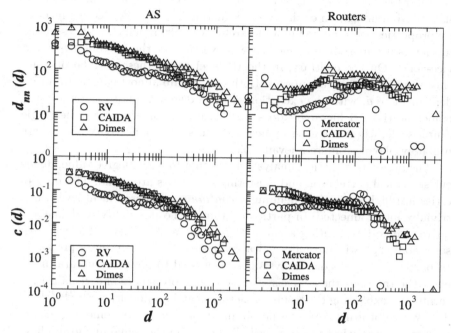

Fig. 58. Average nearest neighbor degrees (top) and clustering spectra (bottom) for the AS and IR Internet maps.

trum follows a behavior that can be approximated by a power law decay. This implies that at the AS level vertices with a small number of connections have larger local clustering coefficients than those with a large degree. This behavior is consistent with the picture described above of highly clustered regional networks sparsely interconnected by national backbones and international connections. The regional clusters of ASes are probably formed by a large number of vertices with small degree but large clustering coefficients. Moreover, they should also contain vertices with large degrees that are connected with the other regional clusters. These large degree vertices will on their turn be connected to vertices in different clusters which are not interconnected and, therefore, will have a small clustering coefficient.

Similarly, for the degree correlation function of the AS maps we observe an approximate power-law decay for more than two decades. This decay indicates the presence of *disassortative mixing*;[41] *i.e.* high degree vertices have a statistical majority of neighbors with low degree, while the opposite holds for low degree vertices. This property is another clear signature of the structural organization of the Internet at the AS level. Vertices connectivity properties are arranged in a hierarchy of levels, in which vertices at the top levels are more interconnected with vertices at the bottom levels and vice-versa. On the contrary, in the IR level graph these correlations and clustering hierarchies are absent. Both spectra are almost constant and independent of d, with the exception of large degrees, due to low statistics. Somehow the AS hierarchy does not leave any fingerprint at the single router scale, where the geographic constraints and connectivity bounds are probably playing a more relevant role.

The previous statistical analysis shows that for each degree value, different statistical correlation and clustering properties are found. These properties are highly variable, defining a *continuum* of hierarchical levels, non trivially interconnected. In particular, there is no possibility to define any degree range representing a *characteristic* hierarchical level. For this reason, more sophisticated hierarchical analysis have been recently proposed. In particular, the k-core analysis has been used to obtain structural models of the Internet, the analysis of its scale-free properties and visualization techniques exploiting the resulting hierarchical decomposition.[204,242,271–275] The k-core of a network can be obtained by recursively removing all the vertices of degree less than k, until all vertices in the remaining graph have degree at least k. It is worth remarking that this process is not equivalent to the simple pruning of vertices of a certain degree. Indeed, a star-like subgraph formed by a node with a high degree that connects many vertices with degree one, and connected only with a single edge to the rest of the graph, is going to belong to the first pruned shell no matter how high its degree. The k-core analysis also uses the following definitions

Definition 1: A vertex i has *shell index* k if it belongs to the k-core but not to the $(k+1)$-core.

Definition 2: A k-*shell* S_k is composed by all the vertices whose shell index is k. The maximum value k such that S_k is not empty is denoted $k_{\max}$. The k-core is thus the union of all shells S_c with $c \geq k$.

The k-core decomposition therefore identifies progressively more and more internal cores and decomposes the networks layer by layer, revealing the structure of the different k-shells from the most external one to the most internal one. The first observation about the structure of the Internet k-cores is that they remain connected. This is not a priori an obvious fact since one can easily imagine networks whose k-core decomposition yields several connected components corresponding, e.g. to various communities. Instead, each decomposition step is just *peeling* the network leaving connected the inner part of the network. Fig. 59 shows a visualization of CAIDA Internet maps that places vertices in 2 dimensions, the position of each vertex depending on its shell index and on the shell index of its neighbors.[274,275]

At the AS level, all shells are populated, and, in a given shell, the vertices are distributed on a relatively large range of the radial coordinate, which means that their neighborhoods are variously composed. It is worth noting that the shell index and the degree are very correlated, with a clear hierarchical structure. Links go principally from one shell to another, although there are of course also intra-layer links. The hierarchical structure exhibited by the autonomous system level is a striking property; for instance, one might exploit it for showing that in the Internet high-degree vertices are naturally (as an implicit result of the self-organizing growing) placed in the innermost structure.

At high resolution, i.e. at the IR level, Internet's properties are less structured: external layers, of lowest shell index, contain vertices with large degree. There are for example 5 vertices with a degree larger than 100 and shell index less than 6. The lowest index shells, containing vertices that are very external, are displayed as quite broad layers, meaning that the corresponding vertices have neighbors with shell index covering a large range of values. The innermost shells are thin rings, which means that the neighbors of the vertices in a given layer have similar shell index.

It seems moreover interesting to apply the previous statistical analysis concerning degree distributions and correlations to the successive k-cores, i.e. to more and more central parts of the networks.[271] Fig. 60 shows the cumulative degree distribution for some k-cores, for various AS and IR maps; namely, the probability $P_>(d)$ that any vertex has a degree larger than d. Strikingly, the shape of the distribution, i.e. an approximate power-law, is not affected by the decomposition. In particular the exponent of the power-law is robust although the range of variation of the degree decreases. This

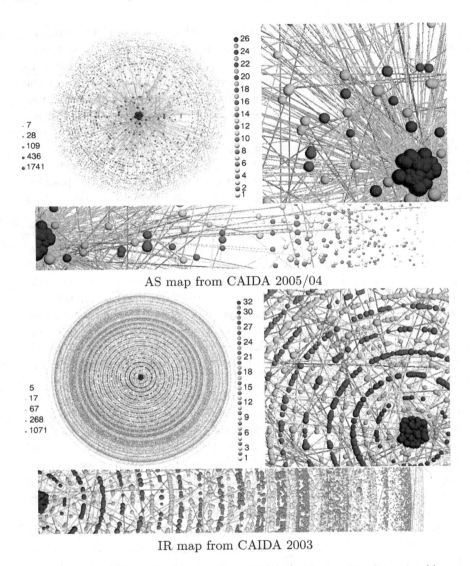

Fig. 59.   LaNet-vi[275] provides images of large scale networks on a two-dimensional lay-out, the position of each vertex depending on its shell-index and on the shell-index of its neighbors. In particular, each k-shell is forming a circular layer, of diameter proportional to $k_{max} - k$, i.e. with the innermost shell at the center and shells of decreasing centrality farther and farther from the center. The left scale gives the correspondence between the size of a represented node and its degree; the scale on the right gives the shell index. The precise position of each node also depends on its neighbors: a node of a given shell is more central in the layout if its neighbors have typically larger shell-index.[275]

feature defines a striking property of statistical self-similarity of the generated k-cores, which resemble one with each other under the opportune rescaling of the average degree. This evidence is strengthened by the inspection of Fig. 61 and 62 where $d_{nn}(d)$ and $c(d)$ are computed for the various k-cores. Also in this case the behavior of the two quantities is preserved as the network is recursively pruned of its low-degree vertices in the case of AS graphs. In the IR case, the curves do not collapse on top of each other, and their global shape is only partially preserved. This points out again the presence of some basic differences in the structure of the Internet at the AS and IR level. On the other hand, it is important to stress that IR maps are just a very partial sample of the full Internet structure at that granularity level and it is possible that this introduces finite size effects during the decomposition process. In general, however, the overall statistical features of the network topology are preserved for k-cores of increasing centrality, and at the AS level the Internet exhibits a statistical scale invariance with respect to the pruning obtained with the k-core decomposition. This hints to a sort of global self-similarity for regions of increasing centrality of the network, and to a structure in which each region of the Internet as defined in terms of network centrality has the same properties as the whole network. The k-core decomposition appears therefore as a suitable way to define a pruning procedure equivalent to a scale-change preserving the statistical properties of graphs and offering an alternative definition of centrality as indicated by the shell-index of each node. This intuitively provides a hierarchy of the vertices based on their shell index that is a combination of local and global properties. Indeed, an approach based on the k-core decomposition has been used to provide a conceptual and structural model of the Internet; the so-called "medusa" model for the Internet.[273]

The hierarchical analysis of the Internet is therefore adding a new dimension to its topological and organizational complexity. The statistical analysis shown in this chapter proposes a structural picture in which the hierarchical properties are extremely interwoven with the connectivity pattern. Yet, concepts like tiers and backbone appears not to be sharply defined, hinting towards a complex and self similar set of hierarchies in which a wide range of correlations and clustering is allowed. On the other hand, the caveats concerning the statistical reliability on the Internet maps might apply also in the analysis of its organizational structure. It is likely that the future research activity will focus on a discussion of this issue in the near future.

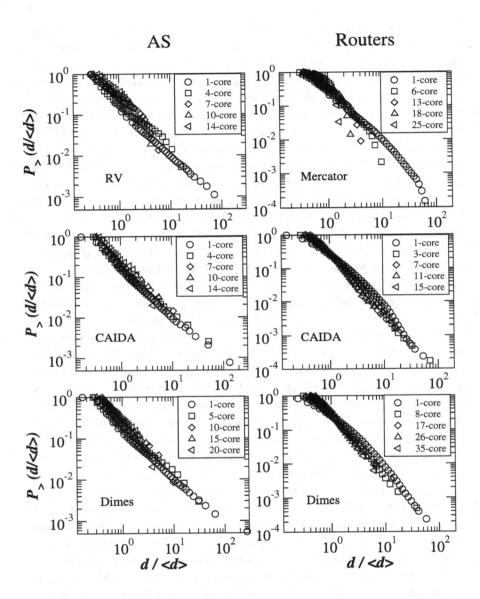

Fig. 60. Rescaled degree distributions of some k-cores of the various Internet maps. The shapes of the distributions are preserved by the successive pruning.

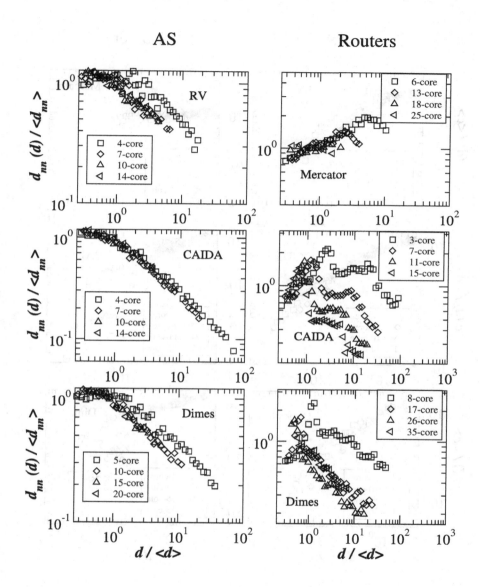

Fig. 61. Rescaled average nearest neighbor as a function of the rescaled degree for some *k*-cores of the various Internet maps.

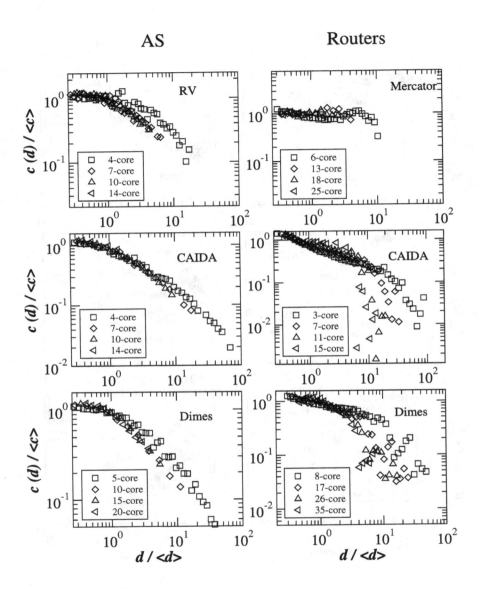

Fig. 62.   Rescaled clustering spectrum for some k-cores of the various Internet maps.

8.6. *Outlook*

The results obtained so far on the Internet structure have highlighted the emergence of a complex structure whose topological properties exhibit many of the features characterizing large scale evolving networks. On the other hand, data gathering processes provide Internet maps which are still incomplete. The biases resulting from the partial sampling of the Internet call for a critical examination of the obtained results and point out the need of mapping strategies able to gather more complete representations of this network. Finally, a more general characterization and understanding of the Internet cannot neglect the traffic properties of this network. Computers have different capacities and each connection is characterized by specific bandwidth and traffic values. These properties are adding an extra dimension to the complexity of the Internet. The evolution of the Internet topology is surely driven by traffic demand, and the traffic is in turn affected by topological changes and increased bandwidth. The understanding of the coupling between topology and traffic is therefore the key element towards a more complete picture of the Internet system and it will surely dominate the Internet research agenda in the years to come.

Acknowledgments

We are grateful to the Internet mapping projects University of Oregon Route Views Project, CAIDA and DIMES for providing maps of Internet at the various granularity levels.

CHAPTER 9

Spanning Trees in Ecology:
Patterns of Trophic and Taxonomic Complexity

Diego Garlaschelli[1], Cecile Caretta Cartozo[2] and Guido Caldarelli[3]

[1]*INFM and Dipartimento di Fisica, Università di Siena,*
Via Roma 56, 53100 Siena, Italy

[2]*EPFL SB ITP LBS, 1015 Lausanne, Switzerland*

[3]*INFM-CNR Centro SMC Dip. di Fisica Università 'La Sapienza',*
P.le Aldo Moro, 00185 Roma, Italy

9.1. *Introduction*

Ecology deals with the description of an extremely large number of biological species organized in complex and highly diverse communities. From a theoretical point of view, an important question is whether the observed complexity of species assemblages can be traced back to relatively simple fundamental principles. One way to answer this question is to characterize the observed 'diversity of life' by means of suitable quantitative properties, to search for possible empirical patterns displayed by these properties across different ecosystems, and finally to understand such patterns in terms of basic underlying mechanisms.

In the neo-Darwinistic paradigm, a powerful and promising hypothesis explaining the complexity of life is the continuous action of *natural selection* as a driving force related to various evolutionary processes such as mutation, speciation and extinction. These processes result in the diversification of species and in their adaptation to the surrounding environment. In the ecological context, the 'environment' experienced by a species is not only determined by the properties and abundance of inanimate entities such as water, light and chemicals, but also by the set of all other living organisms coexisting with the given species. This leads to the concept of *co-evolution*, where each species affects, and at the same time is affected, by the environment determined by all other species. Co-evolution leads to a high degree of complexity, since the behaviour of a single species is coupled to that of the entire community. As a consequence, it is important to introduce suitable quantities at the whole community level and to address the large-scale organization of ecosystems.

In the present work, we focus on two of the most used characterizations of a community of biological species: the *food web* representing in a graph-theoretical fashion the trophic interactions existing among the species, and the *taxonomic tree* wherein the various species are hierarchically arranged according to their observed diversity. We show that both descriptions allow for the study of ecological communities by making use of the concept of *minimum spanning tree* inherited from graph theory. Various properties of the resulting tree-like structures can be analysed in a statistical mechanics perspective, in close analogy with several other examples of complex systems commonly encountered in physics. These properties retain significant biological information and yield interesting insights into the organization of real communities. In particular, the observed patterns suggest how natural selection shapes the structure of ecosystems of co-evolving species. Finally, the study of spanning trees forms a basis for the investigation of more detailed features of ecological systems, which can be thought of as extensions of the spanning tree description.

The Chapter is organized as follows: in Section 9.2 we give some basic graph-theoretical notions and define minimum spanning trees for weighted networks. In Section 9.3 we then apply the concept of minimum spanning trees to ecological networks and use it to define rigorously the relevant subgraphs of food webs and taxonomic trees. The empirically observed topological properties of these structures are then reviewed in Section 9.4, and our summary and conclusions are presented in Section 9.5.

9.2. *Graph-theoretical formalism*

Ecosystems, like many other complex systems, can be fruitfully described by making use of the concepts of graph theory.[8,10,276] A *graph* (or *network*) G is a set of N *vertices* (representing the 'units' of a system) and L *links* or *edges* (representing the connections between the units). In most of the cases of ecological interest, vertices represent biological species and links represent some kind of relationship between them, such as trophic interaction, taxonomic or evolutionary relatedness, *etc.* If a direction is defined on each edge the graph is *directed*, while if both directions are allowed the graph is *undirected*. It is possible to denote each vertex with an integer number

$i = 1, \ldots, N$ and each link from a vertex i to a vertex j with the pair (i, j) (for directed graphs the pair is ordered). The topology of a graph can then be specified by defining an *adjacency matrix* **a** whose element a_{ij} is 1 if the link (i, j) exists, and 0 otherwise (therefore the adjacency matrix of an undirected graph is symmetric, while this is not true in general for directed graphs).

9.2.1. *Basic notions*

In an undirected graph, the number of links of vertex i is called the *degree* k_i of the vertex, and can be expressed in terms of the adjacency matrix as

$$k_i = \sum_{i=1}^{N} a_{ij} \tag{105}$$

In a directed graph, it is possible to define the *in-degree* k_i^{in} and the *out-degree* k_i^{out} as the number of in-coming and out-going links of vertex i respectively, which can be expressed as

$$k_i^{in} = \sum_{i=1}^{N} a_{ji} \qquad k_i^{out} = \sum_{i=1}^{N} a_{ij} \tag{106}$$

The total number of links L in a directed graph is given by

$$L = \sum_{i=1}^{N} k_i^{in} = \sum_{i=1}^{N} k_i^{out} = \sum_{i,j} a_{ij} \tag{107}$$

while in an undirected graph it is given by

$$L = \frac{1}{2} \sum_{i=1}^{N} k_i = \frac{1}{2} \sum_{i,j} a_{ij} = \sum_{i<j} a_{ij} \tag{108}$$

since each pair of vertices must be counted only once.

In what follows, we shall deal with graphs whose links are *weighted*, which means that on the edge (i, j) a weight $w_{ij} > 0$ is defined. Weighted graphs can be thought of as a generalization of unweighted graphs where the adjacency matrix with elements a_{ij} is replaced by a real matrix with elements $w_{ij} \geq 0$. A link from i to j is there if and only if $w_{ij} > 0$, while if $w_{ij} = 0$ the link is absent. In other words, the purely topological information for a weighted graph with matrix w_{ij} can be encapsulated in the adjacency matrix $a_{ij} = \Theta(w_{ij})$ where $\Theta(x)$ is the Heaviside step function. Many quantities can be defined in analogy with the unweighted ones. For instance, the *total weight* W is analogous to the total number of links L defined in Eqs. (107) and (108) and is given by

$$W = \sum_{i,j} w_{ij} \tag{109}$$

for a directed graph and by

$$W = \frac{1}{2} \sum_{i,j} w_{ij} \tag{110}$$

for an undirected graph.

9.2.2. *Connected subgraphs and minimum spanning trees*

Another fundamental concept that we shall encounter in the following analysis is the *connectedness* of a graph.[10,15] A *connected component* (or *cluster*) of an undirected graph is a subset $G' \subseteq G$ of the graph such that from each vertex of the cluster it is possible to reach any other vertex in the same cluster. If the entire graph is a single cluster, the graph is *connected*. For a directed graph, each vertex i has in general an *out-component* defined as the set of vertices which can be reached starting from i, and an *in-component* defined as the set of vertices starting from which i can be reached. Therefore the notion of connectedness is more complicated for directed graphs. A useful case that we shall deal with is when there is a special 'source' vertex from which all other vertices of the graph can be reached. If this is the case, we shall regard the graph as connected, in the sense that the entire graph is the out-component of the source vertex. A subgraph of a connected graph will be considered *connected* if it is connected in the same sense as for the original graph.

For the case of a connected graph G, a very interesting problem is finding, among the connected subgraphs $G' \subseteq G$ spanning all the N vertices of G, the subgraph G^* with the minimum total weight $W(G^*)$:

$$W(G^*) = W_G^* \tag{111}$$

where

$$W_G^* \equiv \min_{G' \in \mathbf{C}(G)} \{W(G')\} = \min_{G' \in \mathbf{C}(G)} \left\{ \sum_{(i,j) \in G'} w_{ij} \right\} \tag{112}$$

where $\mathbf{C}(G)$ is the set of connected subgraphs of G spanning all the N vertices. The above expression holds for both directed and undirected graphs, provided that the pairs (i, j) and (j, i) are considered as different in the former case and as equivalent (thus un-repeated) in the latter. Since the weights are positive quantities, the requirement that G^* is connected and at the same time $W(G^*)$ is minimum means that G^* must be a so-called *minimum spanning tree* of the original graph. A *tree* is a graph with no loops, and a *spanning tree* is a connected tree covering all the vertices of the original graph. Among all possible spanning trees, the *minimum spanning tree* is the one minimizing some specified total weight (or cost function) as in Eq. (112). Adding a link to a minimum spanning tree produces a loop which is unnecessary for the sake of connectedness (since the spanning tree is already connected) and increases the weight of the subgraph. Therefore the minimum-weight connected subgraph G^* must be a minimum spanning tree of G.

In some cases, especially when the weights w_{ij} are integer numbers, there may be a set of *degenerate* spanning trees $\{G_k^*\}_k$ with equal minimum weight:

$$W(G_k^*) = W_G^* \quad \forall k \tag{113}$$

In this case, it is possible to consider the whole ensemble of degenerate spanning trees and perform averages of all the quantities of interest over this ensemble.

9.3. *Graphs and spanning trees in ecology*

In this section we show how the ideas presented above allow to define in a rigorous way minimum spanning trees for two different types of graphs of great ecological interest. We also discuss the implications for the understanding of biological complexity.

9.3.1. *Spanning trees in food webs*

A *food web* is a directed graph representing the observed trophic interactions among a set of N biological species coexisting in a given environment.[277–279] Each species is represented by a vertex and an observed predator-prey interaction is represented by a directed link pointing from the prey to the predator. In this way, the direction of the link corresponds to that of the energy and biomass flow. The abiotic environment supplying water, light and chemicals can be regarded as an additional 'species' represented by a special vertex in the web. In such a way, each species (including primary producers) must prey on at least one species to survive, and all species must ultimately (even through successive predation) feed on the environment. This ensures that food webs are connected, in the sense that all species are in the out-component of the environment vertex. It is then possible to define the minimum spanning tree for a food web by assigning each link a suitable weight, possibly related to the properties of interest to be investigated.

An important choice is finding the spanning tree supplying the largest amount of resources to each species.[280,281] Each link transfers resources from the prey to the predator, however only a small fraction of the prey's energy is transferred in such an interaction.[277-279] In other words, trophic links are *inefficient*. In principle it is possible to measure the amount of resources which is delivered from a prey to each of its predators, however this is in general a very hard task for field ecologists recording the empirically observed trophic interactions. Indeed, most published datasets on food webs report only the topological information. However, the following 'rule of thumb' can be considered as a rough criterion for assessing the energy transfer quantitatively even with no information beyond topology: the longer a food chain, the smaller the amount of resources delivered from the prey at its beginning to the predator at its end, due to the iterated dissipation of energy through successive links.[277] This is the reason why species in a food web are generally layered in *trophic levels* according to their distance l from the environment (see Fig. 63a): each species i feeding directly on the environment is placed on the first trophic level ($l_i = 1$), each species j feeding on species at the first level (but not on the environment)

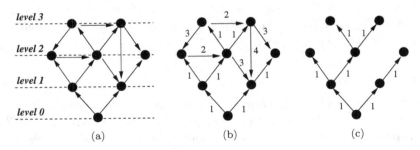

Fig. 63. Schematic construction of spanning trees in food web ecology according to our procedure. (a) Each species in a food web (gray vertices) is assigned a discrete trophic level representing its minimum distance from the environment (black vertex). (b) Each link (i, j) is assigned a weight w_{ij} depending on the trophic levels l_i and l_j, as defined in Eq. (114). (c) For each species, only the in-coming link with minimum weight $w_{ij} = 1$ is selected, representing the final link of the shortest food chain coming from the environment.

is placed on the second level ($l_j = 2$), and so on. The energy supplied by the environment (which is conventionally assigned level zero) is dissipated as it is transferred to higher and higher trophic levels.

The above arguments allow us to suggest a straightforward procedure for assigning a weight w_{ij} to each link in a food web, even if the available original information describes an unweighted network, in such a way that the resulting minimum spanning tree is the subgraph supplying the largest amount of resources to each species. Our choice is the following expression:

$$w_{ij} = (l_i - l_j + 2)a_{ij} \qquad (114)$$

where l_i is the trophic level of species i and a_{ij} is the element of the original unweighted adjacency matrix. With the above choice $w_{ij} = 0$ whenever $a_{ij} = 0$, as requested in the case of no interaction. By contrast, if species j preys on species i ($a_{ij} = 1$), then w_{ij} equals the length of the shortest food chain transferring resources to j *from any species in the trophic level below* j through the link (i, j). To see this, note that

$$w_{ij} = \begin{cases} 0 & \text{if} \quad a_{ij} = 0 \\ 1 & \text{if} \quad a_{ij} = 1 \quad \text{and} \quad l_i = l_j - 1 \\ 2 & \text{if} \quad a_{ij} = 1 \quad \text{and} \quad l_i = l_j \\ \vdots \\ h & \text{if} \quad a_{ij} = 1 \quad \text{and} \quad l_i = l_j + h - 2 \end{cases} \qquad (115)$$

The values of w_{ij} for the food web shown in Fig. 63a are reported in Fig. 63b. For a given predator, the above definition assigns the smallest weight to the in-coming link from the prey at the lowest level, which is also the most efficient link delivering the resources coming from the environment with the minimum degree of dissipation. Note that for each predator j the minimum (nonzero) weight of the in-coming links is always

$$\min_{i:a_{ij}=1}\{w_{ij}\} = \min_{i:a_{ij}=1}\{(l_i - l_j + 2)a_{ij}\} = 1 \quad \forall j \qquad (116)$$

since, by definition of trophic level, if $a_{ij} = 1$ then $l_j \leq l_i + 1$. This is confirmed by looking at Fig. 63b. Therefore a straightforward procedure to find a spanning tree $G^* \subseteq G$ such that its total weight $W(G^*)$ is minimum as in Eq. (112) is given by selecting, for each vertex, only one in-coming link with weight $w_{ij} = 1$, or in other words only one link coming from the level below.[280] In such a way, we are sure that the final subgraph G^* is connected: each vertex receives a link from the level below and therefore all vertices can be reached from the lowest level, in such a way that the entire subgraph is the out-component of the environment vertex. Moreover, we are also sure that the connected subgraph G^* has no loops, since only one link per vertex is selected. In other words, this procedure ensures that the final subgraph is a connected spanning tree of the original food web.[280,281] The spanning tree G^* has also the minimum weight

$$W_G^* \equiv \min_{G' \in \mathbf{C}(G)} \left\{ \sum_{(i,j) \in G'} w_{ij} \right\} = \sum_{j=1}^{N} \min_{i:a_{ij}=1} \{w_{ij}\} \qquad (117)$$

$$= \sum_{j=1}^{N} \min_{i:a_{ij}=1} \{(l_i - l_j + 2)a_{ij} = N$$

where the last equality follows from eq.116. Any other choice for the selected in-coming link would result in some weights w_{ij} being larger than one, and therefore in a larger value of $W(G^*)$. Fig. 63c shows the minimum spanning tree obtained from the food web shown in Fig. 63b according to the above procedure. All selected links have unit weight and $W_G^* = N$.

In some cases, there are vertices with more than one in-coming link with unit weight. This happens whenever a species feeds on more than one prey in the level below. In this case, there is an ensemble of degenerate spanning trees with equal minimum weight $W_G^* = N$ as in Eq. (113). As already mentioned in Sec. 9.2, the relevant quantities can be computed as averages over the degenerate ensemble. The properties of the minimum spanning trees obtained from a set of real food webs are very interesting and will be presented in Sec. 9.4.1.

9.3.2. *Spanning trees in taxonomy*

Taxonomy deals with the classification of the observed biological species into well-defined groups, according to some similarity criterion.[282] From the introduction of the traditional Linnaean classification to the development of modern molecular biology, various possibilities for defining the similarity between two species have been considered, in general based either on their observed phenotypic features or on their genetic sequences. In fact, many taxonomic datasets which are now available rely on a combination of phenotypic and genotypic approaches. A common idea behind all these techniques is that each species i can be assigned a vector $\vec{x}_i$ (a list of phenotypic features, a genetic sequence, or any other convenient set of attributes) representing its coordinates in a D-dimensional space. Any group of N species can then be represented as a set of N points in such space (see Fig. 64a), and for each pair of species it is possible to compute the distance between them. A natural choice is the Euclidean distance

$$w_{ij} = \|\vec{x}_i - \vec{x}_j\| = \sqrt{\sum_{k=1}^{D} \left[x_i^{(k)} - x_j^{(k)}\right]^2} \qquad (118)$$

even if other choices are possible. We can regard the N species as the vertices of a fully connected graph where each link (i, j) is weighted by the distance w_{ij} between i and j (the symmetry property of the distance ensures that the graph is undirected).

Once the weights, or distances, are computed it is possible to obtain an hierarchy of them through a so-called *clustering algorithm*.[283] Clustering algorithms identify groups of 'closest' objects iteratively, and end up with a nested hierarchy of them. To be more explicitly, we illustrate here a particular clustering algorithm of widespread use, the so-called *Minimum Linkage Clustering Algorithm* (MLCA).[283] In this procedure, the two species i and j with minimum distance w_{ij} are first considered, and correspondingly the link (i, j) is selected and drawn explicitly as in Fig. 64b. Contextually, i and j are assigned a common 'branching point' lying on an additional axis representing the distance between i and j. In Fig. 64c this axis is represented as the vertical line, so that the height of the branching point equals the distance between the two selected 'leaves'. Then, all the distances from i and j to any other species k are redefined as the minimum of w_{ik} and w_{jk}:

$$w'_{ik} \equiv \min_{i,j}\{w_{ik}, w_{jk}\} \qquad w'_{jk} \equiv \min_{i,j}\{w_{ik}, w_{jk}\} \qquad \forall k \neq i, j \qquad (119)$$

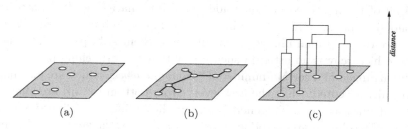

(a)   (b)   (c)

Fig. 64. Schematic construction of spanning trees in taxonomy. (a) The species are embedded in some D-dimensional space in such a way that the coordinates of each species represent the corresponding features (a bidimensional space is shown for simplicity). (b) The spanning tree minimising the sum of the distances between species is constructed, by first linking together the 'most similar' species and then the 'less similar' ones. (c) The dendrogram, or taxonomic tree, associated to the minimum spanning tree is contextually defined, by considering the species as 'leaves' and merging two (groups of) species at a common branching point whose height represents the distance between them.

so that $w'_{ik} = w'_{jk}$. Then, the procedure is repeated: the two closest species are selected again, the link between them is drawn, and they are assigned a common branching point whose height is now greater than the previous one. If one of the two closest species already belongs to a branch (in which case all the species in this branch are at the same distance from all the others), it is the whole branch to be assigned a new, higher branching point.[283]

This iterated procedure ends up with the construction of two distinct tree-like structures: a spanning tree such as that shown in Fig. 64b and a *dendrogram*, or taxonomic tree such as that shown in Fig. 64c. The former is a *minimum spanning tree* of the original fully connected graph since it minimizes the sum of the distances defined in Eq. (118) by construction; note that in this case the minimum weight W_G^* changes from case to case and cannot be computed in general as we did in Eq. (117) for food webs. The latter represents instead the corresponding nested hierarchy of the species, which are the 'leaves' of the tree. In a phylogenetic perspective a branching point could be interpreted as a 'common ancestor' of all the species in its branch, but in a more generic taxonomic view it is simply considered as a 'taxon' (group of species) to which all the 'subtaxa' below it belong. Even if the taxonomic description retains nontrivial information about the species' phylogenetic history, a taxonomic tree cannot be mapped onto a phylogenetic one directly.

The procedure we have described here is by no means unique, for a variety of reasons: different choices other than the Euclidean distance appearing in Eq. (118) exist; also, the MLCA is only one of the possible hierarchical clustering algorithms, even if it highlights the basic ideas behind all of them; moreover, some additional information is often used by taxonomists in defining the dendrogram, including subjective criteria or reference to traditional Linnaean classification schemes. In particular, usually the hierarchy is adjusted in such a way that the branching points are finally arranged in a certain number of *taxonomic levels*, which are also not universally accepted: while the first levels (from bottom to top) are almost always defined as 'species', 'genera' and 'families', different definitions and degrees of resolution are introduced for the higher taxa layered above them up to the final root level. Despite the non-uniqueness of the steps leading to the final taxonomic trees, various empirical results[284–287] show that the structure of the latter obeys some clear regularities (we report some of these results in Sec. 9.4.2). This suggests that various important structural properties of taxonomic trees are robust to the arbitrary choices adopted to obtain them.

We finally note that, unlike food webs, the available taxonomic data do not allow to obtain the explicit structure of the minimum spanning trees such as those shown in Fig. 64b. Indeed, the available information directly concerns taxonomic trees. However we have highlighted that minimum spanning trees determine the structure of taxonomic trees crucially, due to the underlying idea that a meaningful hierarchy is deduced by assuming that the total taxonomic diversity is minimized (in a phylogenetic framework, the resulting tree is the one minimising the number of 'evolutionary steps' required to generate the observed diversity). Even if in most cases they cannot be directly addressed, the 'hidden' minimum spanning trees determine the available taxonomic structure and are implicitly present behind it.

9.4. *Empirical results*

We can now report the empirical properties displayed by the structures we have defined. One important question is whether real ecosystems display particular properties among the possible configurations, and what these properties tell us about the understanding of ecological communities.

9.4.1. *Food webs*

While early studies in ecology[289] defined the 'complexity' of a food web simply as the total number of its links, recent advances in network theory[10,15,276] have shown that the notion of graph complexity requires a much deeper insight into the topology of the network. Graphs with the same number of links may require very different degrees of information in order to be reproduced, depending on whether vertices are connected in an ordered way (such as in a regular lattice), in a stochastic but completely uniform fashion (as in a random graph[10,15,276]), or according to more complicated rules (as in several more recent models aimed at reproducing real networks[10,15]). A similar consideration applies to spanning trees as well. The spanning tree of a food web with $N + 1$ vertices (N species plus the environment) has always $L = N$ links, but — as for the whole web — its complexity is not merely given by the number of links. For instance, there are two instructive examples of 'ordered' spanning trees of food webs.[280,281] One is the *star* where the environment is a central vertex connected to all the other species. This means that all the species belong to the first trophic level, which is thus the maximum value $l_{max} = 1$. At the opposite extreme, there is the *chain* where the environment is directly connected to one species only, which is in turn connected to another species only, and so on in a linear, sequential fashion. In this case each species occupies a distinct trophic level, so that the maximum level is $l_{max} = N$. Clearly, there is a wide range of intermediate possibilities between these two extremes. Therefore it is important to introduce suitable quantities that allow to characterize the particular topology displayed by real ecosystems.

A commonly used and widely popular quantity to be computed on a (tree-like or not) graph is the *degree distribution* $P(k)$, defined as the histogram of the degrees k_i of the various vertices i.[10,15,276] This distribution turns out to display the scale-free (power-law) form $P(k) \propto k^{-\gamma}$ in most real-world networks, with $2 \leq \gamma \leq 3$.[10,15,276] Unfortunately, food webs (and a few other examples) are a remarkable exception to this otherwise universal behaviour. The form of the degree distribution displayed by food webs has been subject to debate,[290-292] and it is now accepted that it is not scale-free, the right tail of the distribution being cut at rather small values of the degree.[291,292] This has been shown for the distributions of the in-degree k^{in} and *out-degree* k^{out} separately,[291] as well as for the distribution of the *total degree* $k^{tot} = k^{in} + k^{out}$.[292] As a consequence, the distribution of degrees $\tilde{k}^{in}$ and $\tilde{k}^{out}$ for the spanning trees of real food webs is not a good candidate to display interesting properties as well. For the in-degrees $\tilde{k}_i^{in} = 1$ by construction, and therefore $P(\tilde{k}^{in}) = N\delta_{\tilde{k}^{in},1}$ trivially. For the out-degrees, $\tilde{k}_i^{out} \leq k_i^{out}$ where k_i^{out} is the out-degree of vertex i in the original food web, so that since $P(k^{out})$ displays no power-law tails, neither does $P(\tilde{k}^{out})$.

Garlaschelli *et al.*[280] proposed to address a different property, the *allometric scaling* of the spanning trees. They extended to food webs a statistical analysis commonly used in other contexts, such as in river network theory[293,294] or in the study of vascular systems.[295,296] This method is based on the calculation of the number A_i of species 'above' each species i (plus i itself) in the spanning tree, and of the integrated quantity

$$C_i \equiv \sum_{j \in \gamma(i)} A_i \tag{120}$$

where $\gamma(i)$ is the set of species above i, plus i itself. The allometric relation is then obtained by plotting C_i versus A_i for each vertex i, which for river networks and vascular systems is found to scale as

$$C(A) \propto A^\eta \tag{121}$$

with $\eta = 3/2$ for river networks[293,294] and $\eta = 4/3$ for vascular systems.[295,296] This empirical result is to be compared with the theoretical one[294,296] that, for a transportation network embedded in a D-dimensional Euclidean space, the most efficient topology corresponds to the value

$$\eta_D = \frac{D+1}{D} \qquad (122)$$

Therefore the empirical values displayed by rivers ($D = 2$) and by living organisms ($D = 3$) correspond to the optimized values η_2 and η_3 respectively, a finding interpreted as the result of the evolution of these systems under the action of some driving force.[294,296] At the opposite extreme, the theoretical value corresponding to the least efficient topology is $\eta = 2$ independently of D, and it is displayed by chain-like graph spanning the D-dimensional lattice.[294]

Garlaschelli *et al.*[280] studied the allometric scaling of several food webs, and found that a relation of the form (121) still holds, but with exponents lying in the narrow range $1.13 \leq \eta \leq 1.16$, with the largest webs displaying the value $\eta \approx 1.13$. The results for the largest webs[297–300] they considered are reported in Fig. 65. One important aspect of this analysis is that the food webs under investigation belong to very different ecosystems, with habitats ranging from terrestrial to aquatic, freshwater to desert, etc. This suggests that the scaling exponent is universal across different food webs, as a result of a common organizing principle.[280,281] Moreover, since food webs are not constrained to any embedding Euclidean space, the value of the exponent is small as compared to that for the Euclidean case reported in Eq. (122). With no embedding space, the value corresponding to the most efficient topology is $\eta = 1$ and is displayed by star-like graphs, which cannot be realized in the Euclidean case with nearest-neighbor connections. Therefore food webs display a scaling exponent close to but different from the optimal one $\eta = 1$.

A detailed discussion of the above results as the effect of evolutionary constraints shaping food web structure has already been presented.[281] Here an interpretation in terms of a trade-off between the maximization of resource input (resulting in the minimization of the number of trophic levels) and minimisation of interspecific competition (resulting in the maximization of the number of trophic level) is suggested. The above results are also important for food web modelling, since they are not displayed by any ecological model. Suggestions about possible improvements of food web models in order to reproduce the observed properties have also been proposed.[281,301]

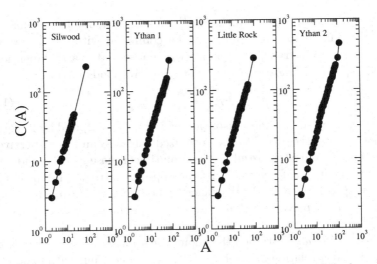

Fig. 65. Allometric scaling relations $C(A)$ for the spanning trees of the largest food webs available:[280] Silwood Park,[297] Ythan Estuary without parasites,[298] Little Rock Lake,[299] and Ythan Estuary with parasites.[300]

9.4.2. *Taxonomic trees*

We now turn to taxonomic trees, which as we mentioned in Sec. 9.3.2 represent the available information about the biological diversity of species. As for spanning trees, taxonomic trees can in principle display very different topological properties. However, now the two extreme possibilities differ from the chain-like and star-like trees, and are shown in Figs. 66a and 66b for a dendrogram with 8 species and 4 taxonomic levels. Fig. 66a corresponds to a 'maximally diverse' community where taxa merge only at the highest possible branching point. By contrast, Fig. 66b shows a 'minimally diverse' community where all taxa merge at the lowest possible branching point (all species belong to the same genus). An intermediate case with uniform branching is shown in Fig. 66c, where all taxa branch in the same number of subtaxa (such a tree is known as *Cayley tree*). Understanding the topology of real taxonomic trees is therefore important for the characterization of the structure of biodiversity.

Perhaps the first topological analysis of taxonomic trees was performed by Willis[284] in 1922. Willis studied the distribution of the number of species per genus in various taxonomic trees, and found that it is well fitted by a power-law with exponent -1.5. This means that real taxonomies are strikingly different from the trivial examples shown in Figs. 66a-b, and also from the Cayley tree with constant branching shown in Fig. 66c. The power-law scaling of the number of subtaxa per taxon was then confirmed by Burlando[285,286] who also extended it to higher taxa by studying the number of genera per family.

Curiously, the property investigated by Willis and Burlando is what we would now call the *degree distribution* for the lowest levels of the taxonomic tree, since the number of subtaxa emanating from each taxon i is simply equal to the degree $k_i - 1$. Therefore it appears that, unlike food webs, taxonomic trees are (loopless) scale-free networks. To address this property more directly, Caretta *et al. cecile* studied the degree distribution $P(k)$ for the *whole* taxonomic trees, not only their lowest levels, describing several plant communities located in different biogeographic regions from all over the world. All species in these datasets have been classified in nine taxonomic levels (*species, genus, family, order, subclass, class, subphylum, phylum and sub-kingdom*) according to the nomenclature proposed by Cronquist.[302] Note that since in principle it is possible to obtain 'extreme' dendrograms such as those shown in Figs. 66a-b by including only suitably chosen species from a large pool, the important property to address is the topology of locally co-evolved communities. For this reason, Caretta *et al.* considered real local communities of coexisting species. They found that the degree distribution is always very broad, and that in most cases it can be fitted with a power-law curve $P(k) \propto k^{-\gamma}$.[287] In particular, the results of this analysis for various North-American *florae*[288] are shown in Fig. 67. In most cases the power-law trend is a very good approximation to the observed distribution. This means that real taxonomic trees are scale-free networks displaying a highly heterogeneous branching of taxa in subtaxa, with some taxa being highly branched and other ones being

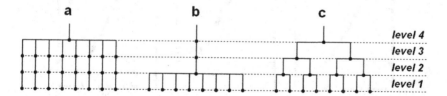

Fig. 66. Examples of possible configurations for a dendrogram with $N = 4$ 'leaves' (species) and $l = 4$ taxonomic levels. (a) Maximally diverse community: taxa merge at the highest possible branching point. (b) Minimally diverse community: taxa merge at the lowest possible branching point (all species belong to the same genus). (c) Intermediate case with uniform branching (Cayley tree).

poorly diversified in subtaxa. These findings confirm the results by Willis and Burlando, and extend them to the whole taxonomic structure of local communities.

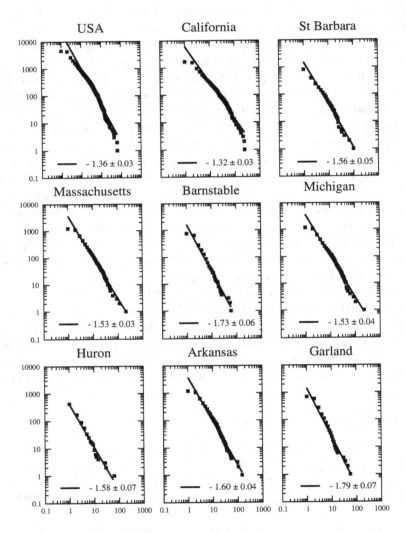

Fig. 67. Degree distribution $P(k)$ for the taxonomic trees describing the *florae* of the USA and of various nested geographic sub-regions, denoted by the name of the corresponding state (California, Massachusetts, Michigan, Arkansas) or county (Santa Barbara, Barnstable, Huron, Garland).[288]

We note that the ecosystems considered in Fig. 67 are the entire USA region plus four subregions corresponding to some of its states (California, Massachusetts, Michigan, Arkansas) and four sub-subregions corresponding to counties of the previous states (Santa Barbara, Barnstable, Huron, Garland), one per state. The various regions are therefore *nested* as follows:

County		State	
Santa Barbara	→	California	→ USA
Barnstable	→	Massachusetts	→ USA
Huron	→	Michigan	→ USA
Garland	→	Arkansas	→ USA

Clearly, species belonging to a county also belong to the corresponding state, and species belonging to a state also belong to the whole USA *flora*. The same is true for higher taxa. From the opposite point of view, each state represents a sample of species from the whole USA pool, and each county represents a sample of species from its state's pool. Such sample are non-random since they all correspond to local communities. An interesting remark is that, except for the Californian taxonomy, the value of the exponent γ for a geographic region is always smaller than that for the nested sub-regions. This indicates that, the smaller the region, the skewer the degree distribution. In other words, as larger geographic regions are considered, the distribution becomes broader and more strikingly different from the regular examples shown in Fig. 66.

As for spanning trees, it is also possible to address the allometric scaling of taxonomic trees. Using the same definitions for A_i and C_i given in Sec. 9.4.1 (with the only difference that now the tree is 'upside down' and subtaxa are 'below' taxa), it is possible to plot C versus A. This is shown in Fig. 68 for the same North-American data considered before. We find again a power-law scaling of the form $C(A) \propto A^\eta$, with $1.15 \leq \eta \leq 1.21$. As for the exponent γ of the degree distribution, the values of η appear to become larger as the geographic region restricts. In this case too, the observed power-law scaling is an interesting signature of the deviation from the regular case shown in Fig. 66c. Indeed, it is possible to show that for a Cayley tree with uniform branching the expected relation is $C(A) \propto A \ln A$. Therefore the empirical observation of allometric scaling, combined with the scale-free character of the degree distribution, gives us a quantitative topological characterization of taxonomic trees.

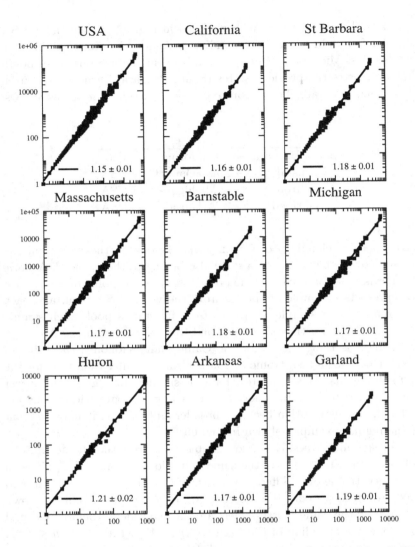

Fig. 68.   Allometric scaling relations $C(A)$ for the taxonomic trees describing the same *florae* considered in Fig. 67.

9.5. *Summary and outlook*

We have reviewed a series of empirical results concerning the topological properties of the spanning trees of real food webs and of the taxonomic trees of real *florae*. We have shown that these structures provide a robust description of communities of co-evolved species. Due to the importance of both structures for the characterization of real ecosystems, we have introduced a general graph-theoretical framework to illustrate how they emerge naturally by isolating minimum spanning trees from more complex weighted ecological networks. These results show that, besides other more popular topological properties, the concept of minimum spanning trees is an additional tool of graph theory that can be used to investigate the structure of real complex networks successfully.

Acknowledgments

D.G. acknowledges support from ISC-CNR. We would like to thank L. Pietronero, C. Ricotta and M. Barthélemy for helpful discussions.

CHAPTER 10

Social and Financial Networks

Stefano Battiston[1], Michele Catanzaro[2] and Guido Caldarelli[3]

[1] *Centre Analyse et Mathématique Sociale, Ecole des Hautes Etude en Science Sociale, Paris, France*

[2] *Departament de Física i Enginyeria Nuclear, Universitat Politècnica de Catalunya, Campus Nord B4, 08034 Barcelona, Spain*

[3] *INFM-CNR Istituto dei Sistemi Complessi and Dipartimento di Fisica Università 'La Sapienza', P.le Aldo Moro, 00185 Roma, Italy*

10.1. *Introduction*

The process of organization of human activities results in sets of social and economical interactions between agents that can be fruitfully represented and studied as a network.

The network paradigm has been used for decades in sociology. Indeed, it conveys the idea that the behaviour of individuals cannot be explained only in terms of psychology, being shaped, on the contrary, by the patterns of social interactions. Even though the first studies of social networks date back to the first half of the XX century, a big change in the field has occurred in the last years: the development of information society has created vast databases about people's relations and habits. The analysis of this information has brought fresh spin to social network studies. Altogether, the new viewpoint of *Network Science* has revealed new features and proposed new questions.

Networks play a relevant role in economics, as well. In classical theories, economic agents are mutually independent, in a first approximation, being perfectly rational at the moment of making a decision, and disposing of a complete information on its consequences. Mutual decisions are influenced by the information conveyed by interactions, so that the utility function of a single agent depends on its links to other agents. In modern world-wide economy, the patterns of interactions are extremely interwoven and scale to a global size. Crisis on bigger and bigger scale (for example, the failure cascade in the East Asia in 1997[303]) show that such strict interdependence has big impact on the welfare of individuals firm and institutions.

The agents involved in social and economical problems are highly complex and heterogeneous. Moreover, their relations can seldom be clearly defined or measured. network science reduces the various systems considered into a graph, i.e. a mathematical object whose elements are nodes connected by edges. In this sense, its approach is heavily reductionist. However, it includes some aspects that classical reductionist ignores. Traditional physics explains the macroscopic behaviour of a system in therms of the properties of its constituents. Quite seemingly, most economic approaches infer macroscopic behaviors by *aggregating* quantities relative to some "representative" agent. Network theory overcomes these approaches, and focuses on the interactions between constituents, rather than on the constituents themselves. The objective is not to predict the behaviour of individuals, but to infer some general trend and compare it with data and "stylized facts". A special relevance is given to the study of the dynamics taking place in top of social and economical networks: indeed they are the substrate for a vast class of processes ranging from epidemic spreading to decision making.

In the first part of this Chapter we review some of the main general findings about social networks. In the second part, we focus on a specific case of economical network: that of the boards of directors of large corporations.

10.2. *Social networks: Examples and general features*

Networks represent a well established paradigm in sociology.[7,304,305] The earlier works on the subject date back to the thirties. Sociological studies have analyzed, for example, friendship networks,[306–308] circles of women,[309] social ties between factory workers,[310] sexual contacts,[311,312] intermarriages between families,[313] and some mathematical models.[314] Indeed, the discovery of the "small-world effect" itself came from a social psychologist, Stanley Milgram.[5,315] The principal method of data collection in traditional social networks studies is the survey. This method generates anyway a series of problems.[316] The most relevant are the small size of the networks, and the subjectivity in the definition of the interactions.

Both problems have been partially overcome by the extraction of the social information encoded in the vast amount of data produced by the information and communication technology. Computerized databases recording the actions, communications and decisions of people have rapidly increased to huge dimensions, in the last years. A careful analysis of this information allows to extract networks involving big numbers of individuals. Moreover, one can define the relation between them according to some kind of measurable parameter. For example, two individuals can be considered to be in relation if they have performed some collaboration act, contacted trough a communication, or formally recognized each other, like in the following cases.

i. *Collaboration networks.* The networks is formed by agents related to each other by a common collaboration. Movie actors relate to each other by co-starring the same movie,[6,57,68,317] and the information about this collaborations can be extracted from the Internet Movie Database (www.imdb.com). Scientists relate to each other by co-authoring a scientific paper,[66,67,119,318–324] as documented by scientific literature archives. Members of the boards of company directors relate to each other by sitting on the same board,[325–328] as recorded in specialized publications. All such structures can be reduced to bipartite graphs[329] (see Section 10.7.1) where one kind of nodes represents collaboration acts, the other actors, and links can be drawn only between nodes of different kind. To obtain the network of actors, one has to take into account the one-mode projection, where two actors end up connected if they are connected to a common collaboration act in the bipartite graph. If two actors share more than one collaboration act, multiple or weighted connections appear in the projection. For simplicity, those connections are usually neglected. In the following, we will take as an example of this kind of networks the scientific collaboration network of 16258 authors sharing 17828 papers in condensed matter physics (*cond-mat*) collected from the preprint archive at Los Alamos (http://xxx.lanl.gov/archive/cond-mat).[330]

ii. *Communication Networks.* The network is formed by agents related to each other by recorded communication acts. For example, the interchange of emails,[152,331] instant messages[332] or phone calls.[333,334] In the following, we will take as an example of this kind of networks the graph constructed using logs from mail servers of the URV University (Spain) over a period of 3 months. In order to focus on real social relations, mails with more than 50 recipients are removed, being considered spam. With the same aim, only bidirectional links are considered, i.e., when a user sends an e-mail to another, the edge is created only if the latter answers.

iii. *Mutual recognition networks*. The network is formed by agents that perform some kind of mutual recognition procedure. In the Internet environment, such procedures are formal and recorded. It is the case of the *Pretty-Good-Privacy* algorithm (PGP),[335,336] a technology for encrypting messages exchanged over the internet in order to guarantee privacy. Each user can create a pair of keys. One is public, and can be used from anybody else to encrypt a message to be sent to the user. The other one is private, and allows the user to decrypt the messages he receives. It is computationally infeasible to deduce the second password from the first. A problem is that somebody could create a public PGP key claiming to be somebody else. The matter of the authentication of the public password has been approached with the *Web of Trust*: users can "sign" the public key of another user, meaning that they trust such user. This creates a network based on trust (www.dtype.org), that has already been analyzed.[75] In July 2001, it included 191.548 keys and 286.290 signatures. The Web of Trust can be "filtered" by considering only mutual signature, thus granting the mutual knowledge between users.[337]

Social networks represent a special class within complex networks. Indeed, it has been shown that they display some features that place them apart from technological, biological and other networks. Such features will be reviewed in the following.

10.3. *Degree distribution*

One of the most interesting findings of network science is related to the degree distribution, i.e. the probability $P(k)$ that a node has a number of connections (or *degree*) equal to k. In most real networks it displays a fat tail that can be approximated by a power-law. This behaviour is not shared by all social networks. On one side, movie actors, scientific collaborations and sexual contacts networks[6,66,67,119,338] do show fat tailed degree distributions. As an example, the degree distribution for cond-mat collaboration network is reported in Fig. 69. On the other hand, other relevant social networks display a wide varieties of functional forms, encoding very different topologies. For example, the PGP Web of Trust has a bounded degree distribution, as shown in Fig. 70. Other networks display exponential degree distributions, like the directors' networks that we will analyze later. The degree distribution of the sexual contacts network[339] can be fitted with a power-law. However, the decay is so fast that an exponential fit would

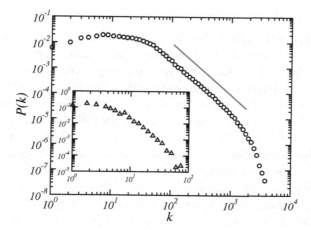

Fig. 69. Degree distribution $P(k)$ of the movie actors collaboration network and, in the inset, of the scientific collaboration network. The full line has slope 2.[330]

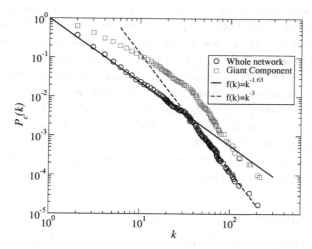

Fig. 70. Cumulative degree distribution of the whole PGP network (circles) and the giant component (squares). A region with a power law decay is followed by a cutoff for low degrees: the degree distribution of the network is not scale-free, but bounded.[75]

be acceptable, also. More precisely, the exponent of the degree distribution is greater than 3, so that the fluctuations around the average degree are bounded, in the limit of an infinite network. Finally, a friendship network,[68] representing a community of Mormons, has a Gaussian degree distribution.

10.3.1. Open questions on degree distribution

The origin of scale-invariance has been often addressed to the presence of *preferential attachment*. Most real networks are dynamical, growing graphs: according to the preferential attachment paradigm, the probability of getting higher connectivity in the future growth is proportional to the connectivity in the present (i.e. "rich gets richer", once richness is measured in number of links). Such mechanism generate networks with scale free degree distribution, as shown by the Barabási-Albert Model.[15] It is reasonable to think that this mechanism acts in some social network. For example, sociologist Robert Merton highlighted that scientific literature is driven by a "Matthew effect".[340] This name refers to an expression in the Gospel ("For to every one that hath shall be given..." Matthew 25:29) taken as a metaphor of the *cumulative advantage* of heavily cited papers, equivalent to preferential attachment, in terms of networks. Deviations from scale invariance observed in some social network can be explained considering that also other mechanisms can play a role. For example, *aging* of nodes and *cost* of links are strong social limitations to the pure preferential attachment. Indeed, the lifetime of an individual in a social network is necessarily limited (at least, because of biological reasons) and the building of a socially significant relation usually implies a huge inversion (at least, in terms of time). It has been shown[68] that the inclusion of aging and cost in Barabási-Albert Model, produces deviations from a pure power-law trend. A completely different approach is associated to *fitness*[19] or *fitness*[58] models. These are models without growth, where the linking probability depends on some intrinsic features of each individual. If this were the case, the shape of the degree distribution would be just a reflection of some other feature distributed through the population and relevant to the construction of a relation.

10.4. Assortativity

It has been recently shown[41,48] that real-world networks display degree correlations, i.e. the degree of two nearest neighbors are non-independent. For example, in most technological and biological networks, one can detect a tendency of high degree nodes to connect with low degree ones. This feature has been called *disassortativity*.[41] This situation is somewhat opposite to what happens in social networks where high degree nodes tend to connect with high degree ones (and low degree nodes with low degree ones) displaying the so called *assortativity*. Correlations can be detected through the measure of the *average nearest neighbour connectivity*, $\bar{k}_{nn}(k)$.[48] Such

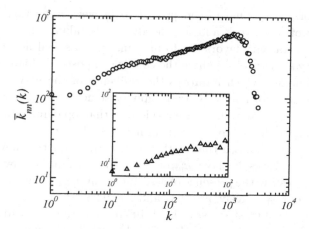

Fig. 71. Average degree $knn(k)$ of the nearest neighbors as a function of the degree k for the movie actors collaboration network (main plot) and the scientific collaboration network (inset).[330]

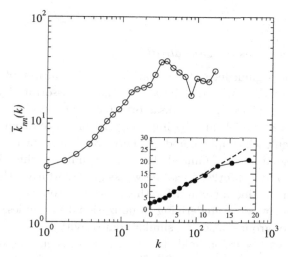

Fig. 72. Average degree of the nearest neighbors as a function of the degree k for the PGP network. This function has an approximately linear behavior for small values of k (see inset).[75]

function measures the average nearest neighbour degree of the nodes with degree k. It is increasing in presence of assortativty, decreasing in presence of disassortativity and flat in absence of correlations. Another measure is the assortativity coefficient r,[41] which is essentially a correlation coefficient.

Degree correlations have been proved to be very important both for
the topology of a network and for the dynamics taking place on top of
it. Indeed, assortativity favors the formation, within social networks, of a
core-periphery structure[159] (where the core is composed by high degree interconnected node), which improves the resilience of the network against
attacks (disruption of nodes). Core-periphery structure are known in epidemiology as well[42] and there are evidences that epidemic spreading is
affected by degree-degree correlations in networks.[43]

In Fig. 71, one can see that both the scientific and the movie actors
collaboration networks display a $\bar{k}_{nn}(k)$ increasing as a power law in a wide
range of k, suggesting the presence of assortative mixing. Their assortativity
coefficients are, respectively, $r = 0.31$ and $r = 0.23$.[330]

The PGP web of trust shows a slight difference with respect to the other
social networks: it is assortative (Fig. 72), but its $\bar{k}_{nn}(k)$ is approximately
linear (at least for not very large values of k), and not power-law.

10.4.1. Open questions on assortativity

The origins and significance of assortativity is still subject of debate. In
some papers[6,341] it has been pointed out that disassortativity could be
a purely random effect. Indeed, disassortativity can be obtained from a
random finite size model, just by imposing the presence of no more than
one link between each couple of nodes. Therefore, disassortativity would be
the result of the absence of multiple linking: a condition which is observed
in many real-world networks. Social networks are assortative, therefore the
previous argument doesn't stand for them. On the contrary, correlations
must be driven by some underlying organizational principles, that favor
the formation of groups based on similar connectivity.

An analogous discussion holds for the subset of social networks represented by collaboration networks.[342] These works focus on the underlying
bipartite graphs. A random bipartite graph is generated, under the only
constraint that the two degree distributions for both kinds of vertices are
given. One can see that the empirical degree distribution of the one-mode
projection can be obtained from this random construction, only by imposing the constraint of absence of self and multiple links. However, this model
fails to reproduce the observed degree correlations, suggesting again that
these are generated by some non-random mechanism.

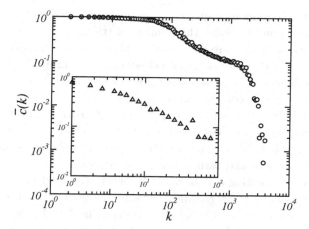

Fig. 73. The Clustering as a function of the degree $c(k)$ for the movie actors collaboration network (main plot) and the scientific collaboration network (inset).[330]

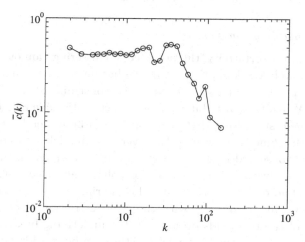

Fig. 74. The clustering as a function of the degree k of the PGP network is a nearly independent function of the degree.[75]

10.5. *Clustering*

One of the first features observed in many networks was their tendency to form groups where the density of links is larger than the average (*cliques*). This property is especially accentuated in social networks. There are various way to measure that property, probably the simplest one is the *clustering coefficient*,[6] $\bar{c}$. This quantity measures the average probability that a pair of vertices with a common neighbor are also connected each other. In other words this correspond to count the number of triangles one vertex belongs to. This pattern of linking are known in social science as *transitive relationships*. One can sort the information on clustering by computing the average clustering coefficient $\bar{c}(k)$ of vertices whose degree is k.[255] From a statistical point of view this corresponds to a higher order correlation measure. While $\bar{k}_{nn}(k)$ gives information about "two point" correlations (degrees at the ends of an edge), $\bar{c}(k)$ gives information about "three point" correlations (triangles). It has been shown that this three point correlation is also related to the presence of modular structures in the network.[62]

In the case of scientific collaboration networks (Inset of Fig. 73) we can see that $\bar{c}(k)$ is steadily decreasing; the same behaviour is observed only after a flat region in the movie actors network (Fig. 73). In the PGP Web of Trust we have a large clustering ($c = 0.4$), but one can see (See Fig. 74) that, in this case, $\bar{c}(k)$ is roughly independent of k. Once again, we detect a wide variety of behaviors in social networks.

10.5.1. *Open questions on clustering*

As in the case of assortativity, the presence of clustering cannot always be reduced to a purely random origin. A model has been presented in Ref. 60, where edges are placed at random under the constraint of a fixed degree distribution. When that distribution is scale-free, noticeable clustering values are obtained, suggesting that clustering could be a merely topological property, in this kind of networks. However, this model does not explain the high values observed in social networks with a bounded degree distribution.[68] On the other hand, a model for collaboration networks[342] (see Section 10.4.1) accounts for the observed clustering coefficient, on the basis of a purely random linking, with the only restriction of given degree distributions of the two kinds of nodes in the underlying bipartite graph. This is reasonable, since the bipartite structure can be considered the main responsible for the presence of cliques.

10.6. *Community structure*

A central problem in social network analysis is the study of their community structure. This reflects the fact that individuals belong to groups with a high density of internal connections and loosely connected among them. An example is given by the informal groups forming within an organization, that are different from the formal chart. Understanding these patterns is a key problem for successful management. In other contexts, communities reflect a spontaneous arrangement developed in order to optimize communication or productivity. Dynamics defined on the network as the flow of goods or information along the edges form a feedback loop with the system topology.

The process of community identification is one of the most studied topic in the field. As a result a whole set of different algorithms and techniques is available in literature. The considerations in the following are all based on a standard procedure by Girvan and Newman (GN),[144] based on the concept of betweenness.[158,344] GN algorithm recursively splits the network into isolated clusters, until the single vertex level. The resulting community structure can be encoded into a binary tree, where the communities are the branches and the leaves are the single nodes (see Fig. 75). It has been also shown[154] for a whole set of cases that the resulting communities, at a certain level of iteration, correspond to "common sense" ones. For example, in the email network of URV University one is able to recover the division in departments.

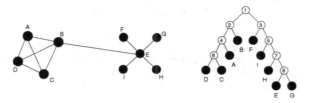

Fig. 75.   Community identification according to the GN algorithm. The link BE in the graph on the left is the first to be cut, splitting the network in two. This process corresponds to the bifurcation at the highest level of the binary tree on the right. The process is iterated generating the whole tree. The numbers written at the bifurcations refer to the size of the communities emerging at each step. These numbers contribute to the community size distribution. Note that a single node belongs to different communities at different levels.[154]

The overall community structure of real social networks can display some interesting patterns.[144,152,345] Groups are nested in higher level "groups of groups": one can reveal a self similar hierarchy in this structure.[152] More specifically, it was found that the distribution of the size of the communities (see caption of Fig. 75) follows a power law. This last property has been claimed to be the distinguishing feature of social networks[6,144,152] able to fully characterize their features. Fig. 76 and Fig. 77 display the size distribution of several scientific collaboration networks (Physicists con-

tributing to the Spanish Fisica Estadistica Conference (FisEs), Mathematical physicists (math-ph), High Energy and Lattice physicists (heplat),
General Relativity and Quantum Cosmology researchers (gr-qc), Quantum
Physics researchers (quant-ph)).[154] While FisEs and math-ph display a
clear power law with exponent about 2, the others show a crossover behaviour to another power law with exponent about 1.5.

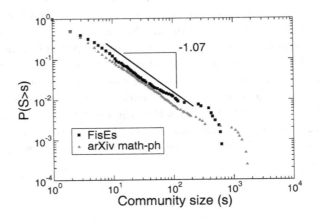

Fig. 76.   Cumulative community size distribution $P(S > s)$ as a function of community
size s for the FisEs and ArXiv math network. The results for the FisEs network are
plotted in full squares, while full triangles correspond to the ArXiv mathematical physics
network. The full line follows a power law with exponent 1.07.[154]

The same study, performed on the giant connected component of the
PGP Web of Trust, is displayed in Fig. 78. Again, a power law distribution
is obtained, and the resulting exponent is 1.8. In Fig. 79, one can see the
community size distribution of the email network of URV, and of the network of jazz musicians. This is obtained from the Red Hot Jazz Archive of
recordings between 1912 and 1940 (www.redhotjazz.com), where musicians
are connected if they played in the same band. The estimated exponent in
both cases is about 1.5.

10.6.1. Open questions on community structure

The broad community size distribution represents a very interesting and
nontrivial feature of social networks. One can build a random counterpart
of the networks analyzed, by generating a random network with degree

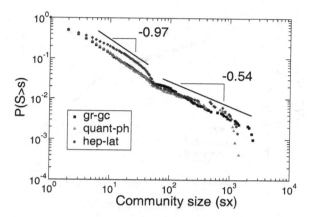

Fig. 77. Cumulative community size distribution $P(S > s)$ as a function of community size s for the ArXiv gr-qc, quant-ph and hep-lat networks. The results for the gr-qc network are plotted in full squares, full triangles correspond to the quant-ph network and diamonds represent the hep-lat network. The full lines follow power laws with exponent -0.97 and -0.54.[154]

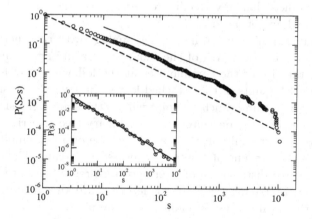

Fig. 78. Cumulative community size distribution of the giant component of the PGP network. The solid line has slope -0.8. The dashed line corresponds to a power law of exponent -1. Inset: Binned community size distribution. The solid line has slope 1.8, in agreement with the slope measured from the cumulative distribution.[75]

distribution equal to the real one. This procedure completely destroys the community structure detected in the real networks, as shown in Fig. 79.

It is interesting, as well, that in some cases the exponent of the size distribution deviates from the value 2. Indeed, in a recent paper,[346,347]

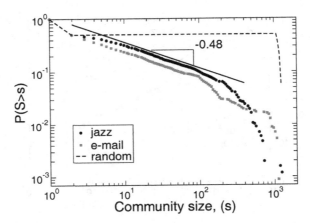

Fig. 79.   Cumulative community size distribution as a function of community size s for the email and jazz musician networks. The results for the e-mail network are plotted in full triangles, while full circles correspond to the jazz musicians network. The dotted line corresponds to the results obtained in a random network with the same degree distribution as the musicians network[154]

it has been argued that any treelike representation should lead to a size distribution with exponent 2.

Finally, one can observe an interesting analogy with river networks.[154] If one attributes to the leaves of the binary tree a unitary quantity, one obtains that the size of the communities at the following level is nothing but the sum of the units of the attached leaves. In general, the size of the community at a certain branching point will be the sum of the sized of the "offspring". Therefore, if one interprets the binary tree as a river network where the sources are only on the leaves, the size of a community can be considered as the amount of "water" generated upstream. The similarity with drainage area distribution of river networks, regarding both the slope and the cutoff, is striking.[348,349] River networks are known to evolve to a state where the total energy expenditure is minimized.[349–351]

Communities within networks might also spontaneously organize themselves into a form in which some quantity is optimized.[154]

10.7. *Economical networks: The case-study of the board of directors*

The field of social networks is widely overlapped with that of economic networks. Indeed, a subset of the social networks studied until now describe the interactions of agents that play a role in business, finance and capital. In economics, agents are not necessarily individuals,; they can be companies, institutions or even countries. Networks have a natural place in modern economics, since they offer a good representation of situations where *partial* or *asymmetric information* is available to the agents. Moreover, they support the social phenomena that act within economy,[352] and provide the substrate for heterogeneous cooperative and competitive phenomena.[353] Network structures can be envisaged in economics in many contexts: business communities,[354,355] capital control structure,[356,357] world trade web,[358] etc.

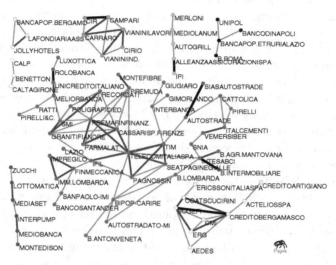

Fig. 80. The Italian Stock Market: the network of boards with two or more shared directors. Gray, dark gray and black links correspond to 2, 3, and 4 shared directors respectively.

In this second part of this Chapter, we will analyze in detail the networks of the *Boards of Directors*. These are the entities that determine, under the direction of Chief Executive Officer (CEOs), the strategies of companies. Directors form a network, where a couple of them are linked if they share a membership in the same board. It is well known that many companies are *interlocked*, i.e. some directors serve on several boards, so that boards are connected by shared directors. Thus, one can create a network of companies, as well. In figure 80 the network of boards with two or more shared directors in the Italian Stock Market is represented. In the following, the boards of the "Fortune 1000" corporations in 1999 (1000 companies) and the boards of the quoted companies in the Milan Stock Market (220-240 companies) are analyzed in detail. The first dataset refers to the most important companies in US,[326] while the others refer to the quoted Italian companies. In the second case, two temporal snapshots are available (1986-2002), so that the data are resolved both in space and time. The data have been collected from technical publications used by stock market operators.[359-361]

The most interesting aspect, in these networks, is that interlock conveys information and power. For example, banks lending money to a firm can use interlocked directors in firms of the same industrial sector to get information about the real risk of the loan. It has been argued that in a capitalistic economy, as a consequence of economic power concentration, "a special social type emerges spontaneously, a cohesive group of multiple directors tied together by shared background, friendship networks, and economic interest, who sit on bank boards as representative of capital in general".[362] Now, while part of the public opinion has been since long ago concerned about the fact that the corporate *élite* would represent a sort of "financial oligarchy controlling the business of the country",[363] stockholders are more concerned about the effectiveness of boards in overseeing management. Boards directors should in fact monitor managers strategies and decisions to the interest of stockholders. Recently, after several cases of financial defaults in the western countries (for example: Enron, Vivendi, Parmalat in 2002-2003), the role of boards in the decision making process is under examination and more sophisticated forms of corporate control are often advocated by the public opinion. Our activity in this field is twofold: firstly, we study the topological properties of such networks and try a comparison across time and countries of these properties in various datasets available; secondly we try to understand how the structure of these networks influences the decision making process in which directors are involved.

10.7.1. *Board and directors network as bipartite graphs*

The exact definition of the networks we are handling is given in the framework of bipartite graphs. A bipartite graph consists of two separate classes of nodes, while an edge connects only nodes within the same class. An example is reported in Figure 81. A node represents alternatively a director or a board. A link between two nodes represents the fact that the director serves on the board. We have an interlock when a director serves on the boards of two companies. If two directors of a given board, serve together as well in another board, we then have a multiple interlock. We call *lobby* the subset of directors of a board who serve on an outside board together with a director of the present board.[364] In fact, the members of such a sub-group will have stronger connections among each other than with the other members of the board, and they will have common interests outside the company under consideration.

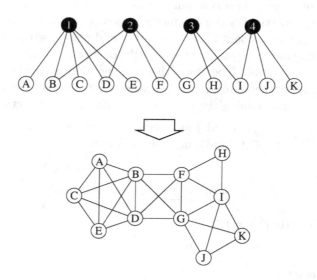

Fig. 81. A bipartite graph and its one-mode projection. Nodes labeled by numbers corresponds to boards, nodes labeled by letters corresponds to directors.

The bipartite graph can be projected into two so called "one-mode networks". In each projection two boards (directors) are connected if they have at least one director (board) in common. The projections will be referred to as the director network and the board network (for an example see Fig. 80). In the operation of projecting, some information is lost: consider for instance three directors connected in a triangle. The links do not specify whether each pair of directors sit in a different board or whether the three directors sit all in the same board. Without interlocks the director network would split up into disconnected clusters each of which completely connected. Clusters would correspond in this case to the boards. The two networks have weighted edges: two boards can share one or more directors and two directors can co-serve in one or more boards.

A bipartite graph can be represented in a compact way by the adjacency matrix:

$$C_{\alpha i} = \begin{cases} 1 \text{ if } \alpha \text{ sits in board } i \\ 0 \text{ otherwise} \end{cases} \tag{123}$$

This is an $M \times N$ matrix, M being the number of directors, and N being the number of boards. This is a binary matrix, and in general it is neither square, nor symmetric. For the one-mode projection relative to the boards, we should take into account that the number of directors sitting in boards i and j, is equivalent to the number of paths of length 2 connecting i and j in the bipartite graph. Therefore, this number, that gives the weight of the connection between i and j, can be expressed in terms of the adjacency matrix. In the end, defining the adjacency matrix of the projection as

$$B_{ij} = \begin{cases} w_{ij} \text{ if } i \text{ and } j \text{ are connected with weight } w_{ij} \\ 0 \text{ if } i \text{ and } j \text{ are not connected} \end{cases} \tag{124}$$

the entries are:

$$B_{ij} = \sum_{\alpha} C_{\alpha i} C_{\alpha j}. \tag{125}$$

In terms of matrix product:

$$B = C^T C. \tag{126}$$

In analogous way:

$$D_{\alpha\beta} = \sum_{i} C_{\alpha i} C_{\beta i}. \tag{127}$$

And,

$$D = C C^T. \tag{128}$$

While the off-diagonal entries correspond to the edges weights, the diagonal entries, are, respectively, the size B_{ii} of board i, and the number $D_{\alpha\alpha}$ of boards a director α serves on.

10.8. *Topological properties of boards and directors Networks*

10.8.1. *Average quantities*

In the following, we summarize the main results of the analysis of the Boards and Directors Networks. In table 7 we report some average quantities concerning the two projections of the boards of directors network. For sake of comparison, we report in the same table the values concerning other two networks that have been well studied in recent years. The first one is *cond-mat* (see sec. 10.2). The second one, *AS99*, describes the Internet map, at the level of Autonomous systems as it appeared in 1999.[255] While the first is a social network and we expect to observe some similarity with the the director network under study, the second one is a technological network and therefore it should present very different features.

Table 7. Average and global quantities for board network (marked with B), the director network (marked with D), cond-mat and Internet. N=number of nodes, E= number of edges, N_c/N=fraction of nodes belonging to the maximal connected component, $\bar{k}/k_c$=average degree over the connected component (in percentage), b/N=average site betweenness, $\bar{C}$=average clustering coefficient, d=average distance.

−	$B86$	$B02$	BUS	$D86$	$D02$	DUS	$C-M$	$AS99$
N	221	240	916	2378	1906	7680	16725	5287
E	1295	636	3321	23603	12815	55437	47594	10100
N_c/N	0.97	0.82	0.87	0.92	0.84	0.89	0.83	−
$\bar{k}/k_c$	5.29	2.22	1.57	0.84	0.71	0.79	0.03	0.07
b/N	0.736	0.875	1.080	1.116	1.206	1.384	1.932	2.21
$\bar{C}$	0.356	0.318	0.176	0.899	0.915	0.884	0.327	0.241
d	3.6	4.4	4.6	2.7	3.6	3.7	6.4	3.7

First of all, we notice that the maximal connected component includes most of the nodes. The fraction N_c/N of nodes belonging to it is over the value of 0.8 for all the projections. The network is a *small-world*,[326] since the average distance between two nodes of the maximal connected component is always of the of the order of $\log(N)$, (N being the total number of nodes), i.e. of the order of a few units. Not only there is a path of acquaintances between almost each couple of directors or companies, but such path is very short, as well, this has clear implications on the diffusion of information and influences on the networks.

Interestingly, both the boards and the directors network are much denser than the comparison networks. A measure of the density of a network is given by the ratio of its average degree $\langle k \rangle$ and the degree k_c it would have if it were completely connected ($k_c = N(N-1)/2$, where N is the number of nodes). The value of $\langle k \rangle / k_c$ for the board network is larger than the one for the director network, which is anyway one order of magnitude higher than the one of cond-mat and Internet.

The clustering coefficient is around 0.9 in the director network and around 0.35 in the board network, suggesting a high density of "cliques". This result can be fruitfully interpreted in relation with the interlock. In the absence of interlock, directors would be connected to all the other directors of their board and to no other directors outside their board. Therefore the clustering would be 1 for the director network and 0 for the board network. If now a director of board i serves also on board j, then his clustering coefficient will be much less than 1 because his neighbors in board i and j are not nearest neighbors among each other. Thus the interlock decreases the clustering coefficient of the director network and increases the clustering of the board network.

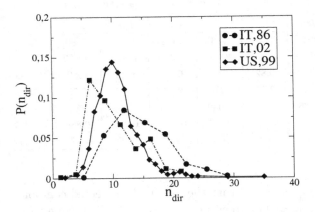

Fig. 82. Boards size distributions (the size is the number of directors sitting in a single board).

10.8.2. Degree distributions and assortativity

The Boards have a typical size of around ten members, inside size distribution (Fig. 82) has bounded fluctuations around about 10, with a maximal size of the order of 30. Most directors serve only on one board. Indeed the probability of serving in a certain number of boards (Fig. 83) decays exponentially as this number grows. One can see from the sizes of the networks that there are more chairs in boards than active directors. Looking at the distributions, one can conclude that exceeding chairs are far from being assigned purely at random. The ratio of the number of available chairs over the number of directors in the three data sets is 1.2297 (US), 1.2769

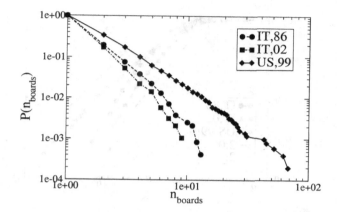

Fig. 83. Cumulated distributions of the number of boards on which a single director serves.

(IT '02), 1.3646 (IT '86). Thus in principle, chairs could be assigned in a way that no director holds more than two chairs. If instead the exceeding chairs were assigned at random, then the distribution of the number of chairs per director would follow a Poisson distribution. In all data sets, starting from 5 chairs the probability of holding m chairs deviates from the Poisson distribution by one or several order of magnitude, meaning that directors with more than 5 chairs are far from being purely random events.

The degree distribution for the network of the directors (boards) is shown in Fig. 84 (85). While the boards show a fast decaying trend, the directors display a tail can be fit with a power law with slope of about 3.5 in the Italian cases and 3.0 in the US case. It should be remarked that such a trend takes place only above a threshold of around 10 directors: it is very unlikely to find a director connected with less than 10 colleagues, essentially because this is the characteristic size of a board. Interestingly enough, the power law tail stretches much further than the maximal size of the boards. This means that whenever a director has more than 10 links in general this is the result of the interlock between different boards.

As observed in the first part of the chapter, social networks typically display degree assortativity: nodes tend to connect with nodes of similar degree. This patterns are confirmed in this analysis. The plots of $K_{nn}(k)$ for the networks under study (Figs. 86 and 87) are increasing. The increase is sub-linear in the boards' networks, while a stronger assortativity is visible in the directors' one. In the Italian case, the increase is approximatively linear.

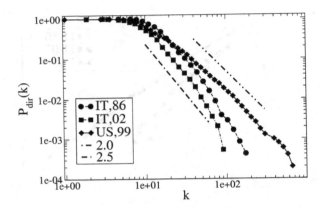

Fig. 84. Cumulated degree distributions of the directors' networks. Power laws with exponent 2.0 and 2.5 are reported for comparison.

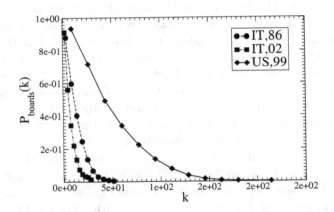

Fig. 85. Cumulated degree distributions of the boards' networks.

At high degrees, a crossover is visible to a smaller slope. The same crossover behaviour is visible in the US case, but the assortativity is generally less intense.

10.8.3. Lobbies

One of the most interesting results of the analysis concerns lobbies. We remind that we call "lobby" the subset of directors of a boards who co-serve

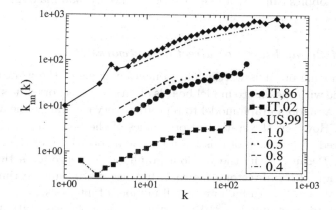

Fig. 86. Average nearest neighbor connectivity of the directors' networks. For the sake of clarity, the results of Italy,2002 and US,1999 has been respectively divided and multiplied by 10. Power laws with exponents 1.0,0.5,0.8 and 0.4 are reported for comparison.

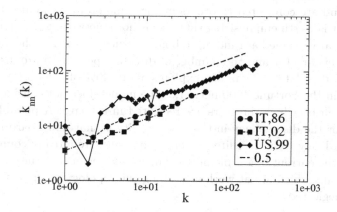

Fig. 87. Average nearest neighbor connectivity of the boards' networks. A power-law with exponent 0.5 is reported for comparison.

on an outside board together with a director of the present board. Thus for instance a lobby of size 2 in board i consists of two directors of the board i who serve as well on board j. We have computed the percentage of boards containing a lobby of size at least 2. It turns out that 35% of US companies and 44% (1986) and 63% (2002) of Italian companies have a lobby of size at least 2, revealing that lobbies are a macroscopic phenomenon. As we will see later, lobbies can play a relevant role in the decision making process of companies.

10.9. *Modeling boards of directors networks*

Before moving on, it is worthwhile to mention some of the work that has been done with the aim to model boards of directors networks. It is possible by using a random graph model to reproduce very accurately the directors' network. However, the statistical properties of the board network are not reproduced. The reason of this failure is the assortativity of the directors' network. Because of it, the random graph model reproduces the degree distribution of the director's network, but necessarily underestimates the number of boards with high ans small number of interlocks.

There are some models[365] that try to explain the assortativity of the system. Nodes belong to one or more groups and have probability p to be connected to another node of the same group. Instead they are never connected to nodes of groups they do not belong to. If groups have heterogeneous size, then nodes who belong to a small group tend to have low degree and are connected to others in the same group, who also have low degree. It is worth emphasizing that this is not a network formation model: directors are assigned at random to board in such a way that the number of boards per director and the number of directors per board are distributed as in the real data. This model explains about 40% of the observed assortativity in the Fortune 1000 network. The model does not consider a local mechanism by which directors are recruited in a board. A possible explanation for the discrepancy in the assortativity is that new board members are more likely to be recruited among those who are already connected to some of the current board members. This would mean that the sociological mechanisms which are at work in shaping the topology of the network can not be neglected.

10.9.1. *Interlock structure and decision making dynamics*

When the directors of a company have to make a decision, they are certainly subject to some kind of social influence. Indeed, usually the subjects they have to consider are very complex, and the information they dispose of is incomplete. Therefore, it is reasonable to assume that they take seriously into account the opinion of their neighbour in the network.

In the following, we study decision making dynamics taking place on the network of corporate directors, both at a single firm level and at a firm network level.[364,366] We distinguish two cases, whether boards make decisions independently or not from other boards:

- For decisions regarding topics specific to the board, such as the appointment of a vice president, we can reasonably assume that different boards don't influence each other. In this case each director has an initial opinion on the topic to decide upon and evolves the opinion according to the social influence.

- By contrast, there are decisions about topics which are relevant to the economical trend. For instance, whether to increase or decrease investments in development or in advertisement, depends upon the belief in economical growth or recession. Decisions of equivalent generality concern the adoption of governance practices. In these cases, decisions previously made in some boards might influence other boards, through the presence of shared directors.

Sociology has already done some field work on phenomena of the second type. It is documented that inter-organizational imitation of managers played a role in the corporate acquisition activity, in the eighties.[367] In the same period, the interlock mediated the diffusion of the *poison pill*[w].

The decision models will address two questions:

1. can a lobby constituted by a minority of well connected directors (in the following we will call it *interlock graph*) drive the decision of the majority of a board and can we predict the impact of the minority based on its topological structure?

2. under which conditions a large majority of boards making the same decision can emerge in the network?

10.9.2. *Single board decision making model*

We want to evaluate the impact of the interlock on the process of decision making in a single board. We model such process by using a standard model in economics, the *Survey Model*. The situation is the following: at the board meeting, the CEO proposes a strategy, the directors discuss it, and then they vote. To understand the role of network structure we put ourselves in the limit assumption that agents take decisions based *only* on the social influence of the neighbors. Such strong social influence is summarized with

---

[w]The poison pill is a counter measure against hostile take-over allowing "target shareholders to acquire shares at a 50 percent. discount if an buyer passes a certain ownership threshold" among US largest corporations.[325]

a majority rule: agents tend to adopt the opinions of the majority of their nearest neighbors. This conformist attitude if known in economics as *herd behaviour*.[368] A further simplification is that directors have binary opinions. For example, their role is restricted only to accepting or refusing a proposal of the CEO. In synthesis, agents update their opinion tending to assume the binary options that is more popular between their neighbors.

In formulas, the model is defined as follows:

i. The opinion of director i is a binary variable $s_i = \pm 1$. The CEO always sticks to opinion $+1$.

ii. Other colleagues' opinions define a field. The field acting on director i is:

$$h_i = \sum_{j=1}^{m} J_{ij} s_j \qquad (129)$$

m being the size of the board, $J_{i,j}$ being the number of boards on which directors i and j sit together.

iii. The new opinion of i depends stochastically on the intensity of the field. The probability that director i takes some opinion ± 1 at time $t + 1$ depends on the field by means of the log-it function:

$$P\{s_i(t+1) = \pm 1\} = \frac{\exp(\pm\beta h_i(t))}{\exp(\beta h_i(t)) + \exp(-\beta h_i(t))} \qquad (130)$$

Off diagonal elements of matrix J_{ij} are equivalent to the adjacency matrix of Section 10.7.1. Diagonal elements are defined as follows. Obviously, directors take into account their own opinion, hence J_{ii} in eq.129 must be non zero. Setting J_{ii} to 1 is not very realistic, since it implies that a director with some interlock ties assigns a larger weight to his colleagues' opinion than to his/her own opinion. We choose to set J_{ij} as the number of boards where director i serves with at least one other director of the same board. The parameter β in the opinion update acts as the inverse of a temperature. It measures the degree of independence of a director's opinion from the field. At T=0 the opinion dynamics becomes deterministic, at infinite T the dynamics becomes random. The fact that the CEO sticks to opinion $+1$ can be regarded as a constant external field: $h_{CEO} = J_{CEO,j} s_j = J_{CEO,j}$.

This model is formally equivalent to a variant of the well known Ising model.[369] It displays a very interesting behaviour: Ising Model is sensible to the topology of the underlying network,[370] and the Survey Model exhibits a phase transition.[364] To the aims of this chapter, we focus on the impact of the interlock on the decision making process as configured by the model.

We consider the probability that the board votes $+1$, conditional to the initial average opinion M^0 in the board being zero:

$$P_+^0 = \{M^* > 0 \mid M^0 = 0\} \tag{131}$$

We want relate this quantity to a scalar quantity that predicts the impact of an interlock graph.

The predictor of the impact we propose is

$$F = \frac{1}{m^2} \sum_{ij \in G} J_{ij} s_j(t = 0) \tag{132}$$

which we call the *force of the lobby*. G is the interlock graph. The quantity J_{ij} encodes its topology. Indeed, the topological structure of the interlock graph makes a difference with respect to its impact on decision making: with the same number of nodes and links, one can build a clique or a chain, two structures with a very different impact. The quantity takes into account the initial opinions of the directors in the interlock, that certainly count a great deal. Indeed, the quantity is equivalent to the intensity of the field exerted at time $t = 0$, by all the directors in the interlock graph on themselves. The field is normalized with respect to the size m of the whole board, because we want to estimate the impact of the interlock graph with respect to the whole board. The same interlock graph will affect more strongly a small board than a large board. To have an intuition of the notion we want to capture, suppose that at time $t = 0$ all the directors of the interlock graph have opinion $+1$, but the board as a whole has magnetization $M = 0$. The stronger the field the interlock members exert on themselves as compared to the field exerted by the directors outside the interlock graph, the more chances that the directors of the interlock graph stick to their initial opinion at $t \geq 0$. They would then act as an external field driving the board toward positive values of magnetization.

By construction, P_+^0 is an increasing function of F. Moreover, it turns that it is linearly dependent on the force. Finally, it results that lobbies with different number of links and different topology but with similar value of F do have similar value of P_+^0, which means that the force is a good predictor of the influence of the lobby on the result of the board decision making.[364] Therefore, the answer to the first question we have made is that a lobby constituted by a minority can indeed drive the decision of the majority, depending on its force, that is, a combination of its topology and its initial opinions.

10.9.3. *Multiple boards decision making model*

In the previous section we have seen how the interlock graph influences a decision within a single board. Now we focus on how interlocks conveys opinions from one board to another, thus influencing the decision of the second. We want to understand what structural parameters of the network determine the number of boards adopting a given decision. The model is defined as follows.[366]

i. The decision making dynamics within each board is that of the Survey Model. The most central board of the networks takes the decision in the first place.

ii. The field acting on each agent is now

$$h_i = h_i^0 + h^e = \frac{1}{n}\sum_{j=1}^{n}(1 + \alpha_1 J_{ij})s_j + \alpha_2 \sum_{l=1}^{deg(k)} J_{kl}^B b_l \qquad (133)$$

i.e. the sum of an internal field h_i^0 taking into account the influence of the lobbies in board k and an external field h_i^e taking into account the influence of other boards l. The quantity n is the size of the board k, $J_{i,j}$ is the number of *outside* boards on which directors i and j sit together, α_1 is a parameter modulating the mutual influence of directors in the lobby. In the second term the sum is running on the boards l interlocked to board k, deg(k) is the connectivity degree of board k, J_{kl}^B is the number of directors shared by boards k and l, b_l is the decision made by the board l (if it has already met, $b_l = 0$ otherwise), α_2 is a parameter modulating the influence of the information about other board's decisions.

The model is designed in such a way that the information flux moves from one board to another through the interlocked directors. When one of these moves from one meeting to another, the director sticks to the opinion acquired in the previous meeting. Then, two behaviors are possible: either the director supports the same decision, keeping confidential the information about the fact that the other board has has made that decision (*Model 1*); or the director reveals this information to the other directors, which will then take it into account when forming their opinion (*Model 2*). It turns out that only in the second scenario there is an avalanche of boards making the same decision. Therefore, the answer to the second question we have made above is that interlock alone does not produce an avalanche of boards taking the same decision. One has to suppose some additional form of information transfer.

10.10. *Conclusion*

Networks are a rich representation of social interaction at all levels: from friendship to sexual contacts, from professional collaboration to sharing of common interests. Moreover, networked social structures are the substrates of a wide variety of dynamical phenomena, ranging from epidemic spreading to diffusion of influence, information and innovation. Within social networks, those related to economics are especially relevant, because of control, governance and efficiency reasons. In this Chapter, we have shown that social and economical networks display many features that put them apart form other networks, like widely varying topological structure, assortativity, high clustering, and complex community structure. The networks of the boards of directors is an example of such a rich behaviour. The strategic decisions of companies' directors are crucial for the evolution of the economy of a country. We have investigated how the interlock structure of the boards influences the decision making process and the spreading of opinions. This work is only a small step in the understanding of such complex phenomena. However, is shows that the networks representation is a powerful tool to organize and interpret information about social systems.

References

1. D. B. West, *Introduction to Graph Theory* (2nd *Edition*), Prentice Hall (2001).
2. B. Bollobás, *Graph Theory, An Introductory Course*, Springer-Verlag, New York, Heidelberg, Berlin (1979).
3. R. Diestel, *Graph Theory*, Springer-Verlag, New York, Heidelberg, Berlin (1997-2000).
4. G. Caldarelli, *Scale-free Networks*, Oxford University Press, Oxford (2007).
5. S. Milgram, *Psychology Today*, **2**, 56-63 (1967).
6. D. J. Watts and S. H. Strogatz, *Nature* **393**, 440 (1998).
7. S. Wasserman and K. Faust, *Social Network Analysis: Methods and Applications*, Cambridge University Press, Cambridge (1994).
8. R. Albert and A.-L. Barabási, *Review of Modern Physics* **74**, 47-97 (2002).
9. S. N. Dorogovtsev and J. F. F. Mendes, *Advances in Physics* **51**, 1079-1187 (2002).
10. M. E. J. Newman, *SIAM Review* **45**, 167-256 (2003).
11. S. N. Dorogovtsev and J. F. F. Mendes, *Evolution of Networks: From Biological Nets to the Internet and WWW*, Oxford University Press, Oxford (2003).
12. R. Pastor-Satorras and A. Vespignani, *Evolution and structure of the Internet: A statistical physics approach*, Cambridge University Press, Cambridge (2004).
13. P. Erdős and A. Rényi, *Publicationes Mathematicae* **6**, 290-297 (1959).
14. P. Erdös and A. Renyi, *Publications of the Mathematical Institute of the Hungarian Academy of Sciences* **5**, 17-61 (1960).
15. A.-L. Barabási and R. Albert, *Science* **286**, 509-511 (1999).
16. E. A. Bender and E. R. Canfield, *Journal of Combinatorial Theory A* **24**, 296-307 (1978).
17. M. Molloy and B. Reed, *Random Struct. Algorithms* **6**, 161 (1995).
18. K.-I. Goh, B. Khang and D. Kim, *Physical Review Letters* **87**, 278701 (2001).
19. G. Caldarelli, A. Capocci, P. De Los Rios and M.A. Muñoz, *Physical Review Letters* **89**, 258702 (2002).
20. M. Boguña and R. Pastor-Satorras, *Physical Review E* **68**, 036112 (2003).
21. V. D. P. Servedio G. Caldarelli and P. Buttà, *Physical Review E* **70**, 056126 (2004).
22. A. Fronczak, P. Fronczak and J. A. Holyst, *Physical Review E* **70**, 056110 (2004).

23. M. Boguña, R. Pastor-Satorras, A. Díaz-Guilera and A. Arenas, *Physical Review E* **70**, 056122 (2004).

24. I. Ispolatov, A. Yuryev, I. Mazo and S. Maslov, *Nucleic Acid Research* **33**, 3629-3635 (2005).

25. H. Tangmunarunkit, J. Doyle, R. Govindan, S. Jamin, S. Shenker and W. Willinger, *Computer Communication Review* **31**, 7-10 (2001).

26. G. Zipf, *Human Behavior and the Principle of Least Effort*, Addison-Wesley, MA (1949).

27. R. Albert, H. Jeong and A.-L. Barabási, *Nature* **401**, 130-131 (1999).

28. P. L. Krapivski, S. Redner and F. Leyvraz, *Physical Review Letters* **85**, 4629 (2000).

29. J. M. Kleinberg, R. Kumar, P. Raghavan, S. Rajagopalan and A. S. Tomkins, *Lecture Notes in Computer Science* **1627**, 1-18 (1999).

30. R. Kumar, P. Raghavan, S. Rajagopalan, D. Sivakumar, A. S. Tomkins and E. Upfal, Stochastic models for the Web graph, in *Proceedings of the 41st IEEE Symposium on Foundations of Computer Science (FOCS)*, 57-65 (2000).

31. S. Ohno, *Evolution by Gene Duplication*, Springer, Berlin (1970).

32. A. Wagner, *Molecular Biological Evolution* **18**, 1283-1292 (2001).

33. A. Vázquez, *Europhysics Letters* **54**, 430 (2001).

34. A. Vázquez, A. Flammini, A. Maritan and A. Vespignani, *ComPlexUs* **1**, 38-44 (2003).

35. R. V. Solé, R. Pastor-Satorras, E. D. Smith and T. Kepler, *Advances in Complex Systems* **5**, 43 (2002).

36. G. Bianconi and A.-L. Barabási, *Europhysics Letters* **54**, 436-442 (2001).

37. G. Bianconi and A.-L. Barabási, *Physical Review Letters* **86**, 5632-5635 (2001).

38. A. Capocci, G. Caldarelli and P. De Los Rios, *Physical Review E* **68**, 047101 (2003).

39. A. Barrat, M. Barthélemy, R. Pastor-Satorras and A. Vespignani, *Proc. Natl. Acad. Sci. (USA)* **101**, 3747-3752 (2004).

40. A. Barrat, M. Barthélemy and A. Vespignani, *Physical Review Letters* **92**, 228701 (2004).

41. M. E. J. Newman, *Physical Review Letters* **89**, 208701 (2002).

42. M. E. J. Newman, *Physical Review E* **67**, 026126 (2003).

43. M. Boguñá and R. Pastor-Satorras, *Physical Review E* **66**, 047104 (2002).

44. R. Pastor-Satorras, M. Rubi and A. Díaz-Guilera (editors), *Proceedings of the Conference "Statistical Mechanics of Complex Networks"*, Springer (2003).

45. O. Frank and D. Strauss, *J. Amer. Stat. Assoc.* **81**, 832 (1986).

46. S. Maslov and K. Sneppen, *Science* **296**, 910 (2002).

47. S. Maslov, K. Sneppen and A. Zaliznyak, *Phys. A* **333**, 529 (2004).

48. R. Pastor-Satorras, A. Vázquez and A. Vespignani, *Physical Review Letters* **87**, 258701 (2001).

49. A. Barrat and M. Weigt, *Eur. Physics J. B* **13**, 547 (2000).

50. A. Vázquez, R. Pastor-Satorras and A. Vespignani, *Physical Review E* **65**, 066130 (2002).
51. P. M. Gleiss, P. F. Stadler, A. Wagner and D. A. Fell, *Adv. Comp. Sys.* **4**, 207 (2001).
52. A. Fronczak, J. A. Holyst, M. Jedynak and J. Sienkiewicz, *Physica A* **316**, 688 (2002).
53. G. Caldarelli, R. Pastor-Satorras and A. Vespignani, *Eur. Phys. J. B* **38**, 183 (2004).
54. G. Bianconi and A. Capocci, *Physical Review Letters* **90**, 078701 (2003).
55. G. Bianconi, G. Caldarelli and A. Capocci, *Physical Review E* **71**, 066116 (2005).
56. M. Boguñá, R. Pastor-Satorras and A. Vespignani, *Physical Review Letters* **90**, 028701 (2003).
57. M. E. J. Newman, S. H. Strogatz and D. J. Watts, *Physical Review E* **64**, 026118 (2001).
58. M. Boguñá and R. Pastor-Satorras, *Physical Review E* **68**, 036112 (2003).
59. S. N. Dorogovtsev, *Physical Review E* **69**, 027104 (2004).
60. M. E. J. Newman, in *Handbook of Graphs and Networks: From the Genome to the Internet*, Ed. S. Bornholdt and H. G. Schuster, Wiley-VCH, Berlin (2003), p. 35.
61. Z. Burda, J. Jurkiewicz and A. Krzywicki, *Physical Review E* **70**, 026106 (2004).
62. E. Ravasz and A.-L. Barabási, *Physical Review E* **67**, 026112 (2003).
63. A. Vázquez, M. Boguñá, Y. Moreno, R. Pastor-Satorras and A. Vespignani, *Physical Review E* **6**, 046111 (2003).
64. A. Capocci, G. Caldarelli and P. De Los Rios, *Physical Review E* **68**, 047101 (2003).
65. G. F. Davis, M. Yoo and W. E. Baker, *Strategic Organization* **1**, 301 (2003).
66. M. E. J. Newman, *Physical Review E* **64**, 016131 (2001).
67. M. E. J. Newman, *Physical Review E* **64**, 016132 (2001).
68. L. A. N. Amaral, A. Scala, M. Barthélemy and H. E. Stanley, *Proc. Nat. Acad. Sci.* **97**, 11149 (2000).
69. M. E. J. Newman, S. Forrest and J. Balthrop, *Physical Review E* **66**, 035101 (2002).
70. H. Jeong, S. Mason, A.-L. Barabási and Z. N. Oltvai, *Nature* **411**, 41 (2001).
71. H. Jeong, B. Tombor, R. Albert, Z. N. Oltvai and A.-L. Barabási, *Nature* **407**, 651 (2000).
72. N. D. Martinez, *Ecol. Monogr.* **61**, 367 (1991).
73. R. Albert, H. Jeong and A.-L. Barabási, *Nature* **401**, 130 (1999).
74. V. Colizza, A. Flammini, A. Maritan and A. Vespignani, *Physica A* **352**, 1 (2005).
75. M. Boguñá, R. Pastor-Satorras, A. Díaz-Guilera and A. Arenas, *Physical Review E* **70**, 056122 (2004).
76. S. Garfinkel, *PGP: Pretty Good Privacy*, O'Reilly and Associates, Cambridge MA (1994).
77. W. Stallings, *BYTE* **20**, 161 (1995).

78. M. Faloutsos, P. Faloutsos and C. Faloutsos, *Comput. Commun. Review* **29**, 251 (1999).
79. A. Barrat, M. Barthélemy, R. Pastor-Satorras and A. Vespignani, *Proc. Nat. Acad. Sci.* **101**, 3747 (2004).
80. M. A. Serrano and M. Boguñá, *Physical Review E* **68**, 015101(R) (2003).
81. A. Bekessy, P. Bekessy and J. Komlos, *Stud. Sci. Math. Hungar.* **7**, 343 (1972).
82. E. A. Bender and E. R. Canfield, *J. Comb. Theory A* **24**, 296 (1978).
83. M. Molloy and B. Reed, *Rand. Str. and Algth.* **6**, 161 (1995).
84. J. Park and M. E. J. Newman, *Physical Review E* **68**, 026122 (2003).
85. M. Boguñá, R. Pastor-Satorras and A. Vespignani, *Eur. Physics J. B* **38**, 205 (2004).
86. M. Catanzaro, M. Boguñá and R. Pastor-Satorras, *Physical Review E* **71**, 027103 (2005).
87. A.-L. Barabási and R. Albert, *Science* **286**, 509 (1999).
88. A. Barrat and R. Pastor-Satorras, *Physical Review E* **71**, 036127 (2005).
89. G. Szabó, M. Alava and J. Kertész, *Physical Review E* **67**, 056102 (2003).
90. S. N. Dorogovtsev, J. F. F. Mendes and A. N. Samukhin, *Physical Review Letters* **85**, 4633 (2000).
91. S. N. Dorogovtsev and J. F. F. Mendes, *Europhysics Letters* **52**, 33 (2000).
92. R. Albert and A.-L. Barabási, *Physical Review Letters* **85**, 5234 (2000).
93. P. L. Krapivsky and S. Redner, *Physical Review E* **63**, 066123 (2001).
94. D. Strauss, *SIAM Review* **28**, 513 (1986).
95. S. N. Dorogovtsev, J. F. F. Mendes and A. N. Samukhin, *Physical Review E* **63**, 062101 (2001).
96. B. Söderberg, *Physical Review E* **66**, 066121 (2002).
97. B. Söderberg, *Physical Review E* **68**, 015102(R) (2003).
98. B. Söderberg, *Physical Review E* **68**, 026107 (2003).
99. G. Bianconi and A.-L. Barabási, *Europhysics Letters* **54**, 436 (2001).
100. S. L. Pimm, *Food Webs*, The University of Chicago Press, 2nd edition, Chicago (2002).
101. A. E. Krause, K. A. Frank, D. M. Mason, Z. R. E. Ulanowic and W. W. Taylor, *Nature* **426**, 282 (2003).
102. M. Granovetter, *American Journal of Sociology* **78**, 1360 (1973).
103. R. Guimerà, S. Mossa, A. Turtschi and L. A. N. Amaral, *Proceedings National Academy Science (USA)* **102**, 7794 (2005).
104. R. Guimerà and L. A. N. Amaral, *European Physical Journal B* **38**, 381 (2004).
105. W. Li and X. Cai, *Physical Review E* **69**, 046106 (2004).
106. C. Li and G. Chen, cond-mat/0311333.
107. D. Garlaschelli, S. Battiston, M. Castri, V. D. P. Servedio and G. Caldarelli, *Physica A* **350**, 491 (2004).
108. E. Almaas, B. Kovács, T. Viscek, Z. N. Oltvai and A.-L. Barabási, *Nature* **427**, 839 (2004).
109. S. H. Yook, H. Jeong, A.-L. Barabási and Y. Tu, *Physical Review Letters* **86**, 5835 (2001).

110. J.-P. Onnela, J. Saramäki, J. Kertész and K. Kaski, *Physical Review E* **71**, 065103 (2005).
111. B. Derrida and H. Flyvbjerg, *Journal Physics A* **20**, 5273 (1987).
112. M. Barthélemy, B. Gondran and E. Guichard, *Physica A* **319**, 633 (2003).
113. S. Eubank, H. Guclu, V. S. Anil Kumar, M. V. Marathe, A. Srinivasan, Z. Toroczkai and N. Wang, *Nature* **429**, 180 (2004).
114. L. Hufnagel, D. Brockmann and T. Geisel, *Proceedings National Academy of Science (USA)* **101**, 15124 (2004).
115. G. Chowell, J. M. Hyman, S. Eubank and C. Castillo-Chavez, *Physical Review E* **68**, 066102 (2003).
116. S. Zhou and R. J. Mondragon, The missing links in the BGP-based AS connectivity maps, *PAM2003 — The Passive and Active Measurement Workshop* (http://www.pam2003.org), San Diego, USA, April 2003.
117. A. de Montis, M. Barthélemy, A. Chessa and A. Vespignani, *Structure of Inter-cities traffic: A weighted network analysis*, submitted to *Env. Plan. J. B* (2005).
118. A. Barrat, M. Barthélemy and A. Vespignani, *Journal of Statistical Mechanics*, P05003 (2005).
119. A.-L. Barabási, H. Jeong, Z. Néda, E. Ravasz, A. Schubert and T. Vicsek, *Physica A* **311**, 590 (2002).
120. H. Jeong, B. Tombor, R. Albert, Z. N. Oltvai and A.-L. Barabási, *Nature* **407**, 651 (2000).
121. A. Wagner and D. A. Fell, *Proceedings Royal Society London B* **268**, 1803 (2001).
122. E. Ravasz, A. L. Somera, D. A. Mongru, Z. N. Oltvai and A.-L. Barabási, *Science* **297**, 1551 (2002).
123. D. Zheng, S. Trimper, B. Zheng and P. M. Hui, *Physical Review E* **67**, 040102 (2003).
124. W. Jeżewski, *Physica A* **337**, 336 (2004).
125. E. Almaas, P. L. Krapivsky and S. Redner, *Physical Review E* **71**, 036124 (2005).
126. K. Park, Y.-C. Lai and N. Ye, *Physical Review E* **70**, 026109 (2004).
127. T. Antal and P. L. Krapivsky, *Physical Review E* **71**, 026103 (2005).
128. S. Wang and C. Zhang, *Physical Review E* **70**, 066127 (2004).
129. A. Barrat, M. Barthélemy and A. Vespignani, *Physical Review E* **70**, 066149 (2004).
130. A. Barrat, M. Barthélemy and A. Vespignani, *Lecture Notes in Computer Science* **3243**, 56 (2004).
131. R. V. R. Pandya, cond-mat/0406644.
132. S. H. Yook, H. Jeong and A.-L. Barabási, *Proceedings National Academy of Science (USA)* **99**, 13382 (2002).
133. M. Barthélemy, *Europhysics Letters* **63**, 915 (2003).
134. S. N. Dorogovtsev and J. F. F. Mendes, cond-mat/0408343.
135. S. N. Dorogovtsev, J. F. F. Mendes and A. N. N. Samukhin, *Physical Review E* **63**, 062101 (2001).
136. G. Bianconi, *Europhysics Letters* **71**, 1029-1035 (2005).

137. W.-X. Wang, B.-H. Wang, B. Hu, G. Yan and Q. Ou, *Physical Review Letters* **94**, 188702 (2005).

138. M. Li, J. Wu, D. Wang, T. Zhou, Z. Di and Y. Fan, cond-mat/0501665.

139. S. H. Strogatz, *Nature* **410** 268-276 (2001).

140. S. Bornholdt and H. G. Schuster (editors), *Handbook of Graphs and Networks - From the Genome to the Internet*, Wiley-VCH, Berlin (2002).

141. M. E. J. Newman, *European Physics Journal B* **38**, 321-330 (2004).

142. P. Holme, M. Huss and H. Jeong, *Bioinformatics* **19**, 532-538 (2003).

143. M. Boss, H. Elsinger, M. Summer and S. Thurner, cond-mat/0309582 (2003).

144. M. Girvan and M. E. J. Newman, *Proceedings of the National Academy of Sciences (USA)* **99**, 7821-7826 (2002).

145. G. W. Flake, S. Lawrence, C. L. Giles and F. M. Coetzee, *IEEE Computer* **35**, 66-71 (2002).

146. J.-P. Eckmann and E. Moses, *Proceedings of the National Academy of Sciences (USA)* **99**, 5825-5829 (2002).

147. H. Zhou and R. Lipowsky, Preprint (2005).

148. M. R. Garey and D. S. Johnson, *Computers and Intractability, A Guide to the Theory of NP-Completeness*, W. H. Freeman, New York (1979).

149. B. W. Kernighan and S. Lin, *The Bell System Tech. J* **49**, 291-307 (1970).

150. M. Fiedler, *Czechoslovak Mathematical Journal* **23**, 298-305 (1973).

151. S. Boettcher and A. G. Percus, *Physical Review E* **64** (2001).

152. R. Guimerà, L. Danon, A. Díaz-Guilera, F. Giralt and A. Arenas, *Physical Review E* **68**, 065103 (2003).

153. P. Gleiser and L. Danon, *Advances in Complex Systems* **6**, 565-573 (2003).

154. A. Arenas, L. Danon, A. Díaz-Guilera, P. M. Gleiser and R. Guimerà, *European Physical Journal B* **38**, 373-380 (2004).

155. F. Radicchi, C. Castellano, F. Cecconi, V. Loreto and D. Parisi, *Proceedings of the National Academy of Sciences (USA)* **101**, 2658-2663 (2004).

156. C. Bron and J. Kerbosch, *Communications of the ACM*, 575-577 (1973).

157. R. Guimerà, M. Sales and L. N. A. Amaral, *Physical Review E* **70**, 025101 (2004).

158. U. Brandes, *Journal of Mathematical Sociology* **25**, 163-177 (2001).

159. M. E. J. Newman and M. Girvan, *Physical Review E* **69**, 026113 (2004).

160. S. Fortunato, V. Latora and M. Marchiori, *Physical Review E* **70**, 056104 (2004).

161. V. Latora and M. Marchiori, cond-mat/0402050 (2004).

162. J. Scott, *Social Network Analysis, A Handbook*, SAGE Publications (2000).

163. A. K. Jain and R. C. Dubes, *Algorithms for Clustering Data*, Prentice-Hall, Upper Saddle River, NJ (1988).

164. J. Hopcroft, O. Khan, B. Kulis and B. Selman, *Proceedings of the National Academy of Sciences (USA)* **101**, 5249-5253 (2004).

165. J. P. Bagrow and E. M. Bollt, *Physical Review E* **72**, 046108 (2005).

166. M. E. J. Newman, *Physical Review E* **69**, 066133 (2004).

167. A. Clauset, M. E. J. Newman and C. Moore, *Physical Review E* **70**, 06111 (2004).

168. C. P. Massen and J. P. K. Doye, cond-mat/0412469 (2004).
169. J. Duch and A. Arenas, cond-mat/0501368 (2005).
170. S. Boettcher and A. G. Percus, *Physical Review Letters* **86**, 5211-5214 (2001).
171. B. Bollobás, *Modern Graph Theory*, Springer, New York (1998).
172. A. Pothen, *SIAM Journal on Matrix Analysis and Applications* **11**, 430-452 (1990).
173. A. Pothen, Graph partitioning algorithms with applications to scientific computing, in *Parallel Numerical Algorithms*, Kluwer Academic Press (1996).
174. L. Donetti and M. A. Muñoz, *Journal of Statistical Mechanics: Theory and Experiment*, P10012 (2004).
175. G. H. Golub and C. F. V. Loan, *Matrix Computations*, Johns Hopkins University Press, Baltimore (1996).
176. A. Capocci, V. D. P. Servedio, G. Caldarelli and F. Colaiori, in *Algorithms and Models for the Web-Graph: Third International Workshop, WAW 2004, Rome, Italy, October 16, 2004, Proceeedings, Lecture Notes in Computer Science* **3243**, 181-188 (2004).
177. M. Steyvers and J. B. Tenenbaum, cond-mat/0110012 (2001).
178. F. Wu and B. Huberman, *Eurpean Physics Journal B* **38**, 331-338 (2004).
179. J.-P. Eckmann, E. Moses and D. Sergi, *Proceedings of the National Academy of Sciences (USA)* **101**, 14333-14337 (2004).
180. H. Zhou, *Physical Review E* **67**, 041908 (2003).
181. H. Zhou, *Physical Review E* **67**, 061901 (2003).
182. H. Zhou and R. Lipowsky, *Lecture Notes in Computer Sciences* (in press) (2004).
183. M. Latapy and P. Pons, cond-mat/0412568 (2004).
184. J. H. Ward, *Journal of the American Statistical Association* **53**, 263-244 (1963).
185. J. Reichardt and S. Bornholdt, *Physical Review Letters* **93**, 218701 (2004).
186. M. Blatt, S. Wiseman and E. Domany, *Physical Review Letters* **76**, 3251-3254 (1996).
187. W. Tutte, *Proceedings of the London Mathematical Society (Third Series)* **13**, 743-768 (1963).
188. D. Knuth, *Communication of the ACM* **6**, 555-563 (1963).
189. International Symposium on Graph Drawing, http://graphdrawing.org
190. G. Di Battista, P. Eades, R. Tamassia and I. G. Tollis, *Graph Drawing. Algorithms for the Visualization of Graphs*, Prentice Hall (1999).
191. J. Michael and P. Mutzel (eds.), *Graph Drawing Software*, Mathematics and Visualization, Springer-Verlag (2003).
192. T. Kamada, *Visualizing Abstract Objects and Relations*, World Scientific (1989).
193. M. Kaufmann and D. Wagner (eds.), *Drawing Graphs: Methods and Models*, Lecture Notes in Computer Science **2025**, Springer-Verlag (2001).
194. Sugiyama, Kozo, *Graph Drawing and Applications for Software and Knowledge Engineers*, World Scientific (2002).

195. P. Eades, *Congressus Numerantium* **42**, 149-160 (1984).
196. U. Brandes, in *Drawing Graphs: Methods and Models*, Springer Lecture Notes in Computer Science, **2025**, M. Kaufmann and D. Wagner (eds.), Springer-Verlag (2001), pp. 71-86.
197. K. M. Hall, *Management Science* **17**, 219-229 (1970).
198. U. Brandes, P. Kenis and D. Wagner, *IEEE Transactions on Visualization and Computer Graphics* **9**, 241-253 (2003).
199. U. Brandes and S. Cornelsen, *Journal of Graph Algorithms and Applications* **7**, 181-201 (2003).
200. U. Brandes and D. Wagner, in *Special Issue on Graph Drawing Software*, Springer Series in Mathematics and Visualization, M. Jünger and P. Mutzel (eds.), Springer-Verlag (2003), pp. 321-340, http://www.visone.de/
201. R. Brockenauer and S. Cornelsen, in *Drawing Graphs: Methods and Models*, Lecture Notes in Computer Science, **2025**, M. Kaufmann and D. Wagner (eds.), Springer (2001), pp. 71-86.
202. V. Batagelj and M. Zaveršnik, *Generalized cores*, Preprint 799, Universtiy of Ljubljana (2002).
203. S. B. Seidman, *Social Networks* **5**, 269-287 (1983).
204. M. Baur, U. Brandes, M. Gaertler and D. Wagner, in *Proceedings of the 12th International Symposium on Graph Drawing (GD'04)*, Lecture Notes in Computer Science, **3383**, Springer (2005), pp. 43-48.
205. I. Alvarez-Hamelin, M. Gaertler, R. Görke and D. Wagner, Halfmoon – A new Paradigm for Complex Network Visualization TR 2005-29, Informatics, University Karlsruhe (2004).
206. S. Brin and L. Page, *Computer Networks and ISDN Systems* **30**, 107-117 (1998).
207. J. Kleinberg, *Journal of the ACM* **46**, 604-632 (1997).
208. S. Dill, R. Kumar, K. McCurley, S. Rajagopalan, D. Sivakumar and A. Tomkins, in *Proceedings of the 27th VLDB Conference*, Morgan Kaufmann (2001), pp. 69-78.
209. M. Adler and M. Mitzenmacher, Tech. Rep. 00-39, University of Massachussets (2000).
210. P. Boldi and S. Vigna, in *WWW '04: Proceedings of the 13th International Conference on World Wide Web*, ACM Press (2004), pp. 595-602.
211. I. H. Witten, A. Moffat and T. C. Bell, *Managing gigabytes (2nd ed.): compressing and indexing documents and images*, Morgan Kaufmann Publishers Inc. (1999).
212. J. Abello, P. M. Pardalos and M. G. C. Resende, *Handbook of massive data sets*, Kluwer Academic Publishers (2002).
213. F. Harary, *Graph Theory*, Addison-Wesley, Reading, MA (1969).
214. M. Mitzenmacher, *Internet Mathematics* **1**, 2 (2003).
215. J. Cho and H. Garcia-Molina, Parallel crawlers, in *Proc. of the 11th International World-Wide Web Conference* (2002).
216. P. Boldi, B. Codenotti, M. Santini and S. Vigna, Ubicrawler: A scalable fully distributed web crawler (2002).
217. J. Vitter and E. Shriver, *Algorithmica* **12**, 107-114 (1994).

218. J. Vitter and E. Shriver, *Algorithmica* **12**, 148-169 (1994).
219. The Stanford webbase project,
     http://www-diglib.stanford.edu/~testbed/doc2/WebBase
220. Cyvellance, 2000, http://www.cyvellance.com.
221. R. Kumar, P. Raghavan, S. Rajagopalan and A. Tomkins, in *Proc. of the 8th WWW Conference*, Elsevier North-Holland, Inc. (1999), pp. 1481-1493.
222. A. Broder, R. Kumar, F. Maghoul, P. Raghavan, S. Rajagopalan, S. Stata, A. Tomkins and J. Wiener, *Computer Networks* **33**, 309-320 (2000).
223. G. Pandurangan, P. Raghavan and E. Upfal, in *Proc. of the 8th Annual International Conference on Combinatorics and Computing (COCOON)*, Lecture Notes in Computer Science, **2387**, Springer-Verlag (2002), pp. 330-339.
224. S. Raghavan, Personal communication (2002).
225. J. Kleinberg, R. Kumar, P. Raghavan, S. Rajagopalan and A. Tomkins, in *Proc. International Conference on Combinatorics and Computing*, Lecture Notes in Computer Science, **1627**, Springer-Verlag (1999), pp. 1-18.
226. L. Laura, S. Leonardi, G. Caldarelli and P. De Los Rios, A multi-layer model for the webgraph, *On-line Proceedings of the 2nd International Workshop on Web Dynamics* (2002).
     http://www.dcs.bbk.ac.uk/webDyn2/onlineProceedings.html.
227. R. Kumar, P. Raghavan, S. Rajagopalan, D. Sivakumar, A. Tomkins and E. Upfal, in *Proc. of 41st Symposium on Foundations of Computer Science (FOCS)*, IEEE Computer Society (2000), pp. 57-65.
228. D. Pennock, G. Flake, S. Lawrence, E. Glover and C. Giles, *Proceedings of the National Academy of Sciences (USA)* **99**, 5207-5211 (2002).
229. B. Bollobas and O. Riordan, *Internet Mathematics* **1**, 1-35 (2003).
230. J. Sibeyn, J. Abello and U. Meyer, Heuristics for semi-external depth first search on directed graphs. in *Proceedings of the fourteenth annual ACM symposium on Parallel algorithms and architectures* (2002).
231. D. Donato, L. Laura, S. Leonardi and S. Millozzi, Tech. Rep. D13, COSIN European Research Project, 2004. http://www.cosin.org.
232. A. Walker, *ACM Trans. Mathematical Software* **3**, 253-256 (1977).
233. D. E. Knuth, *Seminumerical Algorithms*, third ed., Vol. 2 of *The Art of Computer Programming*, Addison-Wesley, Reading, Massachusetts (1997).
234. T. H. Cormen, C. E. Leiserson and R. L. Rivest, *Introduction to algorithms*, 6th ed., MIT Press and McGraw-Hill Book Company (1992).
235. R. E. Tarjan, *SIAM Journal on Computing* **1**, 146-160 (1972).
236. M. Garey and D. Johnson, *Computers and Intractability*, W. H. Freeman (1979).
237. T. H. Haveliwala, *Efficient computation of PageRank*, Tech. rep., Stanford University (1999).
238. R. Kraft, E. Hastor and R. Stata, Timelinks: Exploring the link structure of the evolving web., in *Second Workshop on Algorithms and Models for the Web-Graph (WAW2003)* (2003).
239. R. Govindan and H. Tangmunarunkit, *IEEE INFOCOM 2000*, 1371–1380, Tel Aviv, Israel, June 2000, IEEE.

240. University of Oregon Route Views Project, http://www.routeviews.org/.
241. Router-Level Topology Measurements: "Cooperative Association for Internet Data Analysis".
     http://www.caida.org/tools/measurement/skitter/router_topology/.
242. "Distributed Internet Measurements and Simulations".
     http://www.netdimes.org.
243. Y. Shavitt and E. Shir, Dimes: Let the internet measure itself, Preprint cs.NI/0506099 (2005).
244. B. W. Bush, C. R. Files and D. R. Thompson, Empirical characterization of infrastructure networks, Technical Report LA-UR-01-5784, Los Alamos National Laboratory (2001).
245. D. J. Watts, *Small worlds: the dynamics of networks between order and randomness*, Princeton University Press, New Jersey (1999).
246. A. Broido and K. Claffy, Internet topology: connectivity of IP graphs, in *SPIE International symposium on Convergence of IT and Communication*, Denver, CO (2001).
247. S. Mossa, M. Barthélemy, H. E. Stanley and L. A. N. Amaral, *Physical Review Letters* **88**, 138701 (2002).
248. M. Molloy and B. Reed, A Critical Point for Random Graphs with a Given Degree Sequence, *Random Structures and Algorithms* **6**, 161-180 (1995); R. Cohen, K. Erez, D. ben-Avraham and S. Havlin, *Physical Review Letters* **85**, 4626-4628 (2000); D. S. Callaway, M. E. J. Newman, S. H. Strogatz and D. J. Watts, *Physical Review Letters* **85**, 5468-5471 (2000).
249. R. Pastor-Satorras and A. Vespignani, *Physical Review Letters* **86**, 3200 (2001); R. Pastor-Satorras and A. Vespignani, *Physical Review E* **63**, 066117 (2001).
250. B. Bollobás, *Random Graphs*, Academic Press, London (1985).
251. H. Tangmunarunkit, J. Doyle, R. Govindan, S. Jamin, S. Shenker and W. Willinger, *Computer Communication Review* **31**, 7-10 (2001).
252. R. Pastor-Satorras, A. Vázquez and A. Vespignani, *Physical Review Letters* **87**, 258701 (2001).
253. D. Magoni and J.-J. Pansiot, *ACM SIGCOMM Computer Communication Review* **31**, 26-37 (2001).
254. H. Chang, S. Jamin and W. Willinger, Inferring AS-level internet topology from router-level path traces, in *Proceedings of SPIE ITCom 2001*, Denver, CO, August 2001.
255. A. Vázquez, R. Pastor-Satorras and A. Vespignani, *Physical Review E* **65**, 066130 (2002).
256. H. Tangmunarunkit, R. Govindan, S. Jamin, S. Shenker and W. Willinger, *Computer Communication Review* **32**, 76 (2002).
257. W. Willinger, R. Govindan, S. Jamin, V. Paxson and S. Shenker, *Proceedings of the National Academy Science (USA)* **99**, 2573-2580 (2002).
258. Q. Chen, H. Chang, R. Govindan, S. Jamin, S. J. Shenker and W. Willinger, in *INFOCOM 2002. Twenty-First Annual Joint Conference of the IEEE Computer and Communications Societies. Proceedings IEEE, Volume 2*, IEEE Computer Society Press (2002), pp. 608-617.

259. T. Bu and D. Towsley, On distinguishing between Internet power law topology generators, in *Proceedings of INFOCOM* (2002).
260. H. Burch and B. Cheswick, *IEEE computer* **32**, 97-98 (1999).
261. L. Li, D. Alderson, W. Willinger and J. C. Doyle, A First-Principles Approach to Understanding the Internet's Router-level Topology, in *Proceedings of ACM Sigcomm*, Portland (2004).
262. A. Lakhina, J. W. Byers, M. Crovella and P. Xie, Sampling biases in IP topology measurements, *Proc. IEEE INFOCOM* (2003).
263. T. Petermann and P. De Los Rios, *Eur. Physics J. B* **38**, 201-204 (2004).
264. J.-L. Guillaume and M. Latapy, Relevance of Massively Distributed Explorations of the Internet Topology: Simulation Results, *IEEE* 24th *Infocom'05*, Miami, USA (2005).
265. A. Clauset and C. Moore, *Physical Review Letters* **94**, 018701 (2005).
266. P. Barford, A. Bestavros, J. Byers and M. Crovella, On the marginal utility of deploying measurement infrastructure, in *Proceedings of the ACM SIGCOMM Internet Measurement Workshop 2001*, CA (2001).
267. L. Dall'Asta, I. Alvarez Hamelin, A. Barrat, A. Vázquez and A. Vespignani, analysis. *Lecture Notes in Computer Science* **3405**, 140-153 (2005).
268. L. Dall'Asta, I. Alvarez Hamelin, A. Barrat, A. Vázquez and A. Vespignani, *Physical Review E* **71**, 036135 (2005).
269. R. Govindan and A. Reddy, in *Proceedings of IEEE INFOCOM'97*, April 1997, p. 850.
270. H. Chang, R. Govindan, S. Jamin, S. Shenker and W. Willinger, ACM SIGMETRICS (2002), pp. 280-281.
271. J. I. Alvarez-Hamelin, L. Dall'Asta, A. Barrat and A. Vespignani, k-core decomposition: a tool for the analysis of large scale Internet graphs, Preprint cs.NI/0511007 (2005).
272. S. N. Dorogovtsev, A. V. Goltsev and J. F. F. Mendes, k-core percolation and k-core organization of complex networks, cond-mat/0509102 (2005).
273. S. Carmi, S. Havlin, S. Kirkpatrick, Y. Shavitt and E. Shir (2005). http://www.cs.huji.ac.il/~kirk/Jellyfish_Dimes.ppt.
274. J. I. Alvarez-Hamelin, L. Dall'Asta, A. Barrat and A. Vespignani, k-core decomposition: a tool for the visualization of large scale networks, Preprint cs.NI/0504107 (2005).
275. LArge NETwork VIsualization tool. http://xavier.informatics.indiana.edu/lanet-vi/
276. S. H. Strogatz, *Nature* **410**, 268 (2001).
277. J. H. Lawton, in *Ecological Concepts*, Ed. J. M. Cherret, Blackwell Scientific, Oxford, 43 (1989).
278. S. L. Pimm, *Food Webs*, Chapman & Hall, London (1982).
279. J. E. Cohen, F. Briand and C. M. Newman, *Community Food Webs: Data and Theory*, Springer, Berlin (1990).
280. D. Garlaschelli, G. Caldarelli and L. Pietronero, *Nature* **423**, 165 (2003).
281. D. Garlaschelli, *European Physical Journal B* **38**(2), 277 (2004).

282. C. Jeffry, *An Introduction to Plant Taxonomy*, Cambridge University Press, New York (1982).

283. R. R. Sokal and P. H. A. Sneath, *Principles of Numerical Taxonomy*, Freeman, San Francisco (1963).

284. J. C. Willis, *Age and Area*, Cambridge University Press, Cambridge (1922).

285. B. Burlando, *Journal of Theoretical Biology* **146**, 99 (1990).

286. B. Burlando, *Journal of Theoretical Biology* **163**, 161 (1993).

287. C. Caretta Cartozo, D. Garlaschelli, C. Ricotta, M. Barthelemy and G. Caldarelli, preprint (2004).

288. North-American *florae* are publicly available from the *Plants National Database* (http://plants.usda.gov).

289. C. S. Elton, *Animal Ecology*, Sidgwick & Jackson, London (1927).

290. J. M. Montoya and R. J. Solé, *Journal of Theoretical Biology* **214**, 405 (2002).

291. J. Camacho, R. Guimerà and L. A. N. Amaral, *Physical Review Letters* **88**, 228102 (2002).

292. J. A. Dunne, R. J. Williams and N. D. Martinez, *Proceedings of the National Academy of Science (USA)* **99**, 12917 (2002).

293. I. Rodriguez-Iturbe and A. Rinaldo, *Fractal River Basins: Chance and Self-Organization*, Cambridge University Press, Cambridge (1996).

294. J. Banavar, A. Maritan and A. Rinaldo, *Nature* **399**, 130 (1999).

295. G. B. West, J. H. Brown and B. J. Enquist, *Science* **276**, 122 (1997).

296. G. B. West, J. H. Brown and B. J. Enquist, *Science* **284**, 1677 (1999).

297. J. Memmott, N. D. Martinez and J. E. Cohen, *J. Anim. Ecol.* **69**, 1 (2000).

298. S. J. Hall and D. Raffaelli, *J. Anim. Ecol.* **60**, 823 (1991).

299. N. D. Martinez, *Ecol. Monogr.* **61**, 367 (1991).

300. M. Huxham, S. Beaney and D. Raffaelli, *Oikos* **76**, 284 (1996).

301. G. Caldarelli, D. Garlaschelli and L. Pietronero, in *Statistical Mechanics of Complex Networks*, Lecture Notes in Physics, Vol. 625, Ed. R. Pastor-Satorras, M. Rubi and A. Díaz-Guilera, Springer-Verlag (2003), p. 148.

302. A. Cronquist, *The Evolution and Classification of Flowering Plants*, The New York Botanical Garden, New York (1998).

303. J. Stiglitz and B. Greenwald, *Towards a New Paradigm in Monetary Economics, Raffaele Mattioli Lectures*, Cambridge (2003).

304. J. Scott, *Social Network Analysis: A Handbooks*, Sage Publications, London (2000).

305. N. E. Friedkin, *American Journal of Sociology* **96**, 1478-1504 (2001).

306. J. L. Moreno, *Who shall survive?*, Beacon House, Beacon, NY (1934).

307. A. Rapoport and W. J. Horvath, *Behavioral Sci.* **6**, 279-291 (1961).

308. T. J. Fararo and M. Sunshine, *A Study of a biased friendship network*, Syracuse University Press, Syracuse, NY (1964).

309. A. Davis, B. B. Gardner and M. R. Gardner, *Deep South*, University of Chicago Press, Chicago (1941).

310. F. J. Roethlisberger and W. J. Dickson, *Management and the Worker*, Harvard University Press, Cambridge, MA (1939).

311. P. S. Bearman, J. Moody and K. Stovel, *Am. Jour. Soc.* **110**, 44-91 (2004).

312. A. S. Klovdhal, J. J. Potterat, D. E. Woodhouse, J. B. Muth, S. Q. Muthand and W. W. Darrow, *Soc. Sci. Med.* **38**, 79-88 (1994).

313. J. F. Padgett and C. K. Ansell, *American Journal of Sociology* **98**, 1259-1319 (1993).

314. A. Rapoport, *Bull. Math. Biophys.* **19**, 145-157 (1957).

315. J. Travers and S. Milgram, *Sociometry* **32**, 425-443 (1969).

316. P. V. Marsden, *Ann. Review Soc.* **16**, 435-463 (1990).

317. L. Adamic and B. A. Huberman, *Science* **287**, 2115 (2000).

318. V. Batgelj and A. Mrvar, *Social Networks* **22**, 173-186 (2000).

319. M. Bordens and I. Gomez, in *The Web of Knowledge*, B. Cronin and H. B. Atkins (eds.), Information Today, Medson, NJ (2000).

320. R. De Castro and J.W. Grossman, *Math. Intelligencer* **21**, 51-63 (1999).

321. J. W. Grossman and P. D. F. Ion, *Congressus Numerantium* **108**, 129-131 (1995).

322. G. Mellin and O. Persson, *Scientometric* **36**, 363-377 (1996).

323. J. Moody, *American Society Review* **69**, 213-238 (2004).

324. M. E. J. Newman, *Proceedings of the National Academy of Science (USA)* **98**, 404-409 (2001).

325. G. F. Davis and H. R. Greve, *American Journal of Sociology* **103**, 1-37 (1996).

326. G. F. Davis, M. Yoo and W. E. Baker, *Strategic Organization* **1**, 301-326 (2003).

327. P. Mariolis, *Social Sci. Quart.* **56**, 425-439 (1975).

328. M. S. Mizruchi, *The American Corporate Network, 1904-1974*, Sage, Beverly Hills, CA (1982).

329. G. Chartrand and L. Lesniak, *Graphs and Digraphs*, Wadsworth and Brooks/Cole, Menlo Park (1986).

330. J. J. Ramasco, S. N. Dorogovtsev and R. Pastor-Satorras, *Physical Review E* **70**, 036106 (2004).

331. M. E. J. Newman, S. Forrest and J. Balthrop, *Physical Review E* **66**, 035101(R) (2002).

332. R. D. Smith, cond-mat/0206378 (2002).

333. W. Aiello, F. Chung and L. Lu, in *Proc. of the 32nd Annual ACm Symposium on Theory and Computing* (2000), pp. 171-180.

334. W. Aiello, F. Chung and L. Lu, in *Handbook of Massive Data Sets*, J. Abello, P. M. Pardalos and M. G. C. Resende (eds.), Kluwer Academic, Dordrecht (2002), pp. 97-122.

335. S. Garfinkel, *PGP: Pretty Good Privacy*, O'Reilly and Associates, Cambridge (1994).

336. W. Stallings, *BYTE* **20**, 161 (1995).

337. X. Guardiola, R. Guimera, A. Arenas, A. Díaz-Guilera, D. Streib and L. A. N. Amaral, cond-mat/0206240 (2002).

338. J. H. Jones and M. S. Handcock, *Proceedings of the Royal Society B* **270**, 1123-1128 (2003).

339. F. Liljeros, R. Edling, L. A. N. Amaral, H. E. Stanley and Y. Aberg, *Nature* **411**, 907 (2001).

340. R. K. Merton, *Science* **159**, 56-63 (1968).
341. S. Maslov, K. Sneppen and A. Zaliznyak, cond-mat/0205379.
342. J.-L. Guillaume and M. Latapy, cond-mat/0307095.
343. M. Girvan and M. E. J. Newman, *Proceedings National Academy Sciences (USA)* **99**, 7821 (2002).
344. L. C. Freeman, *Sociometry* **40**, 35 (1977).
345. J. R. Tyler, D. M. Wilkinson and B. A. Huberman, *The Information Society* **21**, 133-141 (2005)
346. G. Caldarelli, C. Caretta Cartozo, P. De Los Rios and V. D. P. Servedio, *Physical Review E* **69**, 035101 (2004).
347. P. De Los Rios, *Europhysics Letters* **56**, 898 (2001).
348. A. Maritan, A. Rinaldo, R. Rigon, A. Giacometti and I. Rodriguez-Iturbe, *Physical Review E* **53**, 1510 (1996).
349. A. Rinaldo, I. Rodriguez-Iturbe, R. Rigon, E. Ijjasz-Vazquez and L. R. Bras, *Physical Review Letters* **70**, 822 (1993).
350. S. Kramer and M. Marder, *Physical Review Letters* **68**, 205 (1992).
351. K. Sinclair and R. C. Ball, *Physical Review Letters* **76**, 3360 (1996).
352. M. O. Jackson and A. Wolinsky, *Journal of Economic Theory* **71**, 44-74 (1996).
353. A. Kirman, *Economic Journal* **99**, 126-39 (1989).
354. J. Galaskiewicz, *Social Organization of the Urban Grant Economy*, Academic Press, New York (1985).
355. J. Galaskiewicz and P. V. Marsden, *Social Sci. Res.* **7**, 89-107 (1978).
356. S. Battiston, G. Caldarelli and D. Garlaschelli, preprint.
357. D. Garlaschelli, S. Battiston, M. Castri, V. D. P. Servedio and G. Caldarelli, *Physica A* **350**, 491-499 (2004).
358. M. A. Serrano and Boguñá, *Physical Review E* **68**, 015101(R) (2003).
359. Mediobanca, *Calepino dell'Azionista*, Milano (1986).
360. Banca Nazionale del Lavoro, *La meridiana dell'investitore 2002*, ClassEditori, Milano (2002).
361. *Fortune 1000* (Fortune 1000, data concerning the first 1000 US companies, raked by revenues. Data kindly provided by Gerald Davis, Michigan University).
362. B. Mintz, and M. Schwartz, *The Power Structure of American Business*, University of Chicago Press (1985).
363. L. D. Brandeis, *Other People's Money: And How the Bankers Use It*, Frederick A. Stokes, New York (1914).
364. S. Battiston, E. Bonabeau and G. Weisbuch, *Physica A* **322**, 567 (2003).
365. M. E. J. Newman and Juyong Park, *Physical Review E* **68**, 036122 (2003).
366. S. Battiston, G. Weisbuch and E. Bonabeau, *Advances in Complex Systems* **6**, 4 (2003).
367. P. R. Haunschild, *Administrative Science Quarterly* **38**, 564-592 (1993).
368. H. Follmer, *Journal of Mathematical Economics* **1**, 51-62 (1974).
369. S. Galam, Y. Gefen and Y. Shapir, *Journal of Sociology* **9**, 1-13 (1982).
370. M. Leone, A. Vazquez, A. Vespignani and R. Zecchina, *European Physical Journal B* **28**, 191 (2002).

Index